Preservation Management

Policies and Practices in British Libraries

PRESERVATION MANAGEMENT
Policies and Practices in British Libraries

John Feather, Graham Matthews
and Paul Eden

Gower

Published by
Gower Publishing Limited
Gower House
Croft Road
Aldershot
Hampshire GU11 3HR
England

Gower
Old Post Road
Brookfield
Vermont 05036
USA

British Library Cataloguing in Publication Data

Feather, John
   Preservation Management: Policies and
   Practices in British Libraries
   I. Title
   025.840941

   ISBN 0–566–07622–5

Library of Congress Cataloging-in-Publication Data

Feather, John.
   Preservation management: policies and practices in British
   libraries/by John Feather, Graham Matthews, and Paul Eden.
     p. cm.
   Includes bibliographical references (p.   ) and index.
   ISBN 0-566-07622-5
   1. Books–Great Britain–Conservation and preservation.
   2. Library materials–Great Britain–Conservation and preservation.
   I. Matthews, Graham, 1953–   . II. Eden, Paul, 1955–   .
   III. Title.
   Z701.4.G7F43   1996
   025.8'4'0941–dc20

                                95–36428
                                  CIP

Typeset in 10/13 Century Old Style by Poole Typesetting (Wessex) Limited, Bournemouth, England and printed in Great Britain by Biddles Limited, Guildford.

Contents

List of tables

Preface

The work on which this book is largely based began as a study of preservation management practices in British libraries in the early 1990s. As we explain in Chapter 1, we were, in a sense, following in the footsteps of the work done by Ratcliffe and Patterson ten years earlier. It soon became obvious to us, however, that the great changes which have taken place in the last decade were forcing us to change our own understanding of our work. We conducted a questionnaire-based survey of libraries in England, Scotland and Wales during the first half of 1993. Between May and July, following a successful pilot study, questionnaires were sent out to 682 British libraries: 173 public, 228 academic and 281 special. The sample was based on entries in the Library Association's *Libraries in the United Kingdom and the Republic of Ireland 1993*, with some additional libraries identified as having heritage collections. A covering letter sent with the questionnaires outlined the main aims of the research and asked librarians to reply in terms of their library system as a whole and not only with reference to special collections (see Appendix 1). A second questionnaire was sent to those libraries which did not respond to the initial mailing. Completed questionnaires were analysed using a Minitab programme resident on the Hewlett-Packard mainframe computer at Loughborough University. Any difficulties in interpreting responses were clarified by follow-up telephone calls. Libraries were coded according to type within their broad categories so that global figures could be broken down and comparisons made between them.

There was an excellent response to the survey with 488 libraries returning completed questionnaires, an overall response rate of 71.55 per cent. Broken down into our three main library sectors, returns and response rates were: 132 returns, 76.30 per cent, for public libraries; 177 returns, 77.63 per cent, for academic libraries; 177 returns, 62.99 per cent, for special libraries. In addition, there were two anonymous returns.

As we analysed the responses, and began to set them in the context of current developments in library and information service provision, it became clear to us that we were really addressing fundamental issues about access to, and use of, books and information. This approach is reflected throughout our study, but especially perhaps in the last chapter where we try to suggest some possible developments as well as delineating our own conclusions. The central concern of library and information professionals is with access by users; but we consider that the preservation and retention of materials and media is the foundation upon which access is built. In analysing preservation practices in British libraries, we have also tried to assess the attitudes of professional librarians towards this aspect of their work. We have not confined ourselves to a single sector: academic, public and special libraries were all covered in our survey and all are represented here. Indeed, we have found a remarkable homogeneity of opinion, if rather less uniformity of practice, across all three of the sectors into which libraries are traditionally, if not always helpfully, divided.

In Chapter 1, we have drawn upon the literature and recent history of preservation management to describe the context in which our work was planned and initiated. In Chapters 2 and 3 we present our major findings in respect of both managerial attitudes and management practices. In Chapter 4, we have tried to provide a broader professional, technological and political context in which these findings can be understood. In Chapters 5 and 6, we have looked at policy issues in the light of our own findings, and more general approaches. We have analysed the prescriptive policy documents which some international and national professional organisations have provided; and we have also analysed the policy documents which we have seen from British libraries. The contrast between the two is often instructive! In a sense, it is in the gap between prescription and practice that we have constructed Chapter 7. We *do not* seek to prescribe, but we have tried to draw some generally applicable conclusions, and to use them, and the broader context which we have delineated, as the basis for some modest suggestions about how individual libraries might develop preservation policies. Less modestly, perhaps, we have not hesitated to suggest what national policies could be considered in the immediate future.

We offer this book not simply as the report on a piece of research, but as a contribution to a debate: a debate about how late twentieth-century Britain can exploit its written and printed heritage while preserving it for those who will come after us.

John Feather
Graham Matthews
Paul Eden

Loughborough University
January 1995

Acknowledgements

First and foremost we thank the Trustees of the Leverhulme Foundation without whose support the bulk of the research on which this book is based could not have been undertaken. Their generosity supported our work in 1993 and early 1994, and enabled us to undertake a large-scale survey of preservation practices in British libraries. We are also grateful to the hundreds of librarians who responded to our requests for information, and in particular to our questionnaire. We were aware that all of them had other and more important calls on their time, and that one large group had only just completed an even more elaborate and much more troublesome document from another source with which ours partially overlapped. It will be apparent to the reader of this book that their responses far exceeded our expectations; many offered comments and opinions which have been invaluable to us in our work. We guaranteed anonymity to all our respondents, and therefore cannot thank them by name; some will recognise themselves here: to all, however, we offer our thanks.

We are also indebted to the members of the *ad hoc* advisory committee with whom we consulted, both collectively and individually at various stages during the project. They were: Dr Mirjam Foot (British Library); Dr Helen Forde (Public Record Office); Irene Gilchrist (City of London Libraries); Anne Matheson (National Library of Scotland); Ian Mowat (Newcastle-upon-Tyne University Library); Robin Price (Wellcome Institute); and Dr F. W. Ratcliffe (formerly Cambridge University Library, who took the chair). We have also, at various times, had helpful advice, information and opinion from many professional colleagues, including Giles Barber, Nicholas Hadcraft, Ann Hobart, Gillian Pentelow, Dr Katherine Swift, Michael Turner, and the present and past staff of the National Preservation Office, especially Valerie Ferris, Marie Jackson and Geraldine Kenny. We are grateful to Carolyn Pritchett for help with copy preparation and to Cynthia Robinson for secretarial assistance.

Papers based on this work have been published previously in the following journals: *British Journal of Academic Librarianship; Library and Information Research News; Library Management; Public Library Journal; Rare Books Newsletter.* We are grateful to their respective editors and publishers for their hospitality. This book incorporates some of the material in the articles, although none of the papers themselves, to which we make reference from time to time.

Finally, we would like to thank our colleagues at Loughborough for their tolerance of our somewhat single-minded conversations during the last 18 months.

JF, GM, PE

1 A decade of development

Much has happened in the world of libraries and information in the last ten years. Political, economic and technological factors have all influenced development and change. Preservation and conservation have not been immune from these. Added impetus to activity in the field of preservation and conservation came at the beginning of the period, with the publication, in 1984, of a report[1] which strongly criticised the state of preservation and conservation in British libraries and made numerous recommendations for improvement. As part of our survey of preservation and conservation in British libraries in the 1990s,[2] we have tried to identify developments which have taken place since the publication of that report. In this chapter, we trace these developments and attempt, in doing so, to assess the influence of the report, usually known, from the name of its principal author, as the Ratcliffe Report.[3]

It is self-evident that preservation and conservation activity in British libraries did not begin in 1984! The Ratcliffe Report, however, was generally felt to have been influential in bringing about an increase in the awareness and discussion of preservation in this country; accordingly, in considering current policy and practices, it is appropriate to go back to the time of the inception, implementation and dissemination of this seminal document, that is, the early 1980s.

Our major source of information for tracking down developments over the last decade or so has been a literature survey and access to the minutes of various committees. These have been supplemented by knowledge from the authors' own professional involvement and activity over this period and informal discussions with those prominent in the field. It should, however, be acknowledged that the literature alone can be no definitive record of actual activity. Some activity may not be recorded in published format and some of the literature may be theoretical or promotional, and not necessarily taken up in practice in the period in question.

To facilitate a review of developments it is worth noting several published accounts which, taken together, provide details of activity and publications over the period. The first of these is the chapter 'Preservation' in the five-yearly review, *British Librarianship and Information Work*.[4] As this covers the period 1981–85, the comment at the beginning of this chapter also serves to underline the significance of beginning our review at this time:

This is the first occasion in which 'Preservation' has been accorded the status of a full chapter in *British librarianship and information work*, a most eloquent testimony of its growing prominence during the years under review.[5]

The same publication covering the next five years, 1986–90,[6] provides a similarly concise account of activity, and, with regard to the level of development since the last five-year account, an equally astute comment:

In 1985 preservation was, for the first time, deemed important enough for its own chapter in *British Librarianship and Information Work 1981–1985*; by 1990 it would have been impossible to imagine how libraries with sizeable or notable collections could be ignorant of their preservation responsibilities or options ... the place of preservation within the library discipline is proven.[7]

It is perhaps pertinent to note at this point, that an annual review, *Librarianship and Information Worldwide: an annual survey*, first published in 1991,[8] includes a separate chapter on preservation for the first time in its 1994 edition.[9] Ratcliffe himself has published informal accounts and overviews of progress.[10] In the late 1980s, a survey of SCONUL members was undertaken to investigate progress[11] and others have outlined and reviewed the growing British literature of preservation[12] which in itself is to some extent a record of actual activity and aspirations. Three textbooks published in the 1990s are also relevant in this context. *Preservation and the Management of Library Collections*[13] provides, in its concluding chapter ('The professional context'),[14] a brief historical overview of the development of preservation in the United Kingdom and puts it in the context of worldwide activity. *Preservation in Libraries: principles, strategies and practices for librarians*,[15] adds to the international perspective, and while not offering a focused review of developments in any one chapter, provides, through its index, the opportunity to trace activity in various major aspects of preservation; this different approach is equally effective. *A Reading Guide to the Preservation of Library Collections*,[16] a cooperative publication between the National Preservation Office and the Library Association, has chapters on ten different aspects of preservation with suggested readings and introductions which in some instances review key developments in these areas. A major inclusion, however, from the point of view of surveying developments, is the introduction by Ratcliffe,[17] which provides not only an overview of activity since publication of the 1984 report, but also highlights key activity before this and pays due credit to influential developments in the United States.

To add to the understanding of what has been achieved and to express it in a helpful way for the library manager, our review attempts to identify key aspects of preservation which now appear to exist as distinct entities, and to summarise their development, acknowledging key individual or organisational movers in doing so. In addition to specific aspects of preservation such as disaster control planning and surrogacy, all-embracing issues (such as the definition of preservation and conservation, and raising awareness) will be addressed. We do not present this chapter as an exhaustive account; rather, key events and publications which have influenced the situation in Britain, or reflect or describe activity here, are noted as representative examples of impact and action during the period. The publications already mentioned are rich in further sources; we do not attempt to duplicate such comprehensive coverage.

A chronological list of key developments over the decade, which helps put the whole subject in perspective, appears at Appendix 2.[18] A glance at this skeletal representation perhaps confirms the authors' initial, informal and somewhat unscientific view of the British literature of preservation during the 1980s and 1990s: that different aspects of preservation have achieved prominence as awareness and promotion have been turned from one topic to another. This was to be expected in what was, at the beginning, a profile-raising exercise. For instance, one of the first specific aspects to be addressed after the establishment of the National Preservation Office (NPO), was preservation policy; collection surveys, disaster control planning, security and the environment have all in turn been addressed as the spotlight has fallen on the next aspect to be promoted. These have been taken up by libraries to varying degrees, irrespective of the guidelines and examples of application that have appeared in the literature and at conferences and seminars; indeed we shall trace the development in Chapters 2 and 3. Much of this, however, while not wholly new in libraries, is in the main a new development and interest of the 1980s and 1990s. The literature does not reveal similar peaks and troughs for more recognisable and long-standing aspects of preservation, such as conservation and substitution. Rather there is a continual, if sporadic, appearance of accounts of developments in conservation techniques, or new uses of microfilm as a surrogate; more significantly, perhaps, in these more traditional areas, the novel element is provided by scientific research which is gradually producing methods of mass de-acidification, new means of surrogacy such as the optical disc, and opportunities for preservation and access through digitisation. These cannot be rushed as they are tried and tested before being developed for commercial application.

DEFINITION

Central to the whole issue are the definitions of preservation and conservation; it is appropriate that this is the first issue to be considered. Various definitions and interpretations of both terms can be found in the literature. Over the last decade, there has been a focus of attention on this; hand in hand with raising awareness goes the need for a clear explanation of the subject of which awareness is being raised. We shall illustrate this with definitions from four sources from the period in question.

In a *Glossary of Conservation Terms* in the Ratcliffe report[19] the following definitions were provided:

Preservation. Strictly, all the steps taken to protect materials, that is including conservation and restoration, but often used in reference to the treatment of materials on first entering the library; it is preventative rather than remedial. *See* Conservation.[20]

Conservation. Strictly, the repair work and binding carried out on items and of an essentially remedial nature. In present general usage 'conservation' and 'preservation' tend to be interchangeable. For example, the Canadian Survey talks of conservation policies and the Australian National Library of its preservation programme. There are numerous similar examples.[21]

The brief working definitions included on the questionnaires sent out in Ratcliffe's survey were:

Preservation. Prevention of environmental damage to stock (shelving, handling, etc.).

Conservation. Repair work carried out on materials.[22]

An IFLA publication of 1986[23] offers an authoritative definition on which others have since been based:

Preservation. Includes all the managerial and financial considerations including storage and accommodation provisions, staffing levels, policies, techniques and methods involved in preserving library and archive materials and the information contained in them.

Conservation. Denotes those specific policies and practices involved in protecting library and archive materials from deterioration, damage and decay, including the methods and techniques devised by technical staff.[24]

The influence of the above can be seen in the definitions from a recent National Preservation Office *Glossary:*[25]

Preservation. A broader term than conservation. It includes all the managerial and financial considerations including storage and accommodation provisions, staffing levels, policies, techniques and methods involved in preserving library archive materials and the information contained in them.[26]

Conservation. Denotes those specific treatments and techniques applied in protecting library and archive materials from deterioration which involves intervention with the object itself. Modern ethics demand respect for the historic integrity of the item.[27]

Similar definitions are found in the recent academic literature:

Preservation is an aspect of the management of the library. Its objective is to ensure that information survives in a useable form for as long as it is wanted … The essential characteristic of preservation is that it is a large-scale operation, concerned with the effective management of a library's stock, or information source.[28]

Indeed, in another textbook,[29] the IFLA definitions are used.

Finally, we note the view of the Director of Collections and Preservation at the British Library:

We consider **preservation** to include everything that is conducive to the well-being of the collections. Not only concerns such as the development of good storage conditions and book handling but also the administrative effort, so even budgeting for conservation work comes under preservation. In fact preservation covers everything that in the end benefits the physical well-being of the collections, whereas **conservation** is the active work carried out on the collections.[30]

Another term found in the literature is **restoration**. Definitions in our sources are similar for this, too, but the NPO definition of this has one obvious and significant difference, adding that 'it does not necessarily include good conservation practices'.[31] This however, reflects differences of the use of the word 'restoration' on either side of the Atlantic. Our concern here is with preservation and conservation, while noting the view of one writer that 'precise terms are unlikely to be resolved satisfactorily'.[32]

We considered these matters carefully in designing our own questionnaire. We wished to give as clear and concise a definition as possible. Those working directly within the preservation field were not sure of the usefulness of the existing 'formal' definitions, yet we had to express our meaning clearly to librarians with varying levels of knowledge and experience of preservation. We also wanted them to be able to relate these definitions to their normal work and their own collections.

The definitions we provided, based on elements of those broadly accepted and authoritative ones identified above, were:

Preservation. The managerial, financial and technical issues involved in preserving library materials in all formats – and/or their information content – so as to maximise their useful life.

Conservation. The maintenance and/or repair of individual items.[33]

Preservation is any activity, largely preventative, which aims to protect and secure library materials to ensure their availability, access and use. In this broad sense, it includes such matters as disaster control planning, education and awareness, and of course, conservation. Preservation is thus a broad umbrella term encompassing many activities. The problem is not just one of definition, but rather of the perception and image of the subject and the application of what we believe to be preservation in our own libraries. We return to this issue in Chapter 2.[34]

AWARENESS RAISING

The Ratcliffe report 'highlighted the lack, on a national basis, of preservation expertise, training facilities, earmarked funds, coordination among libraries and use of [then] new preservation technologies',[35] such as mass de-acidification. As part of the response to the Ratcliffe report, the British Library set up a National Preservation Office (NPO), the aims of which were:

- Promotion of awareness of pressing conservation problems and the need for good practice.

- Provision of information and referral services on preservation issues.
- Investigation and initiation of debate on important national developments.
- Encouragement of cooperative initiatives.[36]

In general terms, awareness raising is probably the field in which the greatest overall level of achievement has been attained. The NPO, despite limited funds, has played a key role in this. It has contributed to the raising of awareness through a whole range of activities and publications. Since 1986, it has organised an annual seminar or conference. Themes addressed have included: conservation in crisis; preservation and collection management; preservation and technology; preservation policies, preservation and publication, security; microforms; housing collections: environment and storage. These seminars (the proceedings of which have been published),[37] have provided an opportunity not just for librarians but also for other players such as archivists, conservators and publishers to come together to listen to papers on a whole range of topics of current interest and share their experiences and ideas both formally and informally. The NPO in turn appears to have listened to the views at these gatherings if its publications and other subsequent activities offered are any indicator.

Other methods the NPO have employed to raise awareness and, in most instances, to inform at the same time, include bookmarks, posters, free leaflets, video cassettes, short courses/seminars, an annual competition, provision of speakers to conferences, a labelled sweatshirt, and, most recently, a pack for trainers of junior staff. In these activities, the NPO has been supported by sponsorship from commercial organisations such as Riley, Dunn and Wilson, and W.H. Smith, and funding from charitable foundations such as the Andrew W. Mellon Foundation and the Wolfson Foundation.

EDUCATION AND TRAINING

One of Ratcliffe's main conclusions was that:

> There is little evidence of conservation training among newly recruited professionally qualified library staff at any level, and there is little provision for conservation in the curricula of library schools ... [38]

The library schools and others were quick to respond.[39] One of the present authors (G.M.) was given the task of responding to this comment in the department in which he then worked by being asked to devise and develop suitable teaching materials and sessions. In due course, a survey was carried out to ascertain the degree to which the schools had indeed responded to Ratcliffe.[40] It was found that:

> there has clearly been a significant advance with regard to the teaching of conservation in the LIS [Library and Information Studies] curriculum on the situation in 1984, as reported by Ratcliffe ... The present coverage of conservation in the professional educa-

tion of librarians and archivists reflects an encouraging level of commitment to finding an appropriate response to the conservation 'crisis' facing many libraries and record repositories.[41]

It was noted that most of the library schools regarded the subject as a managerial issue, while acknowledging technical knowledge as a necessary background for making management decisions and managing conservation programmes; as a result, the subject had developed mainly in the management areas of the curriculum. Educators were making use of local expertise, with student visits to nearby library binderies, binding companies, and archives, for example, and inviting outside experts to address students. The significance and standing of preservation in the curriculum was perhaps further attested by the fact that preservation was the theme of the 1992 Association of Assistant Librarians (UK) student conference.[42]

Support for preservation education was greatly enhanced by the formation, in 1987, of an Education Panel of the National Preservation Advisory Committee (NPAC). It provided a forum for those involved in the teaching of preservation and its development in the library schools. It gave them ready access to the latest proposals and ideas of the NPO which helped in the updating of teaching materials, and also allowed the educators to feed their opinions to the NPO and to NPAC. Members suggested and helped with, among other things, courses, books and training packs.

On an international scale, there has been much activity, with IFLA, through its Preservation and Conservation (PAC) Core Programme, UNESCO and the International Council on Archives (ICA), all committed to promoting preservation through education, training and research. IFLA initiated the development of *Guidelines for the Teaching of Preservation to Librarians, Archivists and Documentalists ...;*[43] UNESCO has published *A Model Curriculum.*[44] Cloonan, in *Global Perspectives on Preservation,*[45] provides a good international overview of preservation education in the context of a critical evaluation of the subject. She also includes suggestions for future development, in areas such as resources, research, the dissemination of information for education and the potential roles of key players.

Linked to education but significantly different from it, is training, which is an essential ingredient of successful preservation management in a library.[46] Many of the leaflets and video cassettes produced by the NPO, while not solely directed at trainers, have indeed proved to be useful training resources. However, the Education Panel of NPAC has for some time been working on a pack aimed at providing library trainers with a ready-made resource. This was published in 1994;[47] feedback on its utility is awaited at the time of writing. In addition, a range of courses on different aspects of preservation has been offered by various British professional bodies.[48] The importance of the need for librarians involved in preservation to be aware of publications aimed at those working in cognate professions is underlined by a UNESCO publication, aimed primarily at archivists, with guide-lines for staff training. This also deals with user education, another aspect which has received some attention in British libraries, though mainly for users working with special collections.[49]

PRESERVATION POLICY

Two documents of international standing cover this area. The first, published by IFLA in 1986, discusses and outlines the principles of preservation and conserva-tion;[50] the other, more focused on policies, was published by UNESCO in 1990.[51] Both have to be seen in the broader context of the work of national and inter-national professional bodies and non-governmental organisations.[52]

In the years immediately after the publication of the Ratcliffe Report, preserva-tion policy was the subject of considerable attention in the United Kingdom. The Standing Conference of National and University Libraries (SCONUL) Working Party on Preservation addressed it, and urged its members to draw up policies;[53] the Library Association's annual conference of 1986, *Preserving the Word*, included several papers which addressed this issue.[54] In the same year, the Library Association reprinted the *IFLA Principles* as one of its own *Guidelines* docu-ments.[55] The NPO's first preservation competition, sponsored by Dunn and Wilson (as the firm was then known), launched in 1987, asked librarians to '... draw up a statement of policy for preservation relevant to the organisation in which you work';[56] the competition was won by the Church of England Children's Society and a brief account of its policy appeared for wider consumption in the pages of the *Library Association Record*.[57] Finally, the theme of the 1990 NPO seminar was preservation policies.[58] The British Library published a report of an internal review of its own acquisition and retention policies for external consump-tion; the Enright Report, as it has come to be known, has played an increasing part in wider thinking on preservation policy and planning.[59] Policy has also been addressed in NPO guidelines.[60] However, all this prompting does not seem to have resulted in published accounts of preservation policies in British libraries; rather the literature of this topic is dominated by preservation policy and programmes in North America.[61]

DISASTER MANAGEMENT

At the beginning of the period under review this activity was usually called 'disas-ter planning'; later it became known more precisely as 'disaster control planning'. Other terms can be found, too, such as 'emergency' or 'contingency' planning. More recently, as the profession looks further afield for advice and guidance, 'risk management' has become a fashionable term. Currently, and reflecting the place of this topic in the overall management of libraries, as well as to persuade managers of its importance, and to emphasise that it involves more than the disaster plan itself, the preferred term is 'disaster management'.

Although the flooding of the Biblioteca Nazionale in Florence in 1966, when the River Arno burst its banks, brought the impact of disasters and their impact to a worldwide professional audience,[62] the most significant event in the UK appears to have been an initiative of the National Library of Scotland. Following the preparation of its own disaster control plan in 1983,[63] this effort culminated in the publication in 1985 of a *Planning Manual for Disaster Control in Scottish Libraries and Record Offices*.[64] Since its publication, this has generally been regarded as a model of its kind and many libraries have used it as the basis of their own plans. One of its authors, John McIntyre, Director of Preservation, National Library of Scotland, is now acknowledged as the international expert in this field and has written several key papers on the subject.[65] From 1985 to the end of the decade much attention was paid to disaster management. Guidelines from respected organisations appeared over this period, which helped to keep it in the forefront of professional attention. In 1987, the British Library produced an outline disaster control plan;[66] UNESCO guidelines were published in 1988.[67] In the same year, the theme of the NPO's annual competition was disaster control planning and the winning entry and two highly commended entries were published the following year.[68] Further impetus had been given by a video on disaster management produced by the NPO in 1988.[69] All this has had some effect, with nearly 40 per cent of British academic libraries, for instance, now having a disaster control plan.[70]

Unfortunately, more catastrophic events also influenced the growing acknowledgement of the need for effective disaster control. In 1986, a fire started by an arsonist devastated Los Angeles Central Public Library, causing millions of dollars' worth of damage, including the destruction of 400 000 volumes.[71] Two years later, a fire in the Academy of Sciences Library in Leningrad had a similar result, with 400 000 volumes destroyed and others damaged by fire, water and smoke.[72] Both of these disasters received considerable international coverage in the professional literature and, indeed, the general press.[73] It is too easy to think that such incidents will not happen. These were major libraries, not small branches or remote sites. Disasters continue to happen and receive brief mentions in professional journals. The IRA bomb in the City of London in 1992 and accounts of its effect on the Commercial Union Library[74] revitalised interest and emphasised the need for disaster plans to take into account electronically stored information as well as hard copy. Most recently, in the summer of 1994, the full impact of a major library disaster was felt in Britain. In August, Norwich Central Library was totally destroyed by fire. As the title of the report in the *Library Association Record*[75] ('Fire rekindles debate') ironically implies, library managers are now taking this aspect of preservation even more seriously. Courses and seminars have been hastily arranged and extremely well attended.[76] The British Library has acknowledged the urgency with which librarians are now viewing their chances of surviving disaster by having awarded a grant to support a survey in 1994–95, of disaster management in UK libraries with a view to producing guidelines, based on best practice.[77]

SECURITY

Security was added to the remit of the NPO in 1989. Since then, the NPO has been a focal point for action in this field. Why is security an aspect of preservation? A simple, and not entirely facetious, answer is that a library cannot preserve books if it no longer has them. Again, there was activity in Britain before this date, but nothing was fully formalised.[78] Until a survey undertaken in a cooperative venture between the NPO and the Home Office, the results of which were reported in 1992,[79] the number of books lost from British libraries could only be estimated or guessed. However, the rising price of books, cuts in bookfunds and an increase in managerial accountability led to growing concern for a more accurate picture of what was actually going on. The NPO/Home Office report painted a depressing picture:

> Overall, the book losses revealed by counts in the libraries surveyed reflect a national loss (though not necessarily a *replacement* cost) in excess of £150 million each year. This figure is 50% higher than previous estimates.[80]

And:

> Few libraries escape the deliberate mutilation of their book stock … Inevitably much goes undiscovered, but six out of ten libraries have cases come to their notice at least monthly.[81]

However in spite of this:

> there is little evidence that the control of theft and mutilation is universally viewed by library professionals as a valued objective. Only about one in five libraries has developed a security policy.[82]

SCONUL has been active in this field, organising, with the NPO, seminars in 1989 and 1990 on security in academic and research libraries.[83] UNESCO issued guidelines.[84] Two key articles in the professional literature assisted the debate in 1990[85] and 1991;[86] in 1990, the NPO produced a video on security matters;[87] it has also produced a bibliography,[88] and initiated a series of leaflets covering security guidelines, surveys, policy and criminal behaviour in libraries.[89] That security is not just concerned with theft of book stock, and indeed equipment such as computers and video recorders, but also with the theft of the personal belongings of staff and users, is clear from the broad coverage of these NPO leaflets. This is also reflected in a book on security with a British perspective, published in 1992,[90] which addresses key areas of the subject such as the law, designing out crime, preventative measures, and policy design and implementation.

SURVEYING THE COLLECTIONS

The literature reveals very clearly that most activity in this field has taken place in the United States, with several important surveys which are frequently cited.[91] Indeed, a chapter in Kenny contains references to ten sources of information, all of which, save one, are of North American origin.[92] Two surveys in the UK national libraries, the British Library,[93] and the National Library of Scotland,[94] were undertaken in the 1980s but full accounts of these were not published. The NPO's *Survival Kit*,[95] published in 1986, contained four pages on condition surveys, including advice on sampling. In 1988, UNESCO published a set of guidelines, *Methods of Evaluation to Determine the Preservation Needs in Libraries and Archives*.[96] The theme of the NPO's 1989 annual competition was collection surveys.[97] Since then, the literature reveals a survey undertaken at Trinity College Library, Dublin.[98] The apparent lack of activity in this area is somewhat surprising given these earlier promptings and the fact that a one-day survey workshop held in October 1992 was so well attended.[99] The most important development has probably been the survey carried out in Oxford libraries in 1993;[100] it will perhaps encourage activity elsewhere. Certainly the survey of monographs and periodicals at the British Library's Department of Humanities and Social Sciences gave cause for concern.[101] The sample survey of 5283 items, which aimed to indicate the general condition of bindings and paper strength of items published since 1850, revealed that 14.28 per cent had paper in poor condition. Given that an effective preservation policy has to be based on reliable needs assessment, which can also be used to justify cases for resources to turn policy into practice, it is perhaps surprising that more condition surveys have not taken place in British libraries, or that the results of those which may have taken place have not been more widely publicised.

STORAGE AND ENVIRONMENT, EXHIBITIONS AND LOANS

Poor environmental conditions (such as fluctuating or inappropriate temperature and humidity levels) and storage (for example, badly designed or badly located shelving) can accelerate the deterioration process in library materials of all kinds. Ratcliffe found that libraries' ability to monitor, and, even more, to control, the environment in which collections are housed, were poor.[102] From its inception, the NPO has provided guidance on environmental conditions and storage,[103] recently addressing the topic in a targeted manner through a seminar,[104] and a video cassette.[105] In 1989, the British Library published a revised edition of a popular standard text on the care of books.[106] Also in that year, a revised British Standard for the storage and exhibition of archival documents was published.[107] Guidance and recommended levels abound in the literature, both British and from elsewhere; they also cover many different kinds of material housed in libraries,[108] not only books.

AUDIOVISUAL MATERIALS

In the same way that the chapters on preservation in *British Librarianship and Information Work*[109] provide a concise overview of developments, so do the chapters on 'Audiovisual materials' in the same volumes.[110] Issues arising from the management of audiovisual archives are discussed in the literature throughout the period,[111] as are the more specific problems of preserving audiovisual materials,[112] some focusing on particular media.[113] The situation in the first half of the 1980s is concisely outlined in *British Librarianship and Information Work*,[114] where attention was drawn particularly to the fact that much had been written about the need for the preservation of audiovisual materials and a national policy for their retention.[115] The significance of legal deposit in achieving this is noted, but it is acknowledged that preservation had received greater attention. Reference was made to the activities of a Working Party of the British Records Association,[116] and those of various committees of the Library Association. The British Institute of Recorded Sound came under the British Library in 1983 and became the National Sound Archive; preservation of holdings is one of its highest priorities.[117]

The second half of the 1980s began with the publication of a British Library report on legal deposit.[118] *British Librarianship and Information Work* noted the increase in new formats and technologies,[119] and the fact that no one organisation can be responsible for the entire national audiovisual heritage. On the other hand, the establishment in 1986, by the British Library, of the National Archival Collections of Audiovisual Materials Forum provided a means for the 'exchange of information and views on how best to preserve the nation's audiovisual heritage, and to explore ways of working together towards achieving this'.[120] Accounts of subsequent developments have been published;[121] *Audiovisual Librarian: the multimedia information journal*, the journal of the Audiovisual Groups of Aslib and the Library Association, reflecting the interests and activities of members of the group, publishes relevant news items and articles, and provides details of publications appearing elsewhere through its regular 'Bibliographic update'.[122]

That there are guidelines and principles on the subject is emphasised in one of the preservation textbooks referred to earlier: 'Further information concerning the handling and storage of non-paper materials can be found in many places.'[123] While this is indeed true, the librarian with little specialist experience of working with such materials may need guidance, interpretation and advice, which is somewhat more difficult to find. The NPO has produced a leaflet in its *Guidelines* series on photographic conservation;[124] there is also a UNESCO publication of relevance to photographs.[125]

SUBSTITUTION

For some time now, the major medium of substitution has been microform, although newer digital technologies are beginning to show that they may be capable of challenging the predominance of microfilm in this area.[126] This is an area which continues to draw professional debate and about which much is written, which a glance through the pages of periodicals like *Audiovisual Librarian* and *Information Media and Technology*, amongst others, will quickly confirm. The NPO seminar, *Preservation and Technology*,[127] in 1988, also addressed the issue.

The NPO has published, jointly with Kodak, a booklet providing guidelines on the establishment of an archival microform programme, which concludes with a list of British standards on micrographics.[128] More recently, in October 1992, as part of the Mellon Microfilming Project,[129] the NPO held a conference, sponsored by Kodak Office Imaging, on preservation microfilming and microforms in libraries.[130] The Mellon Microfilming Project has had a major impact, especially since the filming of newspapers became eligible for grants. Guidance notes on the project, produced in collaboration with NEWSPLAN,[131] are available from the NPO as is a Project Manual.[132] One of the conditions of the grant is that records of film produced must be entered on the British Library's computer-based Register of Preservation Microforms. There is now a European Register of Microform Masters, regarded as a major instrument, by reducing wasteful duplication of master copies, for preservation policy implementation.[133]

DIGITAL TECHNOLOGY

Throughout the period under review, new technology in general, and the development of new electronic media for the storage and retrieval of information in particular, have impinged on preservation. Newer media, like the optical disc, offer possibilities as alternatives to traditional surrogates such as microfilm. On the other hand, these newer technologies have preservation problems of their own; their own durability is still unclear. This had been realised even before the current and apparently never-ending development of new formats.[134] Advantages and disadvantages are usefully summed up in an *IFLA Journal* special issue on 'Preservation and conservation',[135] and in a piece in *Library Conservation News*,[136] which concludes with the significant statement that:

> A preservation strategy for electronic-based information must tackle the problem of machine dependence and provide a 'future proof' path for conversion of data as technology changes. With an average hardware or equipment lifespan of five years and a life of around three years for the software, this is a formidable challenge.[137]

More recently, the growing application of electronic-based information together with advances in worldwide telecommunications, has added even greater complexity to this picture. 'Preservation' and 'access' are now frequently linked terms; the concept relates the ability to store information in electronic, digitised form and to transfer it around the world relatively simply and cheaply. In this way, some items are 'preserved' primarily to improve access to them, rather than to preserve them in the traditional sense. Those involved in preservation have not been slow to notice this.[138]

Another term which has attracted much attention by those looking for ways of adding to the array of measures available for the preservation of information is **digitization**:

> ... the transcription of '(data) into a digital form [i.e."representing data as a series of numerical values"] so that it can be directly processed by a computer.'[139] Smith adapts this to the library context, providing the following working definition: ... the converting of a printed page to digital electronic form through scanning to create an electronic page image suitable for computer storage, retrieval and transmission.[140]

It is a method of surrogacy, which facilitates the compact storage of a vast quantity of information as digital data. The surrogate can only be produced, interpreted, processed and, if desired, printed out, using appropriate software.[141]

It should be noted that it is not only the printed page that can be digitized; microforms also can be treated in this way. Digitized records can be enhanced and edited, thus improving access to the information contained in the original. Nontextual material can, of course, be digitized.[142] While much of the activity is taking place in the United States,[143] projects are also in progress in Britain,[144] and are beginning to address such problems as developing the technology into a reliable and affordable medium, and are identifying major issues such as standardisation and copyright. At the moment, the technology offers exciting opportunities, some specifically driven by preservation, others by increasing access to information with preservation as an additional benefit. This is reflected by one author prominent in the field, summarising the current situation concerning digitization in general:

> ... technological developments can be expected to overcome or, at least alleviate, many of the present constraints while increased user awareness of electronic systems will foster demand for imaging systems. The outlook is very promising although the time scale is difficult to predict.[145]

This is echoed, but in a more cautious manner, by the Head of Advanced Technology at the British Library:

> The lessons learned are that such a concept can be practically implemented but that it is more difficult than many coming to the topic from a more theoretical point of view might imagine.[146]

CONSERVATION

The journal *Library Review*, certainly acknowledged this aspect of the debate re-initiated by the Ratcliffe Report, and, in a most practical and realistic manner, in a special issue on conservation, which also, on reflection, appears to accurately capture the views held by many at that time outside the preservation lobby:

The most public aspect of the crisis in conservation in libraries today is provided by the concerns and appeals issuing from our great national collections ... But the problems exist for many other libraries also, particularly as in times of financial stringency librarians try to achieve the maximum life from their stocks and at a time when public interest in and demands for access to fragile historical materials are burgeoning. Small wonder that we devote much of this issue to the practical problems of and approaches to conservation in libraries.[147]

Conservators, paper restorers and archivists have, of course, not needed the urgings of Ratcliffe and others. Rather, librarians have come to realise that they can benefit from closer links with experts in these fields and it has been encouraging to note the slow but growing recognition of the need for this. Further interaction is needed; one method by which this has been partially achieved has been through the NPO seminars where speakers from different fields have been invited to make presentations and, indeed, through the attendance at these seminars by participants from diverse backgrounds, who often find the informal contact offered by the seminars useful. The NPO, through its *Library Conservation News*, disseminates to librarians information about activities and developments in conservation which they might miss through not having access to specialist journals. A random look at a few issues suffices to illustrate the point. The activities of the Conservation Unit of the Museums and Galleries Commission, for example, feature in several issues.[148] The Preservation and Conservation Group of the Society of Archivists provides an interesting and concise overview of the profession of conservation in the proceedings of a recent annual meeting,[149] in which reference was made to the role and activities of organisations such as the Society of Archivists, the United Kingdom Institute for Conservation and the Institue of Paper Conservation. As a source of information on conservation and related activities, the *Rare Books Newsletter*, the journal of the Rare Books Group of the Library Association, must not be overlooked. While much of its content is inevitably about conservation, in recent years it has included a regular section on preservation.

Although it is not as fashionable as other newer aspects of preservation, ordinary library binding continues to receive attention, if sparsely and irregularly. For example, at the beginning of this review period, a three-year experiment was in progress to test the lifespans of various types of library binding;[150] at the end of it, Clwyd Library and Information Service was undertaking a survey of the role of rebinding in modern stock management.[151] The project included a literature search of library and binding industry publications and, interestingly, but perhaps not surprisingly, this revealed a '... lack of reference in the professional literature'.[152] Another recent account of an attempt to establish the issue life of bookstock in a county library service, and the justification for rebinding, suggests that economic factors may be rekindling that debate.[153] The NPO has recently been actively assessing the demand for a British library binding standard and has been instrumental in the establishment of a UK Panel for ISO/TC46/SC10/WG4 which is drawing up a standard for publishers' bindings.[154] Concern about book-production quality has recently reached the pages of the national press.[155]

Another important aspect of this area is the large-scale treatment of documents. While microforming and digitization can save the content of a book, they do not preserve the book itself. Various mass treatments (among the better known are the Wei-T'O process, and its variants, the DEZ process and the Lithco-FMC process) have been developed to preserve both the book and its contents. Information on this has been published and reviewed throughout the period as research has progressed, or, indeed, run into difficulties. As can be seen from these accounts,[156] different methods have been developed in Europe and the United States. In Britain, in 1980, the British Library commissioned the University of Surrey's Chemistry Department to investigate a mass treatment for the de-acidification of bound books. A concise description of the method and how it has gradually progressed into a test programme with a commercial partner has recently been provided by Mirjam Foot, Director of Collections and Preservation at the British Library.[157] Developments are reported in *Library Conservation News*.[158] From the timescale of these projects, it is clear that we cannot yet judge whether these systems can be developed into safe and cost-effective treatments.

Another response to the problem of poor quality paper is to press for publishers to use 'permanent' paper.

> Modern research has developed bleached chemical wood pulp, which contains little lignin [a prime agent in causing paper to discolour and disintegrate], and has, subsequently introduced neutral synthetic sizes. Paper so manufactured and so treated will last for centuries. That is why acid-free paper is called 'permanent'.[159]

An international standard for permanent paper,[160] developed on the basis of the American Standard, ANSI Z39.48-1992,[161] has now been agreed.[162] However, the existence of standards is one thing; their implementation is another. In Britain, Her Majesty's Stationery Office (HMSO) decided in 1985 to take positive measures to use archival papers in the production of some HMSO publications. By 1990, it was estimated that about 30 per cent of HMSO's 9000 new titles a year were printed on archival paper.[163]

CONCLUSIONS

Can we now begin to assess developments in preservation in the last ten years? We have used a wide range of publications, from many sources and on many aspects of the topic. One immediate response is that if the Ratcliffe Report was instrumental in bringing about the establishment of the NPO, then that very Office, espoused by Ratcliffe, has indeed been influential, not least in raising awareness of preservation and preservation issues in Britain. How much further this has gone beyond awareness raising is more difficult to analyse. It is not easy to ascribe direct responsibilty for specific initiatives solely to Ratcliffe. Other factors and events, and many individuals and organisations both in Britain and abroad, had to have an important impact. Some of these may have been developed by originators who were not even aware of Ratcliffe, or driven rather by the general impetus initiated by Ratcliffe but carried forward by the NPO and others whom it may have influenced to greater or lesser degrees. It is appropriate to acknowledge Ratcliffe's role, in terms of the Report's general impact, as a facilitator and instigator. Developments have taken place since publication of the Report; some involve planned and coordinated activities. The present situation of preservation is very different from that of the early 1980s. We need to build on what has been achieved in the light of current and future circumstances. In 1985, the then Director of the Preservation Service at The British Library, David Clements, concluded a paper on the establishment and aims of the newly formed NPO, perhaps the key recommendation of Ratcliffe, thus:

> The office's role as information provider and focus is seen initially as an enabling and supporting role to initiatives within the UK but its establishment is however, only the first step towards a coordinated national programme, towards increased awareness and towards increased resources at all levels.[164]

In the last ten years, as we will show in the following chapters, preservation awareness in Britain has risen; there is little evidence of increased resources, other than in a few areas of activity, but recent developments, such as the initial meeting of UK Preservation Administrators,[165] instigated by the British Library, suggest that a coordinated national programme is now at last about to be given serious consideration.

NOTES

1. F.W. Ratcliffe with D. Patterson. *Preservation Policies and Conservation in British Libraries: Report of the Cambridge University Library Conservation Project* (Library and Information Research Report, 25). London: The British Library, 1984.
2. See above, p. ix.
3. For a brief account of the historical background to the modern preservation impetus, much of which has been influenced by activities in the United States, see John Feather. *Preservation and the Management of Library Collections*. London: The Library Association, 1991, pp. 2–9. For instance, Feather mentions two reports from the 1930s, one from each side of the Atlantic, concerned with poor quality paper: The Library Association. *The Durability of Paper*. London: The Library Association, 1930; and T.D. Jarrell, ed. *Deterioration of Book and Record Paper*. Washington, D.C.; Department of Agriculture, 1936; he also notes worldwide factors which have affected preservation activity. An interesting overview of the period when current preservation problems were being created is provided in: Barbara Buckner Higginbotham. *Our Past Preserved: A History of American Library Preservation 1876–1910*. Boston, Mass.: G.K. Hall and Co., 1990. Books dealing with the practical aspects of preservation, such as: Harry Miller Lydenberg and John Archer. *The Care and Repair of Books*. New York: Bowker, 1931, and Eric A. Clough. *Bookbinding for Librarians*. London: Association of Assistant Librarians, 1957, have appeared at irregular intervals over the years.

4. Diana Grimwood-Jones. Preservation. In: David W. Bromley and Angela M. Allott eds., *British Librarianship and Information Work 1981–1985*, 2 vols., London: Library Association, 1987, vol. 2, pp. 270–284. (Diana Grimwood-Jones was National Preservation Officer, National Preservation Office, The British Library, during this period.)

5. Ratcliffe, op. cit., p. 270.

6. Marie Jackson. Preservation. In: David W. Bromley and Angela M. Allott eds., *British Librarianship and Information Work 1986–1990*, 2 vols., London: Library Association, 1993, vol. 2, pp. 275–283. (Marie Jackson was National Preservation Officer, National Preservation Office, The British Library, at the end of this period.)

7. Ibid., p. 275.

8. Maurice Line, Graham Mackenzie and Ray Prytherch, eds. *Librarianship and Information Worldwide 1991: an International Survey*. London: Bowker-Saur, 1991.

9. Peter Fox. Preservation. In: Maurice Line, Graham Mackenzie and John Feather, eds. *Librarianship and Information Worldwide 1994: an Annual Survey*. London: Bowker-Saur, pp. 183–202.

10. F.W. Ratcliffe. Preservation: a decade of progress. *Library Review*, 26: 4 (1994), pp. 228–36; and F.W. Ratcliffe. Stopping the rot: a decade of preservation progress. *Library Conservation News*. 44 (1994), pp. 1–3.

11. Brenda E. Moon and Anthony J. Loveday. Progress report on preservation in British universities since the Ratcliffe Report. In: National Preservation Office. *Preservation and Technology. Proceedings of a Seminar at York University 20–21 July 1988* (National Preservation Office seminar paper 3). London: The British Library, 1989, pp. 11–17.

12. See for example, Graham Matthews. Preservation literature review. *Cablis,* 21 (1990), pp. 12–14; Graham Matthews. The literature of preservation: 80s review/90s preview. In: National Preservation Office. *Preservation and Publication. Proceedings of a Seminar at York University 17–18 July 1990* (National Preservation Office seminar paper, 5). London: The British Library, 1991, pp. 9–19.

13. Feather, op. cit.

14. Ibid., pp. 97–109.

15. Ross Harvey. *Preservation in Libraries: Principles, strategies and practices for librarians*. London: Bowker-Saur, 1993.

16. Geraldine Kenny, ed. *A Reading Guide to the Preservation of Library Collections*. London: Library Association Publishing, 1991.

17. Ibid., pp. 1–12.

18. See below, pp. 168–70.

19. Ratcliffe, op. cit., pp. 73–5.

20. Ibid., p. 74.

21. Ibid., p. 73. Interestingly, 'preservation' is now in the title of the recently devised Canadian strategy: The Advisory Committee on a Strategy of Preservation in Canadian Libraries. *A National Strategy for Preservation in Canadian Libraries*. Ottawa: National Library of Canada, 1992.

22. Ratcliffe, op. cit., p. 76.

23. J.M. Dureau and D.W.G. Clements. *Principles for the Preservation and Conservation of Library Materials* (IFLA professional reports 8). The Hague: IFLA, 1986.

24. Ibid., p. 2.

25. National Preservation Office. *Glossary* (Preservation policies). London: The National Preservation Office, 1992.

26. Ibid., p. 9.

27. Ibid., p. 5.

28. Feather, op. cit., p. 2.

29. Harvey, op. cit., p. 5.

30. Mirjam Foot. Interviewed by Edward Simpson. *Paper Conservation News*, 70 (1994), p. 2.

31. NPO, *Glossary*, p. 9.

32. Jackson, op. cit., p. 275.

33. See Appendix 1, below, pp. 157–63.

34. See below, pp. 28-30.
35. David W.G. Clements. The National Preservation Office in The British Library. *IFLA Journal*, 12: 1 (1986), p. 25.
36. Ibid., p. 25.
37. *Conservation in Crisis: Proceedings of a Seminar at Loughborough University of Technology, 16–17 July 1986* (National Preservation Office seminar papers, 1). London: National Preservation Office, British Library, 1986; *Conservation and Collection Management: Proceedings of a Seminar at Loughborough University of Technology, 22–23 July 1987* (National Preservation Office seminar papers, 2). London: National Preservation Office, British Library, 1988; *Preservation and Technology: Proceedings of a Seminar at York University, 20–21 July 1988* (National Preservation Office seminar papers, 3). London: National Preservation Office, British Library, 1989; *Preservation Policies: the Choices: Proceedings of a Seminar at York University, 28–29 June 1989* (National Preservation Office seminar papers, 4). London: National Preservation Office, British Library, 1990; *Preservation and Publication: Proceedings of a Seminar at York University, 17–18 July 1990* (National Preservation Office seminar papers, 5). London: National Preservation Office, British Library, 1991; *Microforms in Libraries: the Untapped Resource?* Papers given at the National Preservation Office conference held 13–15 October 1992 in Birmingham, organised by the British Library National Preservation Office as part of the Mellon Microfilming Project, sponsored by Kodak Office Imaging. London: National Preservation Office, 1993; *Housing our Collections: Environment and Storage for Libraries and Archives.* Papers given at the National Preservation Office conference held at the Wellcome Trust, London, 1–2 December 1993. London: National Preservation Office, 1995. (In preparation).
38. Ratcliffe, op. cit., p. 3.
39. One of us made proposals for incorporating conservation education into the curriculum at the dissemination seminar for the Ratcliffe report. John Feather. Conservation education for professional librarians: a library school view. In: Ratcliffe, op. cit., pp. 114–18; and see, for example, P. Havard-Williams. Library and information studies. *Journal of Librarianship*, 17: 2 (1985) pp. 100–5; and D.W.G. Clements. Preservation and the library school education programmes. *Library Association Record*, 88: 3 (1986), pp. 136–7.
40. John Feather and Anne Lusher. *The Teaching of Conservation in LIS Schools in Great Britain* (British Library Research Paper 49). London: British Library Research and Development Department, 1988.
41. Ibid., p. 31.
42. J. Connor and E. Bowen. A tale from two cities. *Assistant Librarian*, 86: 5 (1993), pp. 77–8
43. John Feather. *Guidelines for the Teaching of Preservation to Librarians, Archivists and Documentalists for a Joint Working Party of IFLA's sections on Conservation and Education and Training.* The Hague: IFLA (IFLA Professional Reports, 18), 1990.
44. Y.P. Kathpalia. *A Model Curriculum for the Training of Specialists in Document Preservation and Restoration: a RAMP Study with Guidelines.* Paris: UNESCO (PGI-84/WS/2), 1984.
45. Michele Valerie Cloonan. *Global Perspectives on Preservation Education* (IFLA publications 69). Munich: K.G. Saur, 1994.
46. John Feather. Staff training for preservation. *Library Management* 11: 4 (1989), pp. 10–14.
47. Education Panel, National Preservation Advisory Committee, in association with National Preservation Office, The British Library. *Preservation: a Training Pack for Library Staff.* London: National Preservation Office, The British Library, 1994. The report was informally launched at a course entitled, Their Life in Your Hands: Collection Care Training Strategies, organised by The Library Association in association with The National Preservation Office, held at the Library Association, on 8 February 1995.
48. For example, *Preservation and the Librarian*: a one-day course organised jointly by the National Preservation Office and the Library Association, 9 December 1987, the Library Association, London; *Preservation Administration*: a one-day seminar organised by the Library Association and sponsored by Dunn and Wilson and B. Riley and Co. Ltd, 27 April 1988, Manchester Polytechnic; *Take Care: the Conservation of Audiovisual Material.* One-day course organised by the Library Association and the Audiovisual Group of the Library Association, 7 December

1988, The Library Association, London; *Disaster Control Planning for Libraries*. Institute of Information Scientists, Northern Branch. Seminar, 16 October 1991, University of Leeds.

49. Helen Forde. *The Education of Staff and Users for the Proper Handling and Care of Archival Materials: a RAMP Study with Guidelines [for the] General Programme and UNISIST*. Paris: UNESCO (PGI-91/WS/17), 1991. See also below, pp. 115–16.

50. J.M. Dureau and D.W.G. Clements. *Principles for the Preservation and Conservation of Library Materials* (IFLA Professional Reports, 8). The Hague: International Federation of Library Associations and Institutions, 1986. Cited as *IFLA Principles*.

51. Patricia Chapman. *Guidelines on Preservation and Conservation Policies in Libraries and Archives*. Paris: UNESCO (PGI-90/WS/7), 1990. Cited as UNESCO *Guidelines*.

52. John Feather. National and international policies for preservation. *International Library Review*, 22: 4 (1990), pp. 315–27.

53. We are grateful to Gillian Pentelow, formerly Secretary, Standing Conference of National and University Libraries, for access to minutes of SCONUL Working Party on Preservation.

54. R.E. Palmer, ed. *Preserving the Word: the Library Association Conference Proceedings, Harrogate, 1986*. London: The Library Association, 1987.

55. The *Guidelines* document is a photographic reproduction of the IFLA document, with the joint imprint of the two organisations.

56. Patricia Chapman. A prize for policy. *Library Conservation News*, 20 (1988), p. 1.

57. Christine Goodair and Christopher Jackson. Developing a preservation policy for the Children's Society. *Library Association Record*, 90: 10 (1988), pp. 570–2.

58. National Preservation Office. *Preservation Policies: the Choices*. London: The British Library, 1990.

59. Brian Enright, Lotte Hellinga and Beryl Leigh. *Selection for Survival. A Review of Acquisition and Retention Policies*. London: The British Library, 1989. For further discussion, see below, pp. 29, 140.

60. National Preservation Office. *Preservation Guidelines*. London: National Preservation Office, 1991. Cited as *NPO Guidelines*.

61. For a fuller discussion, see below, p. 98.

62. See, for example, Sherelyn Ogden. The impact of the Florence flood on library conservation in the United States of America. A study of the literature published 1956–1976. *Restaurator*, 3: 1/2 (1979), pp. 1–36; Peter Waters. The Florence flood of 1966 revisited. In: Palmer, op. cit., pp. 113–28.

63. John E. McIntyre. Disaster planning: a national concern. *Alexandria*, 2: 2 (1990), pp. 54–5.

64. Hazel Anderson and John E. McIntyre. *Planning Manual for Disaster Control in Scottish Libraries and Record Offices*. Edinburgh: National Library of Scotland, 1985.

65. Including, for example, John McIntyre. Disaster control planning. *Serials*, 1: 2 (1988), pp. 42–6; John McIntyre. Action planning for disaster. *Refer*, 5: 4 (1989), pp. 1–7; John E. McIntyre. Disaster planning: a national concern. *Alexandria*, 2: 2 (1990), pp. 51–60.

66. Ian Tregarthen Jenkin. *Disaster Control Planning and Preparedness: an Outline Disaster Control Plan*. London: British Library, 1987.

67. Sally A. Buchanan. *Disaster Planning, Preparedness and Recovery for Libraries and Archives: a RAMP Study with Guidelines*. Paris: UNESCO (PGI-88/WS/6), 1988.

68. National Preservation Office/Riley Dunn and Wilson. *Keeping our Words. The 1988 National Preservation Office Competition. [Disaster Control Planning]*. London: The British Library, 1989.

69. National Preservation Office. *If Disaster Strikes!* London: National Preservation Office, British Library, 1988. (Video cassette.)

70. Paul Eden, John Feather and Graham Matthews. Preservation policies and conservation in British academic libraries in 1993: a survey. *British Journal of Academic Librarianship*. 8: 2 (1993), pp. 71–2. See also below, pp. 54–5.

71. R. Butler. The Los Angeles Central Library fire. *Conservation Administration News*, 27 (1986), pp. 1–2, 23–4.

72. Graham Matthews. Fire and water: damage at the USSR Academy of Sciences Library, Leningrad. *Library Association Record*, 90: 5 (1988), pp. 279–81.

73. See, for example, Art Plotnik. $18 million LAPL fire: salvaged hopes. *American Libraries*, 17: 6

(1986), pp. 384–6; J. Morris. Los Angeles Library fire – learning the hard way. *Canadian Library Journal*, 44: 4 (1987), pp. 217–21; Tom Watson. Out of the ashes: the Los Angeles Public Library. *Wilson Library Bulletin*, 64: 4 (1989), pp. 34–8. Carolyn Hoover Sung, Valery Pavlovich Leonov and Peter Waters. Fire recovery at the Library of the Academy of Sciences of the USSR. *American Archivist*, 53: 2 (1990), pp. 298–312; Valery Leonov. Vekstremalnikh usloviakh. *Bibliotekar,* 1 (1991), pp. 9–13. V. Uporova. Vistoyali … vmesto poslesloviya. *Bibliotekar,* 1 (1991), pp. 13–16.

74. See, for example, Margaret Saunders. How a library picked up the pieces after IRA blast. *Library Association Record*, 95: 2 (1993), pp. 100–1.

75. Fire rekindles debate. *Library Association Record*, 96: 9 (1994), p. 69.

76. See, for example, Hampshire Archives Trust in conjunction with Hampshire County Council and the Library Association. *Planning for Disasters in Archives, Libraries and Museums: Expecting the Unexpected!* Day conference, 4 November 1994, Portsmouth Central Library; *Disaster Management*: a one-day seminar for archivists and librarians, 18 January 1995, Norwich.

77. The British Library has awarded a grant to one of us (G.M.), through Loughborough University, to undertake a survey of disaster management in British libraries. It will run from March 1995 to March 1996. See Graham Matthews and Paul Eden. Heading off disaster. *Library Association Record*, 97 (1995), p. 271.

78. See, for example, Don Revill. Library security. *New Library World*, 79, (1978), pp. 75–7; Alan Jay Lincoln and Carol Zall Lincoln. Library crime in Great Britain. *Library and Archival Security*, 8: 1/2 (1986), pp. 19–58; Herbert C. Keele. *Preventing Library Book Theft*. Ipswich: Access Keeleway, 1987.

79. John Burrows and Diane Cooper. *Theft and Loss from UK Libraries: a National Survey* (Police Research Group Crime Prevention Unit Series paper 37). London: Home Office Police Department, 1992.

80. Ibid., p. 45.

81. Ibid., p. 45.

82. Ibid., p. 47.

83. A.G. Quinsee and A.C. McDonald. *Security in Academic and Research Libraries*. London: National Preservation Office, 1990.

84. D.L. Thomas. *Study on Control of Security and Storage of Holdings: a RAMP Study with Guidelines*. Paris: UNESCO, (PGI-86/WS/23), 1987.

85. Marie Jackson. Please can we have our books back? *Library Association Record,* 92: 5 (1990), pp. 359–63.

86. Marie Jackson. Library security: facts and figures. *Library Association Record*, 93: 6 (1991), pp. 380, 382, 384.

87. National Preservation Office. *Library Security: Who Cares?* London: National Preservation Office, 1990. (Video cassette.)

88. National Preservation Office. *Security Bibliography*. London: National Preservation Office (1991).

89. National Preservation Office. *Security Guidelines*. London: National Preservation Office (1992); National Preservation Office. *Carrying out a Library Security Survey and Drafting a Security Policy* (Security matters, 1). London: National Preservation Office, 1992; National Preservation Office. *How to Deal with Criminal and Anti-social Behaviour* (Security matters, 2). London: National Preservation Office, 1994; a third leaflet in the series, *Designing Out Crime*, is in preparation.

90. Michael Chaney and Alan F. MacDougall. *Security and Crime Prevention in Libraries*. Aldershot: Ashton Gate, 1992.

91. See, for example, Randall Bond *et al*. Preservation study at the Syracuse University Libraries. *College and Research Libraries*, 4: 2 (1987), pp. 132–47; Sarah Buchanan and Sandra Coleman. Deterioration survey of the Stanford University Libraries Green Library Stack Collection. In: Darling, Pamela W., ed. *Preservation Planning Program: Resource Notebook*. Washington, D.C., Association of Research Libraries, Office of Management Studies, 1982, pp. 159–61; Gay Walker. The Yale survey: a large-scale study of book deterioration in the Yale University Library. *College and Research Libraries*, 46: 2 (1985), pp. 111–32.

92. Eiluned Rees and Julian Thomas. Surveying the collections. In: Kenny, G., ed. *A Reading Guide to the Preservation of Library Collections*. London: Library Association Publishing, 1991, pp. 23–9.

93. Michael Pollock. Surveying the collections. *Library Conservation News*, 21 (1988), pp. 4–6; Edmund King. Surveying the printed book collections of the British Library. *Library Management*, 11: 4 (1990), pp. 15–19.

94. Hazel Anderson. *National Library of Scotland: Report on a Book Condition Survey June 1985 – March 1986*. Edinburgh: National Library of Scotland, 1986. (Internal circulation.)

95. National Preservation Office. *Survival Kit*. London: National Preservation Office, 1986.

96. George M. Cunha. *Methods of Evaluation to Determine the Preservation Needs in Libraries and Archives: a RAMP Study with Guidelines*. Paris: UNESCO (PGI-88/WS/16), 1988.

97. National Preservation Office/Riley Dunn and Wilson. *Keeping Our Words. The 1989 National Preservation Office Competition [Surveying of Collections]*. London: National Preservation Office, 1990.

98. Paul Sheehan. A condition survey of books in Trinity College Library Dublin. *Libri*, 40: 4 (1990), pp. 306–17.

99. IPC workshop: books, archives and art on paper. *Paper Conservation News*, 64 (1992), pp. 12–13.

100. See, for example, Bronwyn Evans. The Duke Humfrey's Library project: using an item-by-item survey to develop a conservation programme. *The Paper Conservator*, 17 (1993), pp. 39–44; Katherine Swift. The Oxford preservation survey. 1: The main survey. *The Paper Conservator*, 17 (1993), pp. 45–52; N. Bell. The Oxford preservation survey. 2: A method for surveying archives. *The Paper Conservator,* 17 (1993), pp. 53–5. We are also grateful to Giles Barber for sight of Libraries Board Preservation Committee. *Preservation Report. Part 1: Report on the Extent and Condition of Oxford Library Holdings*. Oxford: Libraries Board Preservation Committee, 1994 (internal document).

101. King, op. cit.

102. Ratcliffe, op. cit., pp. 21–2.

103. Moving from general guidelines, it has achieved this in recent years through *Preservation policies*, a series of leaflets on topics such as mould, boxing and encapsulation.

104. *Housing our Collections: Environment and Storage for Libraries and Archives*. Papers given at the National Preservation Office conference held at the Wellcome Trust, London, 1–2 December 1993. London: National Preservation Office, 1995. (In preparation.)

105. *Controlling your Environment*. London: National Preservation Office, 1992. (Video cassette.)

106. A.D. Baynes-Cope. *Caring for Books and Documents*, 2nd edn. London: The British Library, 1989.

107. British Standards Institution. *Recommendations for the Storage and Exhibition of Archival Documents*. London: British Standards Institution (BS5454:1989), 1989.

108. For illustrative examples of this, see Robert F. Child. Storage and environment. In: Geraldine Kenny, ed. *A Reading Guide to the Preservation of Library Collections*. London: Library Association, 1991, pp. 31–7. See also below, pp. 64–8, 103–4.

109. Grimwood-Jones; Jackson, Preservation, op. cit.

110. Catherine F. Pinion. Audiovisual materials. In: David W. Bromley and Angela M. Allott, eds. *British Librarianship and Information Work 1981–1985*, 2 vols. London: Library Association, 1987, vol. 2, pp. 142–55; and Catherine F. Pinion. Audiovisual materials. In: David W. Bromley and Angela M. Allott, eds. *British Librarianship and Information Work 1986–1990*, 2 vols. London: Library Association, 1993, vol. 2, pp. 158–69.

111. See, for example, Helen P. Harrison. Conservation of library materials: a progress report. Library and Information Services Council (UK) and Office of Arts and Libraries (UK) and Library and Information Services Council Seminar on Conservation. *Audiovisual Librarian*, 9: 4 (1983), pp. 197–9, (attention is drawn in this article to Ratcliffe's research); Helen P. Harrison. Audiovisual archives. *Audiovisual Librarian*, 12: 3 (1986), pp. 133–41.

112. See, for example, Helen P. Harrison. Conservation and audiovisual materials. *Audiovisual Librarian,* 13: 3 (1987), pp. 177–8; Helen P. Harrison. Conservation and preservation of audiovisual materials: realistic or a dream? *IFLA Journal*, 18: 3 (1992), pp. 212–22.

113. See, for example, Klaus B. Hendricks. *The Preservation and Restoration of Photographic*

Materials in Archives and Libraries. Paris: UNESCO (PGI-84/WS/1), 1984; Helen Harrison. Moving images: preservation and access. *Audiovisual Librarian,* 14: 3 (1988), pp. 159–60; C. Cochrane. An overview of trends in the collection and use of moving images in the United Kingdom. *Journal of Documentation,* 49: 3 (1993), pp. 278–91.

114. Pinion, Audiovisual materials ... 1981–1985, op. cit. (See note 110 above.)

115. Margaret Mann. *Archival Problems of Audiovisual Materials: a Selected Annotated Bibliography.* Sheffield: University of Sheffield, 1982; Anthony Hugh Thompson. *Storage, Handling and Preservation of Audiovisual Materials.* Nederlands Bibliotheek en Lektuur Centrum, on behalf of IFLA Round Table on Audiovisual Media, 1983.

116. British Records Association. *Report to the Council of the Working Party on Audiovisual Archives.* London: British Records Association, 1983; and in *Archives,* 16 (1983), pp. 185–95.

117. Jeremy Silver and Lloyd Stickells. Preserving sound recordings at the British Library National Sound Archive. *Library Conservation News,* 13 (1986), pp. 1–3.

118. Catherine F. Pinion. *Legal Deposit of Non-book Materials* (Library and Information Research Report 49). London: The British Library, 1986.

119. Pinion, Audiovisual materials ... 1986–1990, op. cit., p. 158.

120. Ibid., p. 157.

121. Catherine F. Pinion. Preserving our audiovisual heritage: a national and international challenge. *Alexandria,* 4: 3 (1992), pp. 155–67; this is updated in Catherine F. Pinion. Preserving our audio-visual heritage: a national and international challenge. *Audiovisual Librarian,* 19: 3 (1993), pp. 205–19; see also, Helen P. Harrison, ed. *Audiovisual Archive Literature: a Select Bibliography.* Paris: UNESCO (PGI192/WS/2), 1992.

122. For instance, *Stop the Rot: Practical AV Preservation for Small Collections.* Motherwell: AVSCOT, 1993, is mentioned in Bibliographic update, *Audiovisual Librarian,* 21: 1 (1995), p. 31.

123. Harvey, op. cit., p. 99.

124. National Preservation Office. *Photographic Conservation.* London: National Preservation Office, n.d. [1989].

125. K.B. Hendricks. *The Preservation and Restoration of Photographic Materials in Archives and Libraries.* Paris: UNESCO (PGI-84/WS/1), 1984.

126. John Feather. The preservation of information: principles and practice of format conversion. *Library Review,* 40: 6 (1991), pp. 7–12. See also below, pp. 83–4.

127. National Preservation Office. *Preservation and Technology* (National Preservation Office Seminar Papers, 3). London: The British Library, 1989.

128. *Preservation Microforms.* London: National Preservation Office and Kodak Ltd, 1989.

129. For a brief outline of the Mellon Microfilming project and its application in one library, see Toby Kirtley, Setting up a preservation microfilming programme. *Library Conservation News,* 36 (1992), pp. 1–2. See also below, pp. 83–4.

130. National Preservation Office. *Microforms in Libraries: the Untapped Resource.* London: National Preservation Office, 1993.

131. See below, pp. 83–4.

132. National Preservation Office. *Mellon Microfilming Project Manual.* London: Mellon Micro-filming Project, National Preservation Office, 1992.

133. John Feather and Giuseppe Vitiello. The European Register of Microform Masters: a new biblio-graphical tool. *Journal of Librarianship and Information Science* 23: 4 (1991), pp. 171–82.

134. See, for example, Bernard J.S. Williams. Implications for preservation of newer information media. *Information Media and Technology,* 19: 1 (1985/1986), pp. 13–15, and Michael William Day. *Preservation Problems of Electronic Text and Data* (East Midlands Branch of the Library Association Occasional Papers No. 3). Loughborough: EMBLA, 1990.

135. George Boston. New technology – friend or foe? *IFLA Journal,* 20: 3 (1994), pp. 331–7.

136. George Mackenzie. Preservation of electronic media. *Library Conservation News,* 38 (1993), pp. 1–3, 7.

137. Ibid., p. 7.

138. Patricia Battin. From preservation to access: paradigm for the nineties. *IFLA Journal,* 19: 4 (1993), pp. 368–73.

139. *Collins Dictionary of the English Language,* 2nd edn., 1986, revised 1989, p. 340.

140. Geoff Smith. Digitization of newspapers – capabilities and limitations. In: *Current Perspectives on Newspaper Preservation and Access: Report of the 2nd National NEWSPLAN Conference, Durham, 7–8 March, 1994*. Newcastle-upon-Tyne: Information North for NEWSPLAN, 1994, p. 54.

141. Clare Ashley-Smith. Digitization and the Preservation of Library Materials. M.A. dissertation, Loughborough University, 1994, p. 24. We are grateful to Ms. Ashley-Smith for allowing us to make extensive use of her very valuable work.

142. Jennifer Hogarth and Graham Martin. Non-textual archives material and document image processing: results of a survey. *Journal of the Society of Archivists*, 15: 1 (1994), pp. 27–38.

143. For a general overview, see Anne R. Kenney and Lynne K. Personius. The future of digital preservation. *Advances in Preservation and Access*, 1 (1992), pp. 195-212.

144. See, for example, Richard Gartner. Digitizing the Bodleian? *Audiovisual Librarian*, 19: 3 (1993), pp. 220–3; Mark Greengrass. Interfacing Samuel Hartlib. *History Today*, 43: 12 (1993), pp. 45–9; Andrew Prescott. Beowulf on the Superhighway. *Initiatives for Access News* [British Library], 1 (1994), pp. 4–5; Phil Barden. The British Library Image Demonstrator Project. *Information Management and Technology*, 27: 5 (1994), pp. 214–15; Arthur Shiel and Roger Broadhurst. *Library Material Digitisation Demonstrator Project* (Library and Information Research Report 94). London: British Library, 1994; The British Library has also published a guide (loose-leaf for updating) to sources of digital information, which describes over 200 such sources: Marc Fresko. *Sources of Digital Information* (British Library Research and Development Report 6102). London: The British Library, 1994. *Information Management and Technology* (the journal of Cimtech and UKAIIM) regularly includes news items and articles on digitization and its applications.

145. Roger Broadhurst. *The Digitization of Library Material* (Library and Information Briefings, 39). London: Library Information Technology Centre, 1993.

146. Phil Barden. The British Library Image Demonstrator Project. *Information Management and Technology*, 27: 5 (1994), p. 215.

147. Stuart James. Editorial. *Library Review*, 36: 3 (1987), p. 162. The 'Conservation' papers in this issue as can be seen from the following details are indeed representative of conservation activity in different types of library: Robin J. Davis, Laboratory in the library: archival conservation in Stirling University Library, pp. 174–8; Ann Matheson, Scottish newspapers, pp. 179–85; Teresa Januszonok, the role of the Conservation Unit within Sheffield City Libraries; Stuart James, Restoration and conservation of the Wanlockhead Miners' Library, pp. 191–4; there is also an appropriate article on paper: D.J. Priest, Paper and its problems, pp. 164–73.

148. David Leigh. A focus for conservation. *Library Conservation News*, 22 (1989), pp. 1–3; The Conservation Register. *Library Conservation News*, 27 (1990), pp. 3, 6; Peter Winsor. The Conservation Information Network. *Library Conservation News*, 31 (1991), pp. 1–3, 6.

149. C.S. Woods, ed. *Conservation for the Future. Proceedings of the 1993 Annual Instructional Meeting hosted by Dorset County Archives Service*. Society of Archivists, Preservation and Conservation Group, 1994. Section 4 Conservation – the profession contains the following: Patrick Cleary. The Society and conservation, pp. 50–3; Mark Norman. The accreditation and representation of conservators, pp. 54–8; Chris Woods. Conservators and the Society of Archivists: survey report, pp. 59–62.

150. John Turner. Binding arbitration. A comparison of the durability of various hardback and paperback bindings. *Library Association Record*, 88: 5 (1986), pp. 233–5.

151. Alan Watkin. Library rebinding and public library stock management. *Public Library Journal*, 8: 2 (1993), pp. 42–6.

152. Watkin, loc. cit., p. 46.

153. Ian Matthews. The issue life of bookstock. *Public Library Journal*, 9: 5 (1994) pp. 123–5.

154. NPO news. *Library Conservation News*, 44 (1994), p. 3.

155. Jim McCue and Dalya Albereg. Publishers of crumbling hardbacks are told to turn over a new leaf. *The Times*, 31 December 1994, p. 1.

156. See, for example, Harvey, op. cit., pp. 194–9, which provides a brief review of methods and activity, with further references; Anne Lienardy, A bibliographical survey of mass de-acidification methods. *Restaurator*, 12: 2 (1991), pp. 75–103; Anthony Pacey, Canadian libraries and mass de-acidification. *Canadian Library Journal*, 49: 2 (1992), pp. 115–21; Thorarinn Stefansson and Kari

Christensen. Mass conservation of paper: a comparison of methods. *Alexandria*, 5: 2 (1993), pp. 119–26; P. Vallas. Mass de-acidification at the Bibliothèque Nationale (Sable-sur-Sarthe Center): assessment after two years of operation (late 1992). *Restaurator*, 14: 1 (1993), pp. 1–10; R.S. Wedinger, The FMC mass preservation system: enhancement and extension of useful life. *Restaurator*, 14: 7 (1993), pp. 102–22.

157.   Mirjam Foot. Aspects of mass conservation. *IFLA Journal*, 20: 30 (1994), pp. 321–30. This article also presents a concise overview of the different methods and their application.

158.   See, for example, *Library Conservation News*, 43 (1994), p. 3. News items in this issue report the closure in the United States of the Akzo Chemicals Inc. mass de-acidification plant; the development of other processes, such as Preservation Technologies' Bookkeeper System; the construction of a mass de-acidification plant in Germany, a joint venture between the Deutsche Bibliothek and Battelle Ingenieurtechnik GmbH; and progress on the British Library's joint venture with the Canadian company, Nordion.

159.   *Permanent Paper*. London: The Library Association, The National Preservation Office, The Publishers Association, 1986.

160.   ISO 9706:1994. *Information and Documentation – Paper for Documents – Requirements for Permanence*.

161.   ANSI/NISO Z39.48-1992. *American National Standard for Permanence of Paper for Publications and Documents in Libraries and Archives*.

162.   International standard for permanent paper accepted. *Library Conservation News*, 41/42 (1993/94), p. 1.

163.   Bob Barnard. The way ahead. *Library Conservation News*, 26 (1990), pp. 1, 7–8.

164.   Clements, op. cit., p. 32.

165.   One of us (J.F.) was present at the meeting.

2 Perceptions of preservation

The most persistent themes of the Ratcliffe Report were that librarians were generally ignorant of preservation policy issues, or that they underestimated the importance of them. Many of the key recommendations were intended to remedy that alleged ignorance, and the term 'awareness-raising' became a familiar one in journals, meetings and professional discussions on the subject. The National Preservation Advisory Committee, at its first meeting in November 1984, identified the need to increase awareness of preservation issues as one of its first priorities, and began to devise strategies towards that end.[1] These included suggestions for leaflets and the development of educational and training materials. At almost all subsequent meetings during the next four or five years, similar issues were raised, and gradually expanded into the sponsorship of seminars, publications, support for externally funded research and other activities, many of which have been discussed in Chapter 1.

How far have these efforts been successful? Do British librarians of the mid-1990s have a greater understanding or more positive perception of preservation than did their predecessors of a decade or more ago? The opportunities for learning have been provided, but have they been used or indeed useful? These are some of the questions which we address in this chapter. Our answers are based upon parts of the data which we gathered in response to our questionnaire, but not in a crude statistical sense. Perception and understanding does not always lend itself to statistical analysis. We can interpret the factual data which we have collected, and have not hesitated to do so; but, in reaching our conclusions, we have also to take into account the opinions (sometimes trenchant and often highly personal) of our respondents, as well as the unintended revelations of knowledge and attitudes which we have sometimes detected. In this way, we can attempt to build up a picture of how (or perhaps whether) preservation plays a part in our professional thinking.

PRESERVATION: PRACTICAL DEFINITIONS

In Chapter 1,[2] we quoted a number of published definitions of key terms. The essential element in all of them is that of time, the concept that because all the media of information storage have a limited (even if long) lifespan, there is a need to plan to ensure that their useful life is maximised in the context of the overall objectives of the holding institution. Preservation can therefore be argued to be an aspect of general stock management, rather than concerned only with the management of just a part of the stock. Implicitly, this is accepted by many librarians, but perhaps not always fully understood. The perceptions of practitioners differ from the formal definitions offered by academics and researchers. Emphases can be determined by individual circumstances as much as by general professional considerations.

One university librarian commented to us that:

> … our policy really does differ fundamentally as between policy towards special collections and policy towards the rest of the stock.

The librarian of a medium-size college took a similar view:

> I have answered most of these questions as for the [special collections]. The conditions in the general college library, which contains more modern materials … are totally different.

These are not untypical of academic librarians in a wide variety of institutions; there is some limited recognition that perhaps there *ought* to be a general policy for the physical management and maintenance of stock, but, in general, such policies have been developed in terms of rare books, special collections and archival materials, which are seen as the priority. In many cases, indeed, preservation is understood to be relevant only in the context of such collections and materials.

In public libraries, this narrower understanding of the relevance of preservation is particularly noticeable. In general, preservation is seen as an issue for the managers of special collections (the vast majority of them, of course, primarily of local or regional materials) rather than for the system as a whole.[3] Public library priorities are different; one shire county told us that it:

> … does not, as a general policy, have a commitment to the archival aspects of libraries …

Another wrote that:

> We don't really have many items of an 'archival' nature or lending themselves to conservation …

The Chief Librarian of a metropolitan authority said:

> I believe stock disposal is a far more serious problem than conservation/preservation.

Such opinions and policies certainly accord with those famously (perhaps even notoriously) expressed in the lion's den of a National Preservation Office Seminar in 1987, when the County Librarian of Avon asserted that use was far more important than preservation, and that the latter was essentially irrelevant to public libraries.[4] There was, no doubt, an element of deliberate provocation in the choice of context and audience, but the views expressed are clearly widespread among his fellow senior professionals in the public libraries.

There is, however, another way of looking at this issue. The first of the librarians quoted in the previous paragraph was sufficiently concerned about (or interested in) the issue to write us a substantial letter in addition to providing a full and thoughtful set of answers on the questionnaire. He went on:

> The only aspects of preservation and conservation which are widespread in [our] libraries relate to the routine binding and repair of materials to extend their useful working life.

This represents precisely the appreciation of the time factor in preservation which has been stressed by recent writers; motives for preservation may vary from maximising shelf-life to ensuring a reasonable resale value on withdrawal, but, whatever the motives, a systematic policy for the physical management of stock is necessary to achieve the objectives. Similarly, the same metropolitan chief added:

> We need to work towards regional and national stock retention policies.

Indeed, the British Library has already moved some way towards developing such a policy,[5] and the principle has been endorsed by the recent review of university library provision.[6] The objectives of such policies can, of course, only be achieved if there is stock to retain. This is an issue to which we return in Chapter 7.[7]

There is, as we shall see, some uniformity of views within the academic and public library communities respectively, and even on some issues between them; when we turn to special libraries, however, that was not to be expected and was not found. Some special librarians were very explicit:

> As a special scientific library *we actually don't want to keep* a lot of the material for years.

Again, the time factor seems to be an issue here, although in this case a negative one. The policy may well be appropriate, and it is, at any rate, a conscious policy. Its potential dangers are, however, highlighted by the response of the librarian of a very large general college library:

> We have chosen to preserve periodical subscriptions at the expense of binding and are now paying for it in the additional time it takes to re-shelve loose periodical parts and through increased losses.

In other libraries, these dangers are indeed acknowledged. One respondent told us that his was a

> ... heavily used scientific library. The emphasis is on acquiring new and up to date sources of information ... Preservation/conservation is limited to binding journals for permanent retention, repair binding to heavily-used items of bookstock, where replacement is not feasible or possible, and applying common sense ...

As we shall see, this is by no means a unique example of a well-developed preservation policy which is not actually recognised for what it is, or perhaps represents a misunderstanding of what 'preservation' is actually about. The binding of books and journals is a major component of 'preservation' expenditure in almost all libraries, ranging from about 1 per cent of total annual expenditure in public libraries to about 2 per cent in the pre-1992 universities.[8]

Other special librarians expressed their awareness and understanding in a rather different way, which gives some cause for concern. Two examples will illustrate this. In the first:

> I am well aware that some of our stock (particularly ephemera) is unique, but the current level of the book fund is such that it is only just possible to meet demands for new stock …

This is the library of a public-sector agency; the second example is from the voluntary sector:

> Unfortunately, preservation/conservation has an extremely low priority due to monetary constraints … In spite of this there are several works worth preserving.

Such responses make us pause when we then read the comment of the librarian of a very similar small, but uniquely specialised, library:

> As we are a very new organisation we have very little archive material. We do have material which we shall keep for as long as we exist, but this is all published material and is probably available in the BL [British Library].

Have we found a new and wider awareness and understanding of the fundamentals of preservation? There are strong indications here that preservation is still widely regarded as an issue which is principally relevant to special collections, even among some librarians who have actually developed stock management policies which, in fact if not in name, deal with the key issue of ensuring that materials are usable for the time for which it is desirable to keep them. Perhaps the problem is one of terminology; the word 'preservation' does have overtones and implications which are not always attractive to many library managers. We shall address this issue further in Chapter 7.[9]

The opinions which we have quoted are typical of those which were expressed to us. They are not, however, comprehensive, since the great majority of our respondents did not offer general views of this kind. A more detailed analysis of some specific issues is needed before we can draw some more general conclusions.

THE RELEVANCE OF PRESERVATION

We have already quoted some views which suggest that preservation is either a low priority, or only very selectively prioritised (which is a different matter) in many libraries in all sectors. This should, perhaps, be understood in the context of the comment from the librarian of a university founded in the 1960s:

> This unprepossessing return should not be taken as indicative of (a) ignorance or (b) indifference. Good conservation practice is solely determined by the availability of money (which in our case we have not got).

Resourcing is, of course, a pervasive issue, and one to which we shall return. For the moment, however, we should note this librarian's recognition (borne out by the return itself) that preservation, in the right circumstances, would and, by implication, should be a matter of concern to the institution. The perception of the relevance of preservation is fundamental to an understanding of professional attitudes, and we shall explore it at some length.

In one sense, relevance is determined by broader institutional objectives. Such objectives, however, even where they are incorporated into formal mission statements (as is, of course, increasingly the case) are themselves subject to interpretation. In an attempt to find a more objective measure, we asked a question which was perhaps deceptively simple, and which had also been asked by Ratcliffe.[10] It was:

> What percentage (approximately) of [your] holdings is intended for permanent retention?

We deliberately offered no further definitions, although, as we shall see, some respondents offered unsolicited, and sometimes very revealing and informative, comments.

The raw results are found in Table 2.1. Overall, we can broadly say that libraries either intend to keep very little of their stock, or the greater part of it. A more sophisticated analysis clarifies the position, and is based on Table 2.2. Most strikingly, as we have observed elsewhere,[11] public libraries have a fundamentally different approach to this aspect of stock management. Of 73 (out of 132) public libraries who answered this question, 51 consider that less than a quarter of their stock is intended for permanent retention. Among the academic libraries, there is an almost mirror image of this situation, with 66 out of 98 intending to keep between three-quarters and the whole of their current stock in perpetuity. Perhaps the greatest surprise was that the special libraries, overall, yielded an

Percentage of holdings	Number of libraries (percentage of respondents)
0%	4 (0.82%)
1 – 25%	83 (17.00%)
26 – 50%	20 (4.1%)
51 – 75%	18 (3.69%)
76 – 99%	112 (22.95%)
100%	70 (14.34%)

Table 2.1 Retention of Stock. Holdings Intended for Permanent Retention

Percentage of holdings	Number of libraries (percentage of respondents)		
	Academic	Public	Special
0%	3 (1.69%)	0 (0%)	1 (0.56%)
1 – 25%	13 (7.34%)	51 (38.64%)	18 (10.17%)
26 – 50%	7 (3.95%)	1 (0.76%)	12 (6.78%)
51 – 75%	9 (5.08%)	2 (1.51%)	7 (3.95%)
76 – 99%	47 (26.55%)	7 (5.3%)	57 (32.2%)
100%	19 (10.73%)	12 (9.09%)	39 (22.03%)

Table 2.2 Rentention of Stock. Holdings Intended for Permanent Retention by Sector

even higher proportion which expressed such an intention, but all of this has to be considered in the light of a more detailed analysis.

PUBLIC LIBRARIES

The public libraries perhaps present the most uniform picture. We have already suggested that, in that sector, preservation issues are largely seen as a matter for local studies and other special collections rather than for the stock as a whole. This is certainly confirmed by a more detailed consideration of those public libraries which claim to be intending to preserve most or all of their stock. Many of these had replied (of their own volition) *only* in terms of their local studies collections, archives or other special collections, despite our deliberately inclusive definition. We take this to indicate (although, of course, we cannot be certain) that the chief librarians of these authorities (to whom the questionnaires were addressed) take this view of preservation. It is, by and large, in these public library systems, and only in these systems, that there is a declaration of intent to preserve large proportions of existing stock.

This interpretation is confirmed by the returns from authorities which did take the more general view for which we were hoping. One shire county, for example, which said that it intended to preserve about 20 per cent of its stock overall, added that this really meant the retention of local studies material and rare books. Another, much smaller, shire county, said that it intended to retain 'approximately 0.75 per cent', but added:

We would expect to retain material relating to our subject specialisation. We have a few old books of antiquarian value.

A Scottish district showed a similar approach; the approximately 1.3 per cent of its stock which it intended to preserve included 'all local history books and photos etc'. A London borough which returned 'virtually 100 per cent' added that it had:

… answered only for the local studies library as everywhere [else] in the libraries preservation and conservation is virtually non-existent.

One of our most informative shire-county respondents really summarised the general position admirably:

> less than 1 per cent [of their holdings are intended for permanent preservation and] these are virtually all local studies archive stock.

The professional perception of the relevance of preservation to public libraries is starkly defined by these findings: it is a matter for local studies librarians and for archivists; it barely impinges on stock management in the rest of the system. The Welsh district which intends (or hopes) to keep 70 per cent of its total stock is, so far as we know, a unique survivor of an earlier age when such attitudes commonly prevailed. Those attitudes were perhaps still vestigially found in more authorities in the early 1980s when Ratcliffe conducted his survey, and may explain the discrepancy between his figures and ours.[12] We feel it is at least as likely, however, that we have observed a genuine change in public library managers' attitudes to stock; it is now explicitly seen as temporary and impermanent, intended to satisfy the immediate and changing demands of users. There is, of course, also a financial dimension to this. One valuable measure is of expenditure on binding expressed as a percentage of the book fund. Recent research shows consistent decline between 1987–8 and 1990–1, especially in the London boroughs (6.5 per cent to 4.6 per cent) and metropolitan districts (7.9 per cent to 4.7 per cent).[13] Time and again, as our quotations suggest, words like 'archive', 'antiquarian' and 'rare' are associated with preservation.

ACADEMIC LIBRARIES

Academic libraries present a more diverse picture, and it is precisely for this reason that we have attempted a more formal subdivision of the category as a whole.[14] This has enabled us to distinguish broadly between three types of university (pre-1960, post-1960, and ex-polytechnic), and three types of college and institute (Oxford and Cambridge, London University and non-university). The significance of this categorization is immediately apparent when we consider Table 2.3, from which it can be seen that it is the older universities and the Oxford and Cambridge colleges, with their significant holdings of materials of historical importance and (in many cases) a long tradition of collection building, that constitute the great majority of those intending to retain all, or the greater part, of their stock. Even so, attitudes vary. A number of the pre-1960 universities (mainly the mid-twentieth century foundations) at least imply that total or near-total retention policies are being reconsidered, with such comments as 'library at "self-renewing" stage' and '100 per cent at present'. Overall, however, we find little evidence that the self-renewing concept has been particularly important in driving stock management policies since 1976, and it seems almost certain that its philosophy has long since been overtaken by other factors such as funding restraints and the development of alternative information sources and document supply systems.

Category	Number of libraries	Percentage of category
Pre-1960 university	14	51.85%
Post-1960 university	5	29.41%
Ex-polytechnic	6	18.18%
Oxford/Cambridge colleges and institutes	27	49.09%
London University colleges and institutes	16	48.48%
Other HE and FE colleges	2	16.66%

Table 2.3 Rentention of Stock. Academic Libraries: Retention of 76–100 per cent of Stock

This is perhaps exemplified by the Scottish university which keeps 95 per cent at present, but is engaged on an extensive weeding programme as time permits.

Most of the academic institutions which have more recently attained university status, and virtually all of those which still remain outside the university system, have traditionally had little in common with the older-established universities. Many have, indeed, consciously rejected collection-oriented stock management policies. This was perhaps exemplified in the comment of the librarian of one former polytechnic:

> Most of our stock has a shelf-life of between 10 and 25 years at most. We do not 'preserve' but rather 'exploit' our stock.

The librarian of another new university comments that the library

> ... supports a teaching programme primarily: it is not intended to run an archive.

Such an approach, however, is not unique to the new universities. The librarian of a university of the 1960s generation of foundations was one of the few who gave reasons for *not* completing our questionnaire:

> [The] library is primarily concerned with meeting the current needs of teaching and research ... consequently, preservation and conservation are only of limited relevance to our work.

Clearly, the 'research' referred to here must be assumed to be in fields in which scholars do not need the depth of library and information resources normally associated with that activity. The word 'archive' appears yet again, in the comments of a Cambridge departmental librarian:

> This library theoretically has little archive function – we replace what we need, otherwise it's a case of benign neglect.

Finally, we can contrast this with the library of a very specialised Scottish college which 'would retain more if space were adequate'.

As has been widely observed in a more general context, one of the consequences of the creation of new university institutions since 1992 has been a diversification as well as a multiplication of the higher education sector. The range of institutions from the medieval foundations in both England and Scotland through to local authority colleges seeking franchises for access courses from ex-polytechnics has destroyed whatever homogeneity ever existed in British higher education. This position is inevitably reflected in all aspects of library provision, as is clear from the Follett Review.[15] Library policies in universities can never again be monolithic, if they ever were. The research-driven institutions recognised this some years ago when they came together to form the Consortium of University Research Libraries (CURL), but now, more than ever, there are yawning gaps between university libraries in terms of both provision and philosophies. That great and growing diversity is well exemplified in considering attitudes to, and understanding of, the relevance of preservation of materials. Less obvious, however, is my understanding of the issues raised by the preservation of information and access to it. This will be considered in more detail in Chapters 4 and 6.

SPECIAL LIBRARIES

The special library sector is inevitably and avowedly diverse. Indeed, the variety of libraries which are brought together under this heading is so great that we can only report our findings in terms of examples. At one end of the scale are the cathedral libraries (by no means an homogeneous group themselves), and at the other the libraries of science-based industrial and research organisations. The concern for the preservation of early printed books in the former could hardly be more different from the investigations of digital imaging in some of the latter. One common characteristic of most special libraries, however, is that they have small staffs compared to those of public or university libraries. Often there is a single professional, and it is not unusual for that person to be appointed because of his or her subject knowledge rather than because of a specialised interest in a particular aspect of librarianship. It was perhaps partly because of this that it was among special librarians that we found the most overt statements of ignorance of preservation, even where there was an awareness of the issues involved, or at least of the fact that there *is* an issue.

The comments of the librarian of a professional association exemplified the level of awareness:

> I would be interested in knowing to what extent libraries are aware of, or have adopted or conformed to particular standards.

Small budgets and staff are clearly major restraints on all aspects of work in many special libraries. A medical librarian told us that:

> … necessity has forced us to use part of our book budget for binding, but only for absolutely essential items …

The librarian of a learned society encapsulated the feeling of many special librarians:

> Time is the biggest factor in determining what can be done.

35

This does not mean, however, that some special librarians are not aware of the issues. We have already quoted the cases of two libraries in the voluntary sector which seem to have important material worthy of preservation. A government agency library in Scotland told us that in their environment:

> ... the majority of information has a fairly short shelf-life and does not need to be preserved [but added]. ... We have a special collection of in-house research material but as this was started in 1986 the question of preservation has not yet arisen, although it will within the next few years.

We suspect that much of this collection is of grey literature, and that the issue which has been identified here is a significant one, analogous with that of the voluntary sector library which we discussed earlier. Some libraries have already travelled down a part of this road. One major government agency library reports that:

> For the future we are investigating the use of document image processing as a means both of saving space and preserving documents.

A professional association told us that it also was:

> seriously looking at electronic image creation as a means of preservation and increasing access to its collection.

The librarians are sometimes painfully aware of their own limitations. The librarian of one organisation, with some modestly important historical collections, told us that there was 'difficulty in obtaining suitable specialist advice about the conservation priorities for the collection'. In a professional association, the librarian told us that:

> 'Archives' in my institution covers a vast range of artifacts, particularly working models, paintings, silver, etc. I therefore find in trying to introduce policies to cover preservation, I have to extend my own knowledge into painting and these other areas.

This is not an exceptional situation. The following needs little comment, and perhaps emphasises, if emphasis were still needed, the problems which arise in this sector:

> We collect information on conservation and do what we can within our limited resources but do have a concern for the long term. Our building is 256 years old and would require an awful lot of money to make environmentally perfect. Not complacent – just strapped for cash.

This library belongs to an historically important organisation which has fallen on hard times, but the library itself still holds material of great importance, some of it unique!

CONCLUSIONS

There is a perceptible gap between the aspirations and the achievements of many librarians, in all sectors, in this aspect of their work, and it is a gap which is widely recognised by librarians themselves. Resourcing and knowledge have already begun to emerge as major issues, and we shall return to both. For the moment, however, in concluding this section we note that well over half of the libraries which we surveyed – a large and representative sample of those in Great Britain – have expressed the intention of retaining, or at least of not disposing of, more than half their stock, and that outside the public library sector that proportion rises significantly. Some of this, as we have seen, is preservation by inertia: there is no time to weed, or no incentive to do so. But some, perhaps more, seems to be an expression of a genuine belief in the long-term value of the collections and a consequent desire to preserve them for future generations. What is lacking is not the will, but the means. To all of these libraries, whether or not their librarians express it in these terms, preservation is indeed a relevant issue.

PRESERVATION PROBLEMS

In the previous section, we have tried to define and delineate some generalities about British librarians' perceptions of preservation, in particular by looking at their aspirations for the preservation of the contents of their own libraries. We now turn to some more specific problems and issues. In particular, we have tried to identify the problems which library managers have found, or think that they have found, in relation to particular categories of material and media. We asked whether our respondents had experienced any preservation problems with any of a list of 18 specified media, and invited comments should they wish to make them. It is on the basis of the answers to, and comments on, this question that we offer the following analysis.

Table 2.4 presents the basic statistical data which we have assembled from the replies of our 488 respondents. No doubt because they still predominate in the holdings of libraries, it is paper-based media which are most often identified as being problematic. Photographic materials, however, are not far behind, and we note the authoritative comment of a respected and knowledgeable expert in one university library that it is 'only a matter of time before problems arise with electronic media'; indeed, in a few libraries that time has already, apparently, arrived.

BOOKS

Academic libraries

It is clearly consistent with the 'archival' view of preservation which is prevalent, if not uniquely so, in all sectors, that there is an apparent concentration on the more traditional paper-based materials. The basic problems are, of course, well understood and there is a large scientific and professional literature which deals with them.[16] Most librarians certainly seem to be aware of the consequences of such phenomena as paper decay and inadequate binding techniques and

Medium	Number of libraries identifying as problem	Percentage of respondents
Printed books	289	59.22%
Journals	176	36.07%
Newspapers	164	33.61%
Manuscripts	156	31.97%
Photographic prints	114	23.36%
Photographic negatives	80	16.39%
Microfilms	64	13.11%
35-mm slides	48	9.84%
Videotapes	32	6.56%
Audio cassettes	32	6.56%
Vinyl records	21	4.3%
Microfiches	20	4.1%
Filmstrips	20	4.1%
Compact discs	9	1.84%
Microcards	6	1.23%
Optical discs	3	0.61%
Other*	55	11.27%

*Includes sound film, pamphlets, sheet music and musical scores, reel-to-reel tapes, glass slides and negatives, maps, audio tapes, blueprints and plans, ephemera, computer software, multipart kits, tape-slide sets, prints and drawings, lantern slides.

Table 2.4 Problem Materials

materials, even if they have no scientific or technical knowledge of the causes. They also have an empirical awareness of another phenomenon which has been widely discussed in the specialist literature: the effects of heavy and increasing usage on materials, especially when this is contemporaneous with budgetary restraints which have inhibited the repair, replacement and renewal of stock.

Among those who specified what they saw as the causes of the problems which they were describing, by far the largest group picked on heavy use, overuse and misuse. An Oxford college librarian spoke for many in commenting:

Printed books and journals falling apart through heavy use.

Another college librarian wrote of 'excess use', and from one of the larger libraries in London University we were told of 'damage from overuse'. The librarian of another, comparably large, London University library reported almost identically of damage 'mainly through overuse', while a third clearly now regards this as normal:

Usual problems with printed materials of wear due to heavy use.

The theme is persistent; a post-1960 university library is suffering from 'heavy use of certain titles', while the librarian of a medical school told us that:

Books are heavily used and have to last a long time … some become very tatty … it is a very poor situation.

It is important to recognise that all of these examples (and many more which could be adduced) relate to ordinary stock, not to special collections or rare books. Some come from libraries which have no special concern for preservation; probably all are an expression of the frustration of watching the gradual destruction of the library's most valuable material at a time when replacement, or even proper maintenance, has become economically difficult or impossible. It might be argued that what we have here is evidence which might suggest that the working stocks of academic libraries are deteriorating to the point at which they are in danger of becoming unusable under the dual assault of increased usage and diminishing resources. Perhaps, however, we should sound a cautionary note. Librarians in all universities have been very much aware of the impact of the growth of student numbers on all aspects of library work in recent years.[17] The implication that this is also responsible for greater damage to library stocks is perhaps irresistible and logical, but cannot be proven using our findings alone. It seems likely to be the case: but we can put it no more strongly than that.

Public libraries

Public librarians have also been under severe financial pressure for many years. The continuing decline in the purchasing power of book funds, a trend which is well documented and seems unlikely to be reversed,[18] puts greater pressure on existing stock. Turnover of stock is less frequent, and total stock available is often smaller. Public libraries across the spectrum of authorities report concern with the damage caused by heavy usage and handling of books. So far as general stock is concerned, the position was perhaps summarised by the metropolitan district librarian who wrote that:

> Our problems relate to funding levels – there are no funds.

Special libraries

Many special libraries find themselves in a position similar to the public and academic libraries, although there is, as usual, greater diversity. Nevertheless, the libraries of bodies as different as a government agency, a trade union, a research institute and a scientific association noted that heavy use was leading to such problems as pages being lost by wear and tear. Small libraries are perhaps most vulnerable, with their carefully selected and intensively used stock. One such identified 'wear and tear problems from constant usage' as their principal concern.

Summary

We have deliberately begun this analysis of librarians' perceptions of the physical problems of their stock by concentrating on remarks which seem to relate to the general bookstock. In almost all cases this is stock available for loan, and over which the librarian's control is therefore limited. Even if usage is only elsewhere within the same building (as might be the case with a special library in industry, for example), there is no means of supervising or even monitoring the conditions under which use takes place. In the typical case of borrowings from the general stock of public and academic libraries, only the most general rules can be suggested ('Protect books from the rain') and even they are, in practice, imposs- ible to enforce. In extreme circumstances, demonstrable infringement can be penalised, but by then the damage has taken place.

OTHER PAPER MEDIA

When we turn to other parts of the paper-based stock of libraries, however, differ- ent circumstances often prevail. Bound volumes of periodicals are typically read in the library, and unbound parts almost invariably so, although at some universities the latter may be changing in an attempt to increase access without increasing opening hours. Newspapers, rare books and manuscript documents are, almost without exception, confined to the premises, and often have to be read in specially designated rooms or reading areas. At least some of this material is kept in closed access storage, so that the bulk of handling is by library staff, not by readers. Theoretically, all of this should lead to greater protection for the most valuable, and often the most vulnerable, materials. It is, of course, these materials which were the focus of traditional preservation interest, and, although our own inter- ests are wider than that, these materials are indeed the subject of much comment from our respondents. There are some terminological problems which need to be resolved here. Respondents referred to 'rare books', 'old' and 'older' books and 'antiquarian materials', and used various other phrases to describe what we take to be essentially the same thing: old books which have, or may have, some contin- uing interest for present and future users.

In analysing the issues which have been brought to our attention, we shall consider first the particular problems of periodicals; we then turn to the rather different case of newspapers; then we shall look at older books, designated special collections and the like; we next turn to manuscript materials; and finally, we shall consider comments made about storage conditions and buildings as opposed to the materials stored in them.

Periodicals

Significantly, few public libraries made any comments which appear to relate specifically to periodicals, with the possible exception of a London borough which noted, perhaps somewhat ambiguously, 'the stealing of vital parts', and few identi- fied this as a problem area. In academic and special libraries, however, there are clearly some very real problems. Photocopying, so often cited in the preservation literature as a cause of damage, really does seem to be a major culprit. The librar- ian of a London University institute library told us that:

The bulk of our stock is bound journals. Bindings, unfortunately, are designed for reading not for photocopying, and are rapidly breaking up.

A medical library identified exactly this problem, and it was one of the few specific problems in this area highlighted by a public library. General complaints about periodical bindings were, however, common, and we take it that photocopying on flat-platen copiers has exacerbated whatever other causes of decay and deterioration there may be.

The irreversible growth of the practice of photocopying journal articles is a fact of life, which at least some of our respondents have identified as a cause of damage to stock which may be of long-term as well as immediate interest. Another fact of life, at least in academic libraries, is the mutilation of bound periodicals in order to extract single articles of interest to the thief. At least 12 academic libraries chose to highlight this issue (which was not the subject of a specific question). All are universities, including three post-1992 foundations. Those three, however, have comparatively well-developed library services with a fairly long history, and are not unlike some of the post-1960 institutions which raised this issue. In other words, as we might expect, the problem of mutilation of periodicals is at its worst, and becomes a serious issue, in libraries with long runs of periodicals serving institutions with a strong research culture.

Newspapers

Although newspapers are, in a bibliographical sense, periodicals, they are fundamentally different as physical objects. Their daily or weekly publication, often on poor paper, and in large (and sometimes very large) formats, have always created problems for librarians. These have long been recognised, and strategies adopted for their preservation or substitution.[19] We shall deal with some aspects of this in greater detail in Chapter 3 and elsewhere;[20] at this point, we are merely reporting on the problems identified by librarians.

Poor-quality paper, and its consequences such as embrittlement, were noted by many libraries. So too were the problems arising from the size and bulk of newspapers. One special library with a substantial collection of foreign newspapers not widely available in this country, reported that it had experienced:

... damage due to lack of shelving space for keeping them flat.

The same problem, or something close to it, may well be implied by a terser comment – 'size' – from another special library with important historical collections. Four academic libraries, including one of the largest in the country, also drew our attention to this problem.

Older printed materials

A consideration of some aspects of the preservation of newspapers leads naturally into more general questions of the preservation of older printed materials. In some ways, newspapers are merely a special case of this, although made worse by their size, bulk and typically poor paper. Older books, in general, however, are widely perceived as presenting a major problem. This is true across the whole spectrum of libraries, from those which regard their preservation as a major part of their mission to those which clearly regard them as being ultimately disposable. In the latter category, we were struck by the honesty of the librarian who told us:

> We have a very small collection of items that we would like to keep under better preservation conditions, but it is so small, and the library does not have an 'historical' bent that we have not done much about them, except keep them in a locked cupboard, inspect the bindings, etc. from time to time (using commercial binders for any patching up) and hope for the best. They are not separately insured, as their loss would not amount to a disaster.

Even taking a more active line does not always bring success; one London borough told us that some local history items which had been sent to a well-known commercial binder had been returned because they had, in the view of the company, deteriorated beyond rescue.

Indeed, neglect by past generations of librarians or former owners, and the damage caused unwittingly by ill-advised repairs, are a consistent theme in many libraries with collections of older materials. A Welsh district library put it in this way:

> Remedial work carried out in the past has sometimes been the cause of further problems where there has been a lack of understanding of preservation techniques, etc.

A metropolitan district expressed the same sentiment more succinctly: 'poor previous repairs'. Nor is neglect always benign; one special librarian told us that 'the lack of conservation over 100 years was regarded as the cause of the library's current problems with its early printed books. The librarian of a Cambridge college was more specific:

> Problems arise mainly from the work of trade bookbinders undertaken in the 1920s to 1960s.

This is, however, not only a twentieth century problem; this respondent added:

> In addition, rebinding programmes of the eighteenth century have left us with a legacy of ill-suited book structures.

The librarian of a pre-1960 university with very important rare book collections was perhaps more charitable, but identified essentially the same problem, when he wrote of 'mistaken although well-intentioned past approaches to repair'.

The causes of decay and damage in older materials are well attested in the literature,[21] and equally so in our findings. Poor materials are the most fundamental. The local studies librarian of a London borough expressed this succinctly in reporting 'mould; crumbling leather; acidity'. The librarian of a special library with historical collections of international importance, and well aware of its consequential obligations, produced a list which could be headings in a textbook:

Brittle paper; red rot in leather; splitting joints; adhesive stains; tears and marks; unsuitable mountings and containers.

Once again, past errors, whether well-meaning or just ignorant, have contributed their own problems, as we see both from this example, and from the large university library which told us that it is now suffering from the past use of storage boxes made of card which itself had a very high acid content.

Manuscripts

Manuscript materials share many of the characteristics of printed books; although bindings are a less pervasive issue, all the material problems of paper are also reported. The word 'manuscripts', however, is used here in a very general sense to include not only what research libraries have traditionally called manuscripts but also those documents more often designated as archives. While the distinction is perhaps intellectually legitimate, and is certainly a practical administrative convenience, it is of little relevance here. Some of our respondents seem to have used the word 'archive' rather loosely, but in any case, we are interested in physical documents rather than their information content at this stage. Written and often unbound documents (including typescripts and the like) do present special problems, and are usually treated quite separately from printed books. Nevertheless, they share all the characteristics and problems of paper from the period in which they were written, and all the problems which can arise from less than perfect conditions of storage. Again, they are found in libraries of all kinds, and we find similar problems arising in all of them.

One special factor which has been brought to our attention by a number of respondents is that of the condition in which manuscript accessions are sometimes received from former owners. A London borough told us of a 'donation of MS material which was mouldy/water damaged/ripped/burnt'. Their problem was not unique; two metropolitan districts drew our attention to it; one commented:

Manuscript materials often arrive in damaged condition.

The other said much the same:

Manuscript materials donated in poor condition, affected by damp.

The problem is one for all recipients of such material; an Oxford college librarian told us of the 'poor state of … some MSS when received', and the librarian of a Scottish university noted that:

Material may be received in poor condition requiring cleaning and fumigation.

In other words, donations bring obligations, a fact recognised long ago by academic libraries, and noted by both Atkinson and Follett.[22] One university library's operational policy statement includes this statement:

> The Library reserves the right to decline acceptance of any gift or deposit ... which has conditions attached to deposit, loan, storage, conservation or consultation considered unreadable by the Library.

But there is sometimes a greater and overriding obligation to accept the material and the preservation issues which consequently have to be addressed. The library of a trade union organisation, reported in very similar terms:

> Manuscript/archival material - donated material often arrives in poor condition through inadequate storage, etc.

There was, however, no suggestion that this was an inappropriate or unacceptable donation, merely that it presented the librarian with problems when it arrived.

None of this is very startling, in the sense that it is the range of problems which might have been expected. We are, of course, disturbed by the evidence that decay is widespread and that we are forced to live with the results of neglect and error in the past. Again, however, this is not surprising. On a more positive note, it is very encouraging to find that so many librarians in all sectors are clearly capable of identifying these problems and recognising their implications. We have little evidence that respondents who work regularly with older materials are not aware of preservation and conservation issues, even if they would not claim great technical expertise. We are even more encouraged when we find (as we often do) that the senior managers of libraries with significant holdings share that awareness, even if they are not always in a position to follow through the implications of their knowledge and understanding.

PHOTOGRAPHIC MATERIALS

As we have suggested, our emphasis on paper-based materials reflects the responses of librarians (Table 2.4), but there is also a widespread concern about photographic materials which deserves some further exploration. The most common manifestation of photographic reproductions in libraries is perhaps not always thought of in this context: microfilm and microfiche. Physically and chemically, however, they are no different from any other film; the difference lies in the fact that they are usually more heavily used, and often viewed through equipment which is outdated and inadequate. It is relevant to note at this stage, although we shall return to the issue later, that this medium is also in use as a preservation tool in its own right, as one of the main surrogate media for the preservation of the intellectual content of printed and written documents.[23]

Use is isolated by many respondents as a major factor in considering the preservation of films. One large London University library noted specifically microfilms suffered from 'user misuse'; a Scottish university commented that microfilm 'snaps in reader'; another Scottish university expanded on this point:

> Films stored on reels snapping across the width of the film when in use on the reader due to over-tensioning.

These examples are from academic libraries, but comments from both public and special libraries can easily be added to them. One metropolitan borough librarian wrote of 'deterioration and breakage of microfilm', and another of 'tearing through heavy use'. One of the national libraries highlighted this problem, despite the wide range which it encountered among many media and materials. It is clear that microfilm readers are a serious problem, and that there are design issues which still need to be addressed as a matter of urgency.

Other forms of photographic materials have their own problems. Where they are intended for long-term preservation as part of archival collections these can be particularly acute. One shire county told us that it has 1.5 million negatives, and not surprisingly commented on 'the volume of the problem'. General problems of deterioration of photographic prints are widespread, exacerbated by the comparative instability of photographic images compared with print.[24] Poor storage conditions, both now and in the past, are identified as an additional problem by a number of respondents. A library with important historical holdings in science commented on 'earlier poor storage', conditions which apparently still prevail in the medical library which reported:

> ... photos have no proper housing here and have simply deteriorated.

It is clear that single negatives and prints (or rather collections of them) are seen as essentially archival materials in many libraries. Our survey has revealed a real problem in this field, which has perhaps not been articulated as clearly as it should have been in the past: the preservation of photographic materials is often more difficult, and their repair and conservation more specialised, than that of books and manuscripts. Almost a quarter of our respondents identified photographic prints as being of concern to them, and 13 per cent regard the preservation of microfilms as an issue (Table 2.4). Moreover, we have so far confined ourselves to some of the more common characteristics of such materials. Rarer, but sometimes infinitely more difficult, problems which have been drawn to our attention include the London University institute in which:

> glass slides have been transferred to a specialist archive to expedite their transfer to modern formats to prevent spontaneous combustion.

In this case the slides are central to the library's mission, but the college library which recognises 'the need to transfer [photographic negatives] to a ... less inflammatory medium' seems to have identified a problem rather than to have resourced a solution. The classic problem of nitrate-based cinematographic film is not generally reported from libraries, although one special library (in the legal field) did tell us that it had had such film copied and then destroyed the inherently unstable originals. Copying of microfilm and the creation of archival masters is a separate issue, addressed in Chapter 4.[25]

RECORDED SOUND MEDIA

Storage, physical preservation and damage by use are all major issues for libraries which hold and wish to retain photographic materials. As yet, the same is not true – at least in numerical terms – of audio and digital materials, although we have already quoted the views of a preservation manager on the likelihood of electronic media presenting a major problem in the future. So far as audio materials are concerned, the major problem is predictable and probably uncontrollable. Both academic and public libraries comment on damage through use, but with cassette tapes and (especially) vinyl records that is unavoidable. Public libraries, in particular, face an insoluble problem with their loan collections, and indeed generally seem to regard the consequences of use as a running expense rather than a preservation problem. Only two public library respondents mentioned the fact that damage was caused by borrowers' inadequate equipment, but we assume that this phenomenon is so widespread that it no longer provokes comment.

Where audio materials are intended for long-term archival preservation, however, there are real problems. One university librarian wrote of audio cassettes that they:

> ... get chewed or come off the end of the spools. Usually this is easy to rectify but some cassette cases ... are sealed so are more difficult to open up to mend. Print through is common in old cassettes and is going to become more of a problem. Audios tend to get sluggish too after time and sound warped. Long cassettes (120s) are made of tape that snaps *very easily*.

It was, as he added, 'needless to say' that he does 'not like audio tapes much!' The last word on audio media should perhaps go to the same librarian, since it leads us into the last major group of physical and material problems identified by our respondents:

> The advertising exec[utive] who said you cannot damage CDs should be shot! Because of this early advertising ploy people are not careful with CDs. Many of our CDs are badly scratched and some jump.

ELECTRONIC MEDIA AND DIGITIZED DATA

Although the comment quoted above was made with reference to audio CDs, the same applies, of course, to CD-ROM and to the other manifestations of optical disc technology which are now becoming so familiar in libraries. The potential problems of the preservation of electronic media and digitized data have been the subject of research and speculation for some years, but matters are rapidly coming to a head.[26] So far as media are concerned, technological developments are already redefining the problems associated with the most common form of optical disc, the CD-ROM. To some extent, the rapid increase in the networking of CD-ROMs, especially in academic libraries, makes it possible to circumvent handling problems because handling is minimised. The same effect is achieved by the use of equipment which ensures that users do not actually touch discs during the loading process. These, of course, have their own cost implications (for both hardware and licences), as is implicit from this comment from a large pre-1960 university:

> Scratching of discs leading to illegibility. Currently stored in plastic boxes (unsatisfactory due to splitting of boxes) or in caddies for insertion into the player. A charger/player has been purchased recently to minimise handling to prevent scratching.

The preservation of digitized data itself was mentioned by only three respondents, one of whom was the preservation manager whom we have already quoted. The other two, however, also deserve a mention, since they refer to issues which perhaps anticipate more general problems for the future. The librarian of a broadcasting organisation added 'computer tapes' to the list of media in our questionnaire, with a comment on 'the difficulties of planning for the best way to preserve new media', although this was 'not yet a problem'. Elsewhere, in a slightly different form, it is; a university librarian wrote:

> Computer software: making back-up copies, storing discs with books in loan collection.

This cannot be unique to that respondent, and its implications need to be considered seriously.

STORAGE OF MATERIALS

The ultimate limitations on all library activities are, of course, the availability of staff and funding, to which we shall return. We refer to the funding issue now because it cannot really be separated from a consideration of the final issue in this section, that of buildings and storage conditions. Old buildings were identified by many respondents as one of the causes of the preservation problems which they identified, especially when these buildings were of historical importance, and perhaps listed. This problem is not confined to the older universities, as is perhaps sometimes assumed. Unsuitable buildings, not all of them particularly old, are to be found in all sectors, especially, it would seem, where off-site or closed-access storage is being provided. Many respondents have commented on lack of space, 'incorrect' storage, and space which is inappropriate to the purposes for which it is being used. Several public libraries made this point, at least two of which have apparently been forced to reconsider their retention policies for space reasons.

The librarian of a specialised college with a medium-sized collection reported:

> No suitable storage available. Humidification levels, security, adequate space, suitable storage facilities most inadequate.

We are not graphologists, but feel that we can detect indignation in our respondent's handwriting! The final comment is:

Reasons: (1) lack of funds (2) top management unconvinced.

Serious issues are highlighted here, especially the fact that remedial measures on a scale appropriate to the problem will inevitably involve large-scale expenditures, and have to be assessed against institutional priorities. We shall return to this issue in Chapter 6 and elsewhere.

Meanwhile, we note some of the consequences of problems of this kind. Again, all the textbook examples are reported to us, including mould, insect infestations and the consequences of inappropriate or uncontrollable environments. This is not, however, purely a technical problem. More than one respondent referred to the human element, whether in identifying the potential conflict between conservation and exploitation (a shire-county library) or the analogous conflict between the right temperature for books and an acceptable temperature for readers (in an Oxford college).

CONCLUSIONS

In asking librarians about the problems which they are experiencing with the materials in their libraries, we expected fairly predictable answers. For the most part, these have emerged: poor-quality paper; inadequate bindings; poor storage conditions, the consequences of past ignorance and neglect. We have, however, uncovered a concern for photographic materials which, although not as great as that expressed about paper-based materials, is clearly significant, and needs to be addressed. Our respondents are not, with rare exceptions (which we have not quoted) complaining: they are reporting on facts and phenomena and drawing on their knowledge and experience to explain them.

We have not quantified the problem of damaged, decayed and deteriorating materials in British libraries; indeed, such quantification would have been impossible within the scope of our project. We have, however, uncovered attitudes and approaches which inform our understanding of the problem, not as we see it, but as it is seen by those whose daily tasks are influenced and perhaps circumscribed by its consequences.

CONCLUSIONS

In this chapter, we have tried to analyse the understanding and the experiences of preservation revealed by our respondents. We have used both statistical data based on an analysis of the responses to our survey, and the comments that were made to us by a large representative sample of library managers throughout Great Britain and in libraries of all kinds.

Librarians are confronted by a whole range of problems which arise directly from the inherently unstable and impermanent nature of almost all of the materials used for books and documents, for the recording of images and of sound, and for storing digitized data. A clear majority of our correspondents is aware that their most basic tool – the bookstock – is under continuous and perhaps growing pressure from both use and storage. At a time of diminishing resources, the stock itself is also in danger of unplanned and undesirable diminution. This perception, and the problem which it embraces, is almost universal across the whole spectrum of libraries from the most specialised research institutions to the most advanced of multi-media public libraries.

If there is a considerable, and encouraging awareness, of the issues, there is also a sense of frustration. Inadequate and aging buildings, increases in demand from users and unsympathetic funders share the responsibility for this. At the root of it all is the question of resources. In both the private and the public sectors, and in libraries of all kinds, the general trend of recent years has been a decline in the real value of budgets. At the same time, the demands on those budgets - from new technology and simply from pressure of numbers of users – has inexorably increased. Those librarians who do care about the state of their stock and its effective exploitation – and they seem to be the majority – have more than a little to justify that sense of frustration.

In the next chapter, we shall explore in more detail how librarians have responded to the problems which they and others have identified, and consider the current preservation policies and practices in British libraries.

NOTES

1. NPAC minutes, 1 November 1984. We are grateful to Mirjam Foot for giving us access to a file of minutes of the Committee.
2. See above, pp. 3–5.
3. Paul Eden, John Feather and Graham Matthews. Of special concern? Preservation in perspective. *Public Library Journal*, 9: 2 (1994), pp. 33–8.
4. David Liddle. Conservation: the public library view. In: National Preservation Office, *Conservation and Collection Management*, op. cit., pp. 29–39.
5. Enright, Hellinga and Leigh, op. cit.
6. Joint Funding Councils' Libraries Review Group. [Chair: Sir Brian Follett]. *Report*. Bristol: HEFCE, 1993, pp. 53–4.
7. See below, pp. 141–3.
8. John Sumsion, Helen V. Pickering and Pamela J. Berridge. *LISU Annual Library Statistics 1993*. Loughborough: LISU, 1993, pp. 15, 117. See also below, pp. 82–4.
9. See below, pp. 79-80.
10. See Ratcliffe, op. cit., p. 76, for the equivalent question.
11. See note 3, above.
12. Ratcliffe, op. cit., p. 17.
13. Watkin, op. cit., pp. 5–6.
14. Eden, Feather and Matthews, Preservation policies, loc. cit.
15. See note 6, above.
16. See above, pp. 14–16.
17. John Feather and Richard Marriott. Unchartered territory. Academic libraries and the growth in student numbers. *Library Review*, 42: 3 (1993), pp. 20–30.

18. Sumsion, Pickering and Berridge, op. cit., p. 16.
19. See, for example, Wresell, op. cit.
20. See below, pp. 83–4, 91–2.
21. See above, p. 11.
22. This is implicit in paras 214–31 of the Follett Report (see note 6 above).
23. See above, pp. 12–14, and below, pp. 82–4.
24. See above, p. 12.
25. See below, pp. 82–4.
26. See above, pp. 8–10.

3 Preservation in Practice

In Chapter 2, we have discussed the attitudes of British librarians towards preservation, and tried to present and assess their perceptions of it as a policy issue. In broad terms, it is clear that, at one level, many librarians still understand it primarily as a necessity for the custodians of older and rarer material, and material generally considered to be of longer-term research significance. At another level, however, a substantial number of comments from library managers and policymakers can be interpreted to show that there is a realisation that a wide range of information media, including some of the most technologically advanced, present preservation problems of their own, even if these are, because of the nature of the information and the media, comparatively short-term. In this chapter, we take our investigation further, and in a slightly different direction. Having tried to answer questions concerning what librarians think about preservation, we now turn our attention to what they *do* about it.

PRESERVATION INFRASTRUCTURE

The practical implications and applications of an understanding of the preservation issue, and of the development of preservation policies, can best be judged by considering the results. In general terms, we have suggested elsewhere that six broad criteria can be applied in assessing the significance of preservation to a particular library or sector of libraries.[1] These are:

- having a preservation policy;
- having a disaster prevention, recovery or control policy;
- designating a member of staff as having responsibility for the development, implementation and management of preservation policy;
- running training programmes in preservation awareness for existing and/or newly appointed staff;
- undertaking systematic surveys of stock and storage areas for preservation purposes; and
- using systematic procedures for cleaning and treating stock on the shelves.

We take this to represent what we shall call the infrastructure of the preservation policies of a library, whose presence or absence indicates the library's approach to the basic issues of policy, management and resourcing of preservation.

PRESERVATION POLICY DOCUMENTS

Historically, British librarians have perhaps been more reluctant than their American counterparts to produce written statements of library policy, either generally or in relation to specific activities. This has perhaps been particularly true among academic libraries, where control by the parent body, especially in universities, was comparatively remote. Public libraries, responsible to committees of elected members of Councils, were somewhat more prolific in the production of such documents, but these were often written in very general terms. In recent years, there have been some important changes. In both the private and the public sectors, the concept of accountability has become a major factor in the determination of policy. Mission statements, and the establishment of indicators of performance as targets against which achievements can be measured, have become commonplace. If such methods are to be applied effectively in service delivery agencies such as libraries, written statements of objectives and agreed and generally available statements of policy and methods of implementation are indispensable. In general terms, therefore, formal statements of policy, whether internal or for wider circulation, have become more familiar in British public-sector institutions since the mid-1980s.

Despite this, only 51 of our 488 respondents initially told us that they had written preservation policies. Of these, a marginally higher proportion of the 51 (10.6 per cent) was in public rather than academic libraries (7.34 per cent), but the highest percentage was actually among special libraries (13.56 per cent). The numbers involved, however, are so comparatively small that the significance of these percentage differences is doubtful. It is clear that, across the board, very few British libraries have a written preservation policy.

There is, however, some evidence to suggest that there are policies in place in many institutions which have not yet been recorded in this form, or which are not recognised or identified as 'preservation' policies. Once again, the rather narrow understanding of the idea of preservation which seems to prevail among some librarians has perhaps influenced their responses to us. One shire-county library, for example, told us that it had:

... most of the parts of a policy, but not a document that pulls them all together.

In fact, it was clear from the very detailed letter from this respondent that the county actually has one of the most advanced and sophisticated preservation policies of any library of its kind in the country. Similarly, another shire county and a post-1992 university both told us that, while they did not have a preservation policy, they did have a 'retention' policy; in the latter case this was part of a broader collection management policy. Perhaps the best summary of this position is from the post-1960 university which reported that preservation policy is

> … covered by library's collection development policy and statement of operational policy on binding.

It seems reasonable to infer that the number of policy documents reported to us is a bare minimum. Much more lies hidden in more general policies for the management of collections, but these are not identified as preservation policies by library managers. Moreover, there are some libraries which took our broad definition of preservation to exclude their own policies, such as the university which told us that it had a binding policy but no preservation policy, and the metropolitan district which reported no preservation policy, but 'written procedures only'. There are also some indications that more libraries are developing preservation policies, although the numbers are still small. In the academic sector, seven libraries told us of policies in active preparation as an unsolicited comment on their reply to this question. An even smaller number of public libraries, and a solitary special library, gave similar information. A number of respondents, however, suggested what may be a significant reason for the apparent dearth of activity. One pre-1960 university, with important historical research collections, commented that:

> The willingness to develop policies is present, but time is difficult to find.

No doubt this sentiment would be widely echoed by other managers.

In general terms, however, it is disappointing, although perhaps not entirely surprising, to find that so few British libraries appear to have made much progress in this direction in the last decade. Indeed, there is some evidence that momentum which was gained in the mid-1980s has not been sustained, at least in the academic sector. As part of its response to the Ratcliffe Report, SCONUL established a Working Party on Preservation in 1984; this group immediately decided that the preparation of a 'model preservation policy statement' should be one of its primary objectives. Indeed, a persistent concern of the Working Group throughout the six years of its active life was to provide means of helping libraries to prepare and record their policies for preservation and related issues. This initiative had some effect. A survey in 1988 found that 17 SCONUL libraries had written preservation policies against the two who had reported them in 1982, and another seven institutions had them in draft form.[2] A more comprehensive survey in 1986 had found that 13 per cent of university and polytechnic libraries had prepared a preservation policy statement 'within the past five years'.[3]

Although there is some evidence, as we have suggested, that there are preservation elements in some more general collection management policies, identifiable discrete preservation policy documents are certainly not a major feature of the landscape of British librarianship. The policy documents which do exist, however, are very instructive in helping us to analyse the practice of preservation in British libraries in the mid-1990s. They can provide an insight into the priorities and preoccupations of librarians, as well as revealing the existence of good practice. We shall return to these issues in Chapters 4 and 6.

DISASTER PLANS

Disaster preparedness planning has long been recognised as an integral part of a preservation policy. The literature is extensive,[4] ranging from the theoretical,[5] through the advisory,[6] to the exemplary.[7] Its implications go far beyond the comparatively narrow issues of preservation or indeed of collection management. It encompasses ergonomic and design issues, as well as health and safety concerns; it consequently has a major legal dimension both for employers and for the owners and managers of public buildings.[8] Quite apart from these legal formalities, effective measures to prevent avoidable damage is an integral element in insurance protection, and has wide-ranging financial implications for institutions and parent organisations. The narrower professional aspects include the ability to respond rapidly during, and more particularly immediately after, some event has taken place. Indeed, one of the most striking lessons from the literature is how good planning can help to minimise the damage caused by flood or fire. There are, however, few formalised standards which relate to the safety of materials as opposed to people.[9]

Against that background, we read this comment from the librarian of a government department in Whitehall:

My predecessor ... discussed having a disaster plan with library staff and with ... management. There was enthusiasm in the library, but I believe that the idea stumbled when it was put to management. Finance and security were among the considerations.

Fortunately, this was not typical, although it is still the case that fewer than one-third of our respondents reported that they had a disaster preparedness plan of any kind (Table 3.1).

It is among the academic libraries that the largest percentage with disaster plans is to be found. This represents a marked advance on the position ten years ago (Table 3.2). Clearly the concept has become a familiar one to British academic librarians, especially in the universities, perhaps as a result of persistent pressure

Sector	Number of libraries	Percentage of respondents
All	143	29.3%
Academic	66	37.29%
Public	24	18.18%
Special	53	29.94%

Table 3.1 Libraries with Disaster Preparedness Plans

1986[3]	1988[2]	1993[1]
9%	35.84%	37.29%

Table 3.2 Academic Libraries with Disaster Preparedness Plans 1982–93*
*See respective note numbers.

from SCONUL and elsewhere during the last decade. Much of the high profile of disaster planning, however, should have impinged on all sectors of librarianship, and many of the factors which can be suggested as possible reasons for the change in academic library attitudes are equally applicable in other libraries, especially in the public sector.[10]

On the other hand, there is evidence in the comments of some of our respondents that disaster planning is undertaken at a higher level in the parent body. One Scottish district, for example, told us that there was such a plan

> … for [the] Council as [an] organisation not for the library service.

We take this to be a general response plan for natural and civil disasters and major incidents rather than a plan to protect specific parts of the Council's property such as the contents of its libraries. The response of a London borough is more explicit about the distinction:

> At present, only the Archives Department has a disaster plan in hand, although, obviously, all managers are involved in planning for dealing with disasters of all kinds.

There are also a few alarming examples of naivety; the university library which informed us that it:

> … has a copy of the National Library of Scotland planning manual for disaster control and would follow its guidelines.

might find life a little more complicated than that implies if some disaster were to occur!

Within libraries, it is clear that some which do not currently have disaster plans are developing them. A number in all sectors told us of their progress. This was noticeable among public libraries, where nine were reported to us as being in preparation, but again it was in the academic library sector (ten reported out of 177 respondents) that activity was most marked. Moreover, it should be remembered that these figures are derived from the voluntary comments of respondents; there was no question asking for this information.

In general, it seems reasonable to conclude that librarians are increasingly aware of the need to prevent disasters and the need to prepare for coping with the consequences of those which cannot be prevented. On the other hand, actual plans still seem to be comparatively rare.

PRESERVATION STAFF

The apparent reluctance to commit library policies to paper is starkly illuminated when we consider the number of library staff in Britain who have a managerial or administrative role in preservation activities. As we have seen, only about 10 per cent of British libraries have a written preservation policy, and less than a third have a disaster preparedness plan. These figures may need some marginal modification along the lines we have suggested in the two previous sections, but they still stand in sharp contrast to the overall finding that well over half of our respondents have a member of staff with some responsibility for the management and implementation of preservation. The raw statistics are in Table 3.3, but stand in need of considerable amplification and commentary.

By no means all of the 283 librarians and others recorded in Table 3.3 are concerned with preservation on a full-time basis, or have any special expertise or interest in the field, or regard preservation as one of the principal components of their responsibilities. In many small libraries, for example, the responsibility lies with the librarian, who may even be the only professional. The situation of this Cambridge college librarian is arguably atypical in one sense, but defines a general issue for libraries with few staff:

> As the Assistant Librarian, I run the library on a day-by-day basis. I have one part-time term-time only assistant. My librarian is a busy academic. So any responsibility for these areas falls on my time. I am aware of the problems in conservation and do what I can.

In a different context, the Sub-Librarian (Planning and Resources) in a pre-1960 university library, or the Principal Librarian (Bibliographic Services) in a large English public library, can clearly take only a general overview responsibility.

A more detailed analysis of our data suggests that there is, however, a significant number of librarians with preservation management responsibilities for whom those responsibilities are indeed a major concern, and who can be presumed to have both interest and expertise. This is perhaps especially true in the public libraries, where the concentration of preservation efforts on local studies and other special collections seems to put the local studies librarian in the front line of preservation management. Among others, a shire county, a metropolitan district, a Welsh district and a Scottish district all reported that it was the Local Studies Librarian who had responsibility for preservation management. Comparable posts do not, of course, always have the same job title, but we take the

Sector	Number of libraries	Percentage of respondents
All	283	57.99%
Academic	96	54.24%
Public	82	62.12%
Special	104	58.76%

Table 3.3 Preservation Management Staff

Local Studies Officer of one authority to have much the same range of duties and expertise as the Local Studies Librarian or Local History Librarian of another. On this pragmatic basis, an analysis of staff responsibilities for preservation in public libraries strongly confirms the suggestion made throughout Chapter 2 that senior management in public libraries sees preservation as an issue which primarily impinges upon only this aspect of the library's work. Conversely, it follows that, in many cases, specific preservation expertise may *only* be available in the local studies department.

In some libraries, there are officers for whom preservation and conservation is their core task. This is, of course, most common in the major national institutions and the largest academic libraries. These include the British Library, the National Library of Scotland, the National Library of Wales, the Bodleian Library, the Wellcome Institute and the National Maritime Museum.[11] Elsewhere, we find that archivists play an important role in this aspect of library activities. In the library of one professional body, for example, and in that of a learned society with major historical collections, there are professional archivists who have a general responsibility for preservation. There are other examples of this practice. The significance of this is, of course, that preservation and conservation feature more prominently in the professional education of archivists than they now typically do in that of librarians;[12] in other words, archivists bring to these library posts an area of expertise which comparatively few librarians can offer.

So far, we have considered posts which are normally held by professional librarians. There are also, however, institutions in which responsibility for preservation policy development and implementation apparently lies with senior technical staff. From the job titles reported to us, it is not always possible to make this distinction; for example, we have no means of knowing whether the 'Conservation Officer' of one of our public library respondents is a librarian or a conservator. On the other hand, we assume that such titles as 'conservator' or 'binder' refer to technical staff rather than professional librarians or archivists. On this basis, there seem to be comparatively few such staff with overall responsibility for preservation. No doubt this partly reflects the fact that only about ten per cent of our respondents have an in-house bindery or conservation workshop, and that the number of persons employed in them is typically very small (Table 3.4). We also, however, take it to mean that preservation management is recognised as a professional responsibility in the vast majority of libraries in which it is undertaken at all.

STAFF TRAINING

The need to raise awareness of preservation issues among staff and readers alike was one of the pervasive themes of the Ratcliffe Report and of other contemporary and subsequent writing on the subject in Britain and indeed internationally.[13] It was argued that a knowledge of preservation issues had dramatically declined

Staff numbers*	Binderies	Workshops
Less than 5 staff	38	39
6–19 staff	12	3
More than 20 staff	2	2
Total	52 (10.66%)	44 (9.02%)

*Total bindery staff = 284.　　　　Total workshop staff = 156.

Table 3.4 Libraries with Binderies and Conservation Workshops

among British librarians. Some of the blame for this was laid at the door of the library schools, but it was also recognised that the trainers of non-professional staff had to bear some of the responsibility.[14] The library schools responded fairly quickly to the newly expressed (or, perhaps more accurately, reiterated) wish of some professional leaders for entrants to the profession to have some understanding of preservation management. By 1988, there was evidence that the subject was being taught again in a number of the schools, and that it was increasingly contextualised with management rather than with its traditional companion of historical bibliography.[15] The National Preservation Advisory Committee established an Education Panel in 1987, which has actively pursued the issue, and continues to do so, most recently by the compilation of a pack for use by trainers in libraries.[16]

Staff training within libraries, however, is less easily addressed than initial professional education. Training is still neglected in many libraries, and in others is necessarily constrained by small numbers and other calls on staff time. All libraries have resourcing problems, and it is only too easy to neglect training in favour of the more immediate demands of providing services to users. One in five of our respondents provide some in-house training schemes for existing staff which are intended, wholly or partly, to increase their awareness of preservation issues, or to give them some appropriate basic training in prevention and repair of damage. Rather more, just over 25 per cent, include some mention of preservation in their induction programmes for newly appointed staff.

Much of this training, whether for new or existing staff, is concerned with the day-to-day practicalities of stock maintenance. A shire-county librarian commented:

> It is not a planned programme, but we have regularly held sessions about catching books before they are unable to be bound as well as generally maintaining stock physically.

So far as newly appointed staff are concerned, the same shire county trains them:

> … in the sense that all staff in branch libraries are made aware of binding and preservation policies.

58

This is an unusually full answer, but fairly typical in its substance. Another shire-county librarian, for example, told us that it has:

> no specific regular training but occasional seminars have been held.

This respondent wrote that it does not formally include preservation awareness in induction courses, except:

> ... in a basic sense in being covered generally in induction routines.

These two public library responses call for some discussion. They are typical of those who provided us with comments as well as a simple response to our questions. They both suggest that, despite some of what has been deduced from the answers to other questions, the basic care and maintenance of lending stock is seen as an issue of enough importance to warrant some training, however limited in scope. The almost apologetic tone of the comments quoted in the previous paragraph is again not untypical of many public library responses. Such a tone is quite inappropriate; for a public library whose principal mission, expressed through its network of branches, is to provide reading matter and information to its majority client groups, the maintenance of a loan and reference stock in an acceptable condition is a prime means towards the fulfilment of a major institutional objective. At that level, managers clearly do recognise the significance of the physical care of the stock. As we have suggested in Chapter 2, it may be that the very word 'preservation' carries connotations which are not always associated with this essential day-to-day routine work of the library. We shall return to this in Chapter 7.[17]

Some respondents elaborated on what was actually taught on their training programmes and induction courses. For the most part, these confirm the supposition that much of this training is very basic indeed. Much of it is concerned with the handling of materials, and with the identification of materials which need some attention. A shire county, for example, says that 'all staff [are] trained to identify material suitable for repair/rebinding'. This is echoed in the response of yet another shire-county librarian who noted that new staff were given:

> ... basic information to enable them to identify items which require and are capable of binding and repair.

In the context of public libraries, this is essential. It is, after all, the non-professional staff, often part-time or short-term, who are principally involved in handling books when they are issued, returned and shelved. Many libraries clearly recognise the need to provide training of this kind.

This perception is not confined to public libraries. A pre-1960 university, for example, trains 'issue desk staff in general repair work', and a medical school library noted:

> Senior Library Assistant trains Library Assistant in basic book repair.

Similar practices are reported from other academic libraries, and some have indeed taken the matter a little further. One Oxford college reports that it has prepared a list of 'dos and don'ts' for its junior staff, and in another the Library Assistants are given informal instruction by the Librarian. Much of this is also reflected in the smaller special libraries, especially in those with historical collections.

Not all staff training, however, is at this very basic level. In Oxford, Cambridge, London and perhaps elsewhere there are training courses organised by consortia of libraries for their mutual benefit, which can, of course, draw on a far wider range of expertise than any one small library could offer. There is widespread evidence of the use of videos and other training material, not least that prepared by the National Preservation Office, among those libraries who do offer some staff training; again, this allows a wider perspective and exposes trainees to expertise which may not easily be available institutionally or locally. In some libraries, the whole matter is clearly taken very seriously indeed. Where there is a preservation manager in post, or an identifiable person with responsibility for preservation policy, that postholder is often used as a trainer. One example comes from a pre-1960 university with an internationally important library; our respondent wrote:

> Head of Bookbinding and Conservation [leads the training] in association with a member of staff in Special Collections building. All members of staff, from management level to cleaners, receive instruction – a two-way educative programme.

So far as new staff are concerned:

> All levels of staff instructed: details of how a book is made; different styles of binding; general handling techniques; use of book cradles and similar conservation aids, etc.

This is exceptional, although wholly appropriate to the institution; indeed, as an example of best practice we shall return to it in Chapter 6.[18] For the moment, we quote it to reiterate the point that it is in libraries which hold major historical and research collections that such policies and practices are most fully developed.

Between basic and sophisticated training, there is a continuum rather than a sharp divide. A Scottish college, for example, ensures that 'awareness of issues involved [is] passed on to staff', adding 'but no formal programme'. A special library reports that it gives instruction 'as and when such matters arise'. Examples could be multiplied, but it is needless to do so. The picture which emerges is a mixed one, but suggests that there is indeed a general awareness of the existence of an issue to be addressed, and that many librarians are taking such steps as they can to address it.

PRESERVATION SURVEYS

Like disaster preparedness planning, preservation surveys have been the subject of much literature in recent years, although a large part of it is American rather than British.[19] Indeed, it was from such surveys that the extent of the preservation problems in research libraries was first identified;[20] there are now elaborate guidelines available which can be used to assist in the planning and execution of such surveys, which are widely regarded as the essential basis of the development of an effective preservation management policy.[21]

Of our 488 respondents, 172 (35.25 per cent) indicated that they had systematic arrangements in place for making preservation surveys of their stock; the proportion was substantially the same in all three major sectors. Obviously, practices vary greatly between libraries, but in many cases it is clear that, with differing degrees of formality and systematisation, visual inspection of stock to establish its condition is a fairly widespread practice. Both academic and public libraries reported that books were checked when they were returned by borrowers; we assume that appropriate action is then taken. In any case, this explains the need for the training of junior staff at circulation desks.

More systematic surveys at the shelves are also undertaken in many libraries, although respondents often commented on the time involved, and the sheer scale of the problem. The librarian of a large special library, with major historical holdings told us that:

> Surveying is done on a 'painting the Forth Bridge' approach, but over a longer cycle! Treatment involves basic first aid, tying up damaged volumes and setting aside for conservation or repair.

A shire-county librarian reported that in its local studies library:

> Part of the open shelf stock [which is, we understand, the bulk of the collection] is surveyed each year – 'victims' are removed for paper repair, rebinding, or transfer to reserve stock.

An academic library more tersely notes a similar practice, involving a 'rough survey undertaken with annual stocktaking'.

Stock surveys and inspections on this level are common, and perhaps even more common than the responses to our questionnaire revealed; much work of this kind is so routine, especially among loan stocks in both academic and public libraries, that it is barely noticed even by those undertaking it. There is, however, comparatively little evidence of the systematic comprehensive or sample surveys which are so eloquently commended in the literature. In public libraries it is, once again, in the local studies and other special collections that we find the greatest evidence for activity. One shire county surveys all its local history collections on an annual basis; a Scottish district notes the same practice. We suspect that there are others with similar policies, who have not enlarged on the 'yes' or 'no' response invited by our question. In academic libraries, comparable regular surveys are also to be found, especially in dealing with rare books and special collections. Some libraries select particular sections of stock, or particular areas of the building, for attention as part of a regular cycle. The pattern of the academic year inevitably dictates that much of this work takes place during the summer, so that comparatively long cycles are created in some of the larger libraries. Cyclical surveys were also reported by a number of our special library respondents, ranging from annual checks, to selecting journals for binding (a scientific special library), to a systematic triennial survey (in the library of a professional association).

In general, an analysis of how libraries survey their stock confirms the emerging picture of the practice of preservation in British libraries: on one level, current lending stocks have to be maintained in a usable condition; at another, collections believed to be of permanent importance are recognised as being in need of more elaborate management. The context of this, however, is that few British libraries have actually undertaken conditional surveys, even at the level of sampling, and are therefore unable to arrive at reasoned estimates of the scale of their problems and of the cost of solving them.

CLEANING AND REPAIR

Routine surveys carried out at the shelves or when stock passes across the circulation desk are useful only if they lead to the identification of items in need of repair or replacement, and if some action is then taken as a result. Some of these actions will be taken with respect to individual items; probably the most common would be the repair of a damaged or weak binding. In addition, however, there are basic housekeeping tasks which help to ensure that stock does not deteriorate, or at least that the rate of deterioration is minimised. The most basic of all is cleaning, a form of stock maintenance which is so common that we suspect it has often not been reported to us. Only 35 per cent of our respondents reported that they regularly cleaned or treated stock on the shelves, but we do not doubt that in many more libraries books are, at the very least, dusted as part of the normal process of cleaning.

More specialised forms of cleaning and treatment are, however, to be found. These are largely, although not entirely, confined to special collections in libraries of all kinds. The application of various forms of dressings to leather bindings is still a widespread practice, reported, for example, from various university and college libraries, and from some of the larger special libraries with historical collections, as a regular part of their routine. A number of libraries use volunteers, especially those organised by NADFAS, for this and similar purposes; presumably if these people were not available, no such work would be done at all.

CONCLUSIONS

The six criteria which we have suggested for a preliminary assessment of the extent to which preservation policies have been developed and implemented suggest some modifications to the tentative conclusions which we reached at the end of Chapter 2. We suggested there that the understanding of preservation among British librarians was still comparatively narrowly based, and indeed, to some extent, that is confirmed by an analysis of their current practices. On the other hand, it is clear that there is much activity in libraries which is not actually labelled 'preservation' but which is, nevertheless, concerned with the physical care and maintenance of the stock. As we suggested in Chapter 1,[22] these broader criteria are now generally accepted as defining the proper scope of the concept of preservation.

Many librarians clearly do make efforts to maintain the physical condition of the stock in their charge, and to ensure that it is available for the users for whom it exists. Such maintenance practices have, in some cases, been formalised as part of preservation or collection management policies, or as disaster preparedness plans. In many libraries where formal policies do not exist in written form, there is substantial evidence for some staff training, regular inspection of both lending stock and research materials, and simple cleaning and care programmes. In broad terms, about a half of the very large sample of British libraries in our survey are involved in one or more of these activities. These libraries cover a wide range from the largest to the smallest, and are found in all three sectors into which libraries are customarily divided.

It is, however, increasingly apparent that the greatest preservation efforts are concentrated on collections of materials which are identified by their owners as being 'special' in some way. Some of these are the formally identified special collections which are held in many libraries. Much of this material is of historical interest, and much of it is believed to be of long-term significance to users and potential users of the holding library. In a few libraries, as we have seen, there is a genuine intention to preserve all holdings in perpetuity; even in those with lesser ambitions, there are often parts of the current stock which are earmarked for long-term preservation. It is natural and sensible that formal preservation policies should concentrate on those parts of the stock.

The most clear-cut examples of such concentration of efforts are to be found in public libraries. There is a striking similarity of approach in this sector, no doubt because of the broadly similar missions of all public library systems. In general terms, our public library respondents identified their local studies collections as being the principal focus of their preservation policies. For other stock, they have simple maintenance programmes, backed up by limited but adequate staff training. Many academic libraries, especially among the universities, show a similar approach, although their special collections have a much wider coverage that those in the public libraries. The special libraries are, of course, very diverse, but there is encouraging evidence that those which have historical collections of long-term significance do recognise the obligations which that fact imposes upon them. Almost all libraries in all sectors are operating under serious financial restraints, and it may be that preservation is not always a high priority; we shall return to this issue in Chapter 4. Despite resource restraints, however, there is clearly a comparatively high level of preservation activity, and evidence that it is concentrated in areas of greatest need.

THE IMPLEMENTATION OF PRESERVATION POLICIES

In the first part of this chapter, we have analysed what we consider to be the basic indicators of preservation policies, which show whether or not a library has such a policy in place. In this section, we turn to aspects of the implementation of preservation policies at a somewhat less basic level. We have already, for example, referred to library binderies and conservation workshops; we need to pursue this matter a little further and consider the role which they play in preservation. Logically, that leads us to consider the use of commercial binders and conservators, and, in thus going beyond the walls of the individual library, to look at the sources of advice and information available to librarians seeking to develop and implement preservation policies.

Before venturing outside the library, however, there is one critical internal issue which we need to consider. We have already suggested that preservation policies are largely focused on collections of special materials considered to be of historical and long-term importance. Almost all materials of this kind are available for consultation on library premises only, and are normally kept in closed access stores. Since such materials are often used only intermittently, they spend the greater part of their time on the shelves. The ambient environment of the storage areas is, therefore, critical to the long-term preservation of the material. As we have seen in Chapter 1,[23] there has been a growing awareness of this over the last 30 years, and a growing understanding of the optimal conditions for the storage of the various information media. This is a fundamental issue for the custodians of research collections. We shall, therefore, consider this before moving on to the other matters which concern us in this section.

THE STORAGE OF LIBRARY MATERIALS

The storage question has both a wide and a narrow dimension. At the wider level, we are concerned with library buildings, and such major issues as the climatic and environmental conditions of the location of the library. At the narrower level, we focus on more specific concerns such as the storage equipment used in the library, the security and environmental control of storage areas, and the like. We shall consider each in turn.

There are standards and recommendations for library buildings, and many examples of good practice. Until comparatively recently, however, preservation has probably not been a major consideration in much library building planning. Indeed, librarians have, rightly, emphasised the convenience of the users and the staff rather than creating the ideal conditions for the books. The new British

Library building at St Pancras is a rare exception to the rule that preservation issues are often not prioritised at the planning stage; there is an interesting contrast here with the Bibliothèque de France whose critics have argued that a fine architectural design will be wholly unsuitable for the storage of rare books.[24] In practice, of course, few librarians will have the opportunity to influence the building of a new library, although there are some good recent examples.[25]

For most librarians, however, the buildings in which collections are housed are simply another restraint within which they have to work. This can present some real problems. There are scores of late medieval and early modern buildings in Britain still in use as libraries, and hundreds which date from before 1945. The last great period of library building was the 1960s and early 1970s, a period when preservation was certainly not a major priority for many library planners and policy-makers. Many libraries are housed in buildings which are themselves important monuments, and are consequently subject to many restrictions on alterations and change of use. As one respondent commented:

> A seventeenth century Jacobean mansion is far from ideal in terms of housing a library collection.

The situation in which such libraries find themselves is succinctly summarised in a document from one major institution:

> This range of buildings dates from the middle of the fifteenth century to the late twentieth century. They include buildings of great historic and architectural importance, which are not necessarily suited to the convenience required by a modern and efficient library service.

The problem which this implies is widespread, even though not always so extreme. Several public libraries made the obvious point that they have many buildings, of different ages and sizes, and that the quality and suitability of these vary significantly.

Turning from the general to the specific, we find that many librarians are indeed making serious efforts to create appropriate storage conditions for their stock. The best conditions for paper-based materials are well known and well documented. Essentially, they are constituted by an appropriate combination of temperature and relative humidity; for research materials, light levels can also be important in ensuring long-term survival, and for all organically based materials the level of environmental pollution can be a factor in certain circumstances.[26] On the other hand, paper is tolerant of a rather wider range of conditions than the ideal prescriptions might suggest; one respondent made the point that the ideal temperature for books is distinctly chilly for staff and readers accustomed to normal contemporary standards of heating!

In formulating our specific questions on such matters, we confined ourselves to asking whether or not it was possible to control the four basic constituents of the ambient environment: heat, humidity, light and air quality, although we also invited (as we did throughout) any additional comments which our respondents might chose to make. Perhaps the least surprising finding was that most libraries can control the temperature of their buildings (Table 3.5), and all of them regularly monitor it. Other environmental controls are less common, although monitoring of relative humidity (perhaps the most important factor in the preservation of paper) is reported from about 60 per cent of libraries. The differences between academic, public and special libraries are insignificant. Underlying these bare statistics, however, are some very real problems. We have already quoted the librarians of two collections housed wholly or partly in historic buildings. In both cases the collections themselves are of sufficient importance to ensure that steps are taken to mitigate the possible effects of this as far as possible. This is not always the case. One local studies librarian told us that 'water pours into our archive stores whenever it rains'. Even superficially adequate buildings are often far from perfect; from a former polytechnic, we were told that conditions in the library are 'too hot', and this is, inevitably, causing 'glue and binding materials to dry out'. This is a persistent problem in modern buildings, as the librarian of a professional body reminded us:

> Air conditioned building for last 17 years has led to brittle paper, [and] glue in binding drying out.

From another special library, we were told of an air-conditioning system which was described as 'very rudimentary' and as being 'not satisfactory for materials or for library users/staff'.

There is alarming evidence of neglect of buildings and storage facilities, often no doubt as a result of lack of funds rather than ignorance. In one pre-1960 university library:

Parameter	All		Academic		Public		Special	
		%		%		%		%
Relative humidity								
Monitor	305	62.75%	117	66.1%	87	65.9%	101	57.06%
Control	242	50.02%	96	54.23%	66	50.0%	80	45.19%
Temperature								
Monitor	486	100.00%	177	100.00%	132	100.00%	177	100.00%
Control	393	80.86%	135	76.27%	98	74.24%	148	83.61%
Light								
Monitor	244	50.2%	87	49.15%	64	48.48%	92	51.97%
Control	305	62.75%	109	61.58%	78	59.09%	118	66.66%
Pollution								
Monitor	52	10.69%	13	7.34%	19	14.39%	20	11.29%
Control	72	14.81%	24	13.55%	19	14.39%	29	16.38%

Table 3.5 Libraries with Environmental Monitoring and Control Facilities

... the ventilating system has not functioned for many years. We look to improvements with the installation of a new air-conditioning system ... Generally the Reading Room and Gallery areas are worse, two stack levels, where the major collections are housed, better.

This is a typical order of priorities in many libraries; as far as possible, librarians seem to have striven to protect the collections which are deemed to be of greatest importance. Monitoring of the conditions in which such collections are housed is, as we have seen, comparatively common. The mechanisms vary from simple thermometers to much more sophisticated equipment such as thermohydrographs. Generally, however, it is clear that the environmental conditions in which many important collections are stored are still far from ideal, and often fall below an acceptable level. Considerable efforts are being made to monitor such conditions, which at least makes it possible to identify and perhaps to quantify the problem. Librarians, however, are too often confronted by a situation which they know to be unsatisfactory without having the means to address it effectively. Remedies vary from the simplest (keeping the heating 'as low as possible') to the most sophisticated ('activated carbon filters to reduce dust pollution'). The majority in between make what use they can of heating and lighting systems designed with other priorities in mind, and use such resources as are made available for preventative measures such as ultra-violet filters for windows or portable dehumidifiers for use in small storage areas.

Finally, we turn to the actual equipment used for the storage of materials. To keep this within reasonable bounds, we concentrated on the provision of special equipment or facilities for collections identified by the institutions as being of particular importance. Just under half of our respondents have such facilities, and again there is little difference between sectors (Table 3.6).

So far as facilities are concerned, the most common is a designated room or area in which special collections are shelved. No doubt security is part of the motive for such separation, but it does, of course, also allow these collections to be treated differently in other ways if that is felt to be desirable. Such storage areas were reported from a very large number of libraries, some of which specified that they had been able to create conditions which conform to the requirements of BS5454.[27] More typical, however, is this London University institute:

Sector	Number	Percentage
All	232	47.54%
Academic	91	51.41%
Public	71	53.79%
Special	70	39.55%

Table 3.6 Libraries with Dedicated Storage for Special Collections

... a strongroom which houses most manuscripts and less than 50 per cent of the rare books and archives – the strongroom is environmentally controlled for temperature and humidity.

A pre-1960 university has a:

... strongroom for very valuable material, and three secure 'special collections'.

From a Scottish university we were told of:

Special collections housed in secure strongroom equipped with large fans to assist air circulation and control mildew.

In all three cases, appropriate conditions have clearly been created for the most valuable and vulnerable items in the library; these are, as we have suggested, typical of libraries of their kind.

Among public libraries, however, we suspect that the situation is somewhat different. We have suggested at several points both in this chapter and in Chapter 2 that the preservation activities of public libraries are, for the most part, concentrated on their local studies collections. Many of these collections, however, are on open access, although older and more valuable material, as well as manuscripts and archives, are in many cases kept in secure closed-access storage areas. These practices are revealed through, and reflected in, the comments of public librarians on storage facilities. The word 'archive' is commonly used, and it is, we suspect, archives which are most often found in the strongrooms which are reported by many authorities. These rooms are, of course, comparable with those in the university libraries. A London borough which has a 'separate strongroom for unique MSS, photos, films, rare books' notes that it conforms to BS5454'; a metropolitan district has a similar room 'conforming (almost) to HMC standards'.[28] These arrangements are typical of the more than 50 per cent of public libraries which reported special storage facilities of some kind.

The provision of such facilities indicates an awareness of the issues involved, and a willingness to devote some resources to the protection of important materials in these libraries. We should not, however, succumb to complacency: about half of the libraries in Britain apparently have no such facilities. Some, as we have seen, have identified their needs but have no means of meeting them. Some others, no doubt, have no such needs. We suspect, however, that there are still libraries in all sectors in which special storage facilities are needed for parts of the stock, but such needs have either not been identified, or, if they have, are not being met.

BINDERIES AND CONSERVATION WORKSHOPS

So far, we have been largely concerned with preservation at the policy level, and with the 'passive' aspects such as storage and damage prevention. We now turn to one aspect of active preservation and conservation work: binding and repair. We have already noted (in Table 3.4) that only about 10 per cent of libraries have binderies, and slightly fewer have conservation workshops. Most of these operations are very small indeed, consisting of one or two persons.

For some years now there has been a concern, expressed in the Ratcliffe Report, that the number of trained bookbinders and conservators was insufficient.[29] It is not, however, clear that jobs would necessarily exist for them even if trained personnel were available. Some of the major commercial firms in the field, always an important source of both training and employment, have been downsizing during the 1980s, partly as a consequence of continued mechanisation of some of the routine work for publishers.[30] In fact, only 25 libraries told us that they had experienced difficulties in recruiting suitably trained conservation staff, although this does, worryingly, constitute more than half of those who actually employ conservators. The comments made on this issue suggest that there are a number of separate problems, although these do intersect at various points.

The first, and perhaps the most important challenge, is money. Some libraries who wish to employ binders simply do not have the funds to do so. There are, however, others which do have funds available but have experienced difficulties of a different kind. A metropolitan district with a substantial bindery and conservation workshop noted that 'competition from private binders' made it difficult for them to recruit; this may be a result of local circumstances, for it so happens that a very large commercial bindery is located in the area. A more explicit comment came from the librarian of a post-1960 university in a region where unemployment is below the national average:

Trained binders hard to recruit on university technician pay scales.

It should be added, by way of balance, that one of our respondents told us that their large bindery had no difficulty in recruitment because of the closure of commercial binderies in the town. This was, however, a place with a strong tradition of bookbinding, where there is a disproportionately large pool of trained people.

The second problem which was identified was the difficulty in finding people with the right skills. A shire-county librarian with a substantial bindery commented:

We have had difficulty in recruiting Class I binders with a full range of binding skills.

A pre-1960 university commented on the 'lack of suitable personnel'; this was in a town with high unemployment and two major libraries! The obvious questions about training which arise from these and other comments are not, however, universally perceived in the same way. One shire-county librarian told us that in its experience there are:

... staff readily available through contacts in Camberwell and Gateshead Colleges.

This comment is, however, unique, while several libraries have told us that they have had to set up their own training programmes, or make external arrangements, to try to provide themselves with suitable employees.

In fact, the two issues of wages and training cannot be treated entirely separately. Although we have no direct evidence to support this, it is our supposition that the low wages typically paid to manual staff, especially in the public sector, and the long training for a not particularly prestigious trade, are a deterrent to potential recruits. A few are, of course, still coming forward, but not enough to sustain the national training programmes which would be ideally desirable. There is a spiral of decline in the availability of skilled personnel; a metropolitan district librarian who employs both binders and conservators commented:

Shortage of craft binders/conservators being trained due to limited job opportunities.

As a result, training facilities are simply not available, except in a very few colleges, and through special courses such as those sponsored by the Society of Archivists.[31] Where the skills still exist in libraries, they can, of course, be passed on. The metropolitan district librarian who provided the first comment in this section, added:

We are now instituting a programme to train at least one assistant at a time to Class I.

Securing an adequate supply of people trained to an appropriate standard, and providing jobs for them when they have been trained, is a key issue to which we shall return in Chapter 7.[32]

This is not, however, the only problem experienced by libraries which are trying to run in-house binding and conservation facilities. Fifteen or twenty years ago, it was a common complaint that some essential conservation materials were not readily available, or available only either in impractically large quantities or at disproportionately high prices. This was perhaps especially true of some of the more specialised supplies, such as acid-free card and paper, which were by no means as common then as they have subsequently become. In the early 1980s, the National Preservation Advisory Committee, the SCONUL Working Party on Preservation and the Library Association Sub-committee on Conservation all concerned themselves with this in one way or another. There were some joint initiatives with the printers, publishers and paper manufacturers and importers, which led to the publication of some brief guidelines,[33] and to the increased use of acid-free paper by publishers. In turn, this made such paper more widely available in Britain. There was also some discussion of joint buying of some very specialised materials by several institutions in order to gain the cost benefits of bulk purchase.

Some of these problems still residually exist. It was, however, noticeable that they were drawn to our attention almost entirely by smaller libraries; as one put it to us:

We are a small library – hard to obtain some materials in small enough quantities.

Of course, cost is also a problem. A special library in which there is a strong sense of the historical importance of the stock commented on its difficulties in obtaining 'decent/cheap archival repair tape [and] archival boxes'. A learned society library has had problems in obtaining A3-size acid-free photocopier paper; other specific instances were also brought to our attention. Finally, there has been, as we also know from anecdotal evidence, a problem with instability among suppliers in recent years; this is reflected in several answers. The problem of supplies is a very real one. The most specialised materials, such as acid-free paper and card (and indeed good quality leather, as the librarian of one Cambridge college reminded us) are not easy to obtain, not least because the demand for them is so small. Although some materials are more readily obtainable than 10 or 15 years ago, and suppliers' catalogues do seem to contain more variety of the materials which binders and conservators are seeking, there is still a mismatch between demand and economic supply.

So far, we have confined ourselves to some of the issues raised by libraries which have their own facilities for bookbinding or conservation work. We now turn to the majority whose work is done by commercial binderies. It is important to recognise that some of the largest and most prestigious libraries, including some with their own facilities, make use of these companies. It is a matter of public record that the British Library uses various firms for its routine work, including some simple work on older materials, and uses its own employees for more difficult work and for work on items of special value, rarity or importance.[34] Some other libraries have similar policies, although many inevitably have to use outside companies for all their work because they have no facilities of their own. Indeed, the commercial binders are clearly the cornerstone of library binding activity in Britain. This is where most ordinary binding work is done, as well as much important work in the conservation and repair of archival and other historical materials.

Finally, we turn to the work which is actually undertaken in binderies and conservation workshops, whether in libraries or elsewhere. It is not our intention to make qualitative judgements on this work, but rather to try to give some impression of its range and variety. 'Binding' is a word which covers a multitude of forms and practices, some of which would be regarded as normal in one institution and wholly unacceptable in another. There are, at present, no formal standards, although International Standards for both publishers' and library bindings are at present being negotiated.[35] Binding is not, however, the only means by which library materials, even printed and written materials, can be protected. Indeed, in some cases it is aesthetically or bibliographically inappropriate. In recent years, many substitutes for binding have been developed, and we find widespread evidence for their use in libraries of all kinds. Acid-free boxes, folders, portfolios and the like are common in many libraries. Indeed, there is encouraging evidence that librarians in all sectors with responsibility for historical materials have absorbed the importance of using appropriate methods. We also find evidence for the widespread use of temporary palliatives, such as the taping of damaged books, and the use of phase boxes, although the latter are, we suspect, in many cases inevitably going to be a permanent measure.

KNOWLEDGE AND ADVICE

It is clear from much of what has been written in this chapter, and not least at the end of the previous section, that there is a widespread awareness of at least the basic principles of preservation practice. There is also, however, perhaps a sense of inadequacy in the face of the scale of the problem in many libraries: the lack of necessary skills, the difficulties in obtaining materials, and, above all, the vast shortfall in the resources needed to deal with these problems on anything like an appropriate scale. In this section, we turn to how and where librarians learn about these issues, and how to deal with them, and, by implication, begin to assess how successful the much-vaunted awareness-raising initiative have actually been.

A key player here is the NPO, which, as we have seen in Chapter 1, was established as a direct outcome of the publication of the Ratcliffe Report, and has been active across the whole range of preservation and conservation policy at national level ever since.[36] Without attempting to evaluate the work of the NPO (although there is perhaps a case for an objective evaluation), we tried to assess its impact, by asking about the use made of it. Of our 488 respondents, 218 (44.7 per cent) had used at least one of its services; this may be an underestimate, since it is at least possible that the person completing the questionnaire would not necessarily know, for example, if there had been such consultation several years ago. Not surprisingly, it was the free services, and particularly the free leaflets, which attracted the greatest attention, but a significant number of libraries have also made use of priced services. Nearly 20 per cent had obtained one or more priced publications, and 15 per cent had used the various training videos which the NPO has produced. Seen in the light of our general findings about the priority accorded to preservation in libraries, we suggest that the NPO can be satisfied with (although we are sure that it would never be complacent about!) the level of coverage which it has achieved.

The central concept in the proposal which eventually led to the establishment of the NPO was that of a referral and advisory centre which would go some way towards plugging the gaps created by the widespread ignorance and misunderstanding of preservation and conservation which was perceived among professional librarians.[37] Indeed, there was a suggestion that such a service might eventually be self-funding, or even profit-making. That suggestion has not been tested in practice, perhaps fortunately, for we found that, while only 15 per cent of our respondents had drawn on the expertise of the NPO, or used its advisory services, more than 60 per cent had turned to commercial binders for this purpose (Table 3.7). Unfortunately, we were offered few comments on the answers to our questions about sources of information, but anecdotal evidence suggests that many librarians still follow the long-established practice of asking their binders for advice, a procedure which has much to commend it. It will also be noted that more specialist advice is sought from conservators, and from fellow professionals in other libraries, in record offices and in museums.

CONCLUSIONS

In the second part of this chapter we have tried to put some flesh on the bare bones of preservation awareness and preservation policies. In general terms, as we have suggested, there seems to be a fairly high level of awareness at least of the major issues involved, and of the need to seek specialist advice, specialist skills and specialist materials. The problems lie not in understanding but in implementation. The creation and sustenance of a proper environment for research materials in libraries is a long-term and high-cost investment. Many librarians are doing what they can in straightened circumstances, sometimes with little understanding and support from their parent bodies. Moreover, there is some skill shortage in the two basic crafts of conservation – bookbinding and conservation work – partly because of a shortage of jobs and limited training opportunities. This is not a happy situation. On the other hand, there is evidence that specialist materials can be more easily obtained than used to be alleged to be the case, and it is clear that they are being used by many librarians whenever they can afford to do so. Finally, librarians have become aware of their limitations; perhaps they always were, but we have clearly revealed the extent to which they turn to sources of expertise outside their own organisations to counterbalance the imperfections in their own knowledge.

Source	All	Academic	Public	Special
	%	%	%	%
National Preservation Office	218 44.67%	89 50.28%	59 44.7%	70 39.55%
Commercial binders	304 62.3%	108 61.02%	102 77.27%	93 52.54%
Other libraries	200 40.98%	85 48.02%	45 34.09%	70 39.55%
Record offices	158 32.38%	31 17.51%	81 61.36%	46 25.99%
Private conservators	148 30.33%	52 29.38%	38 28.79%	57 23.2%
Museums	146 29.92%	37 20.90%	61 46.21%	48 27.12%
University departments	109 22.34%	67 37.85%	15 11.36%	27 15.25%
Government departments	57 11.68%	13 7.34%	16 12.12%	28 15.82%
Industrial laboratories	25 5.12%	11 6.21%	7 5.3%	7 3.95%

Table 3.7 Sources of Advice on Preservation

CONCLUSIONS

The main purpose of this chapter has been to present, with some commentary but little qualitative interpretation, the information available to us about the existence and implementation of preservation policies in British libraries at the present time. Some conclusions emerge strongly and consistently:

- A general recognition that preservation policies are essential if collections of historical importance are to be maintained.
- Major financial obstacles to the implementation of the implications of this perception.
- Widespread evidence that librarians, far from being discouraged, are doing what they can to remedy the defects and to protect those parts of their collections which they recognise as having a long-term significance.

Preservation is indeed a part of the way in which many librarians think about their libraries. Under whatever name, there are aspects of preservation policy – in terms of collection management, resource allocation, physical planning, and disaster preparedness, for example – which have entered the mainstream.

In essence, this and the previous chapter represent the factual foundation of this book. We now turn to more interpretative approaches, building upon that foundation. In particular, two major questions can be posed on the basis of the conclusions suggested here. The first concerns the impact of the changing professional and political environment on preservation, including some issues of particular pertinence at the present time. The second question centres around the impact of technological change, and the fundamental changes in the role of libraries and information agencies which that is allegedly driving. We shall formulate, and attempt to answer, these and some subsidiary questions in the next chapter.

NOTES

1. Paul Eden, John Feather and Graham Matthews. Preservation policies and conservation in British academic libraries in 1993: a survey. *British Journal of Academic Librarianship*, 8: 2 (1993), pp. 65–88.
2. Brenda E. Moon and Anthony J. Loveday. Progress report on preservation in British libraries since the Ratcliffe Report. In: National Preservation Office. *Preservation and Technology. Proceedings of a Seminar at York University, 20–21 July 1988*. London: The British Library, 1989, pp. 11–17, at p. 13. Our own findings on this topic are discussed on pp. 137–8 below.
3. Ian R.M. Mowat. Preservation problems in academic libraries. In: R.E. Palmer, ed. *Preserving the Word. The Library Association Conference Proceedings, Harrogate 1986*. London: The Library Association, 1987, pp. 37–42, at pp. 38–9.
4. See J.M. Lancaster. Disaster control planning. In: Geraldine Kenny, ed. *A Reading Guide to the Preservation of Library Collections*. London: The Library Association, 1991, pp. 63–71; and National Preservation Office. *Disaster Planning: a bibliography*. London: The British Library, 1993.

5. G.W. Joseph and G.W. Couturier. Essential management activities to support effective disaster planning. *International Journal of Information Management*, 13: 5, 1993, pp. 315–25.

6. Such as Ian Tregarthen Jenkin. *Disaster Planning and Preparedness: an outline disaster control plan* (British Library Information Guide, 5). London: The British Library, 1987; and Sally A. Buchanan. *Disaster Planning: Preparedness and Recovery for Libraries and Archives: a RAMP Study with guidelines*. Paris: UNESCO (PGI-88/WS/6), 1988.

7. Such as Graham Matthews. Fire and water at the USSR Academy of Science Library. *Library Association Record*, 90: 5, 1988, pp. 279–81; Margaret Saunders. How a library picked up the pieces after the IRA blast. *Library Association Record*, 95: 2, 1993, pp. 100–1; or K. Green. The case of the Pilkington Technology Centre fire. *Aslib Information*, 21: 2, 1993, pp. 72–5.

8. H. Donnelly and M. Heaney. Disaster planning – a wider approach. *Aslib Information*, 21: 2 (1993), pp. 69–71.

9. John E. McIntyre. Disaster planning: a national concern. *Alexandria*, 2: 2 (1990), pp. 51–60.

10. See our comments in Preservation policies and conservation (note 1, above).

11. We break our usual rule of anonymity here because these appointments are a matter of public record from annual reports and the like.

12. Helen Forde. Education and archive conservation. In: National Preservation Office. *Conservation in Crisis*. London: British Library, 1987, pp. 23–7.

13. Ratcliffe, op. cit., pp. 44–5.

14. Ratcliffe, op. cit., pp. 25–8; B.C. Bloomfield. Education and training for conservation work in the UK. In: Ibid., pp. 105–13; and John Feather. Conservation education for professional librarians: a library school view. In: Ibid., pp. 114–18.

15. John Feather and Anne Lusher. Education for conservation in British library schools: current practices and future prospects. *Journal of Librarianship*, 21: 2 (1989), pp. 129–38.

16. See above, Chapter 1, note 47.

17. See below, pp. 136–7.

18. See below, pp. 115–16.

19. Eiluned Rees and Julian Thomas. Surveying the collections. In: Kenny, op. cit., pp. 23–9. See also, above, p. 11.

20. Feather, op. cit., pp. 3–4.

21. George M. Cunha. *Methods of Evaluation to Determine the Preservation Needs in Libraries and Archives: a RAMP study with guidelines*. Paris: UNESCO (PGI-88/WS/16), 1988.

22. See above, pp. 3–5.

23. See above, pp. 1–3.

24. G. Grunberg. La bibliothèque de France, de l'intention à la réalisation. *Bulletin d'informations de L'association de bibliothecaires français*, 161: 4 (1993), pp. 63–7; B. Lang. La British Library à St. Pancras. *Documentation et bibliothèques*, 39: 2 (1993), pp. 65–8; David Clements. The British Library building at St. Pancras as a major new centre. In: C.S. Woods, ed. *Conservation for the future: proceedings of the 1993 Annual Instructional Meeting hosted by Dorset County Archives Service*. London: Society of Archivists, Preservation and Conservation Group, 1993, pp. 1–5; and Anne Pasquinon. The project of the Bibliothèque nationale de France. In: Ibid., pp. 6–8.

25. See, for example, Michael Dewe and Robert Williams. Public library buildings. *Public Library Journal*, 7: 2 (1992), pp. 45–8, 7: 6 (1992), pp. 152–5.

26. See above, p. 11.

27. British Standards Institution. *Recommendations for Storage and Exhibition of Archival Documents*. London: BSI, 1989 (BS5454: 1989).

28. We take this to mean Historical Manuscripts Commission, and to refer, *de facto*, to the British Standard.

29. Ratcliffe, op. cit., pp. 28–30.

30. We derive this from conversations with senior personnel in the industry.

31. See above, note 12.

32. See below, pp. 138–9.

33. Library Association, National Preservation Office and Publishers' Association. *Permanent Paper*. London: LA/NOP/PA, 1986. A new standard for permanent paper (ISO 9706) has just been published (November 1994), and has been recommended by both the Publishers'

Association and the National Preservation Office in guidance with and press releases which we have seen.

34. Information from D.W.G. Clements.
35. Personal information; one of us (J.F.) serves on the relevant UK advisory committee.
36. See above, pp. 3–6.
37. Ratcliffe, op. cit., pp. 36–9.

4 Priorities in Preservation

In the first three chapters of this book we have described the recent history of preservation as a professional issue in British librarianship, and have used both the results of our own research and the published literature to give a reasonably comprehensive overview of current practices and attitudes among libraries and professional librarians. We now turn to broader issues, and in this chapter we shall suggest the broader context within which our earlier findings and conclusions must be seen. There are essentially three paths which need to be followed, and then brought together:

- Changes in professional attitudes to information service provision.
- Political developments which have had financial and other consequences for the provision of libraries services.
- Technological developments which have both introduced new materials and media into libraries and changed the ways in which libraries work.

All of these themes could, of course, be pursued on many levels and in many contexts. Our concern is specifically with their impact on preservation and management of collections of library materials. That issue, central as it is to this book, cannot, however, be wholly divorced from the wider implications of these matters. Some of those implications inevitably, therefore, have to be considered here, and following our general discussion we shall look more specifically at strategic and technological issues in preservation policy.

THE WIDER CONTEXT

THE PROFESSIONAL DIMENSION

One of the most important changes in British librarianship since 1945 has been the changes in librarians themselves. The librarian is no longer simply a custodian; libraries overtly proclaim their mission of making books and information available and accessible to readers in response to demand. Perhaps this can best be understood in the deep, but often unintended, symbolism of library architecture. The oldest library room in Britain still in constant use for its original purpose is Duke Humfrey's Library in the Bodleian; its arrangements and furnishings are still those which were installed when the books were chained to the shelves. Three centuries later, the Reading Room of the British Museum proclaimed its own message: books could be freely read, but they were to be stored elsewhere, found through a catalogue and fetched for the reader. In the first half of this century, the new building designed for the University Library at Cambridge was profoundly different: all but the most valuable books at one end of the scale, and the least academically useful at the other, were to be accessible to readers who could browse the shelves as well as search more systematically with the aid of catalogues and bibliographies. The Cambridge model (which was actually imitated from contemporary American approaches and indeed designs) has become the norm: at the end of the twentieth century, we expect libraries of all kinds to be primarily open access.

It is perhaps now forgotten, except by the diminishing band of library historians, that public libraries in Britain went through a similar evolution. When the first libraries were built under the 1850 Act, they too were closed access. Borrowers selected their books from lists and catalogues, and may sometimes have had their choices restricted by the judgement of the librarian. Open access to lending stock did not become common until after World War One, or universal until the middle of the twentieth century. As in the academic libraries, these changes were symbolised in architecture. In the nineteenth century, the buildings of the great urban public libraries were designed primarily as book stores and, in many towns and cities, as civic monuments. Only in the early decades of the present century did many of the libraries built from the generosity of the Carnegie Trust begin to take on a different appearance. They were lighter and less forbidding, but also places for reading as well as for keeping books and conducting the transactions connected with the lending and borrowing of them. Since 1945, public libraries have changed beyond recognition; even older buildings have had to be adapted to provide not only open access to lending stocks and reference areas, but also facilities for children, for visually impaired users and indeed for the more general cultural and educational use of the library space.

These changes can, as we have suggested, be taken as symbolic of the changing attitude of librarians to both stock and readers. With rare exceptions, readers are no longer seen as the privileged users of a valuable resource, but as the owners and legitimate users of a public good. They are encouraged to use the library; among many librarians, usage of stock is regarded as the major indicator of success. Stock is consequently seen as something to be used rather than protected, an approach exemplified by several of the librarians whom we quoted in Chapter 2. One of those comments bears repetition here:

We do not 'preserve' but rather 'exploit' our stock.

These are the words of a university librarian, but they are typical of many in all sectors. The implication of this librarian's words, and of comparable comments from others, is that because readers are more important than stock, it is the demands of the readers which must always take priority. The implication might be that there is an inherent and irreconcilable conflict between preservation and use, between stock and readers.

That alleged conflict, however, is increasingly a matter of perception rather than reality. It has been cogently argued that digital technologies have the potential to offer both preservation *and* access, and that they should be exploited to that end.[1] Such a strategy encompasses not only the digitization of the information content of documents, but also the development of databases which give distant access to their contents, or to information about the location of conventional materials. The concept of a distributed collection, developed collaboratively and perhaps jointly owned by several libraries, is already established in Australia,[2] and, as we shall see, is the implicit conceptual underpinning of some current developments in the UK. The availability of information over networks is already heavily influencing collection development policies in individual libraries,[3] and has been generalised into the concept of 'just-in-time' provision of electronic documents rather than 'just-in-case' purchase of the printed equivalent.[4]

THE POLITICAL DIMENSION

Libraries in Britain which depend on public funds for the bulk of their income have been subjected to a long period of restraint in growth, and in some cases a decline in funding in real terms. In the UK as a whole, public library expenditure per head of population has increased from £11.33 in 1981–2 to £12.94 in 1991–2. This increase is real, but very small, and has to be measured against the diversification of expenditure, particularly, as we shall see, on information technology products. The percentage spent on books has decreased slightly in the same period, from 14.9 per cent of total expenditure to 14.4 per cent.[5] Comparable figures for academic libraries are not so easily calculated, but one measure is that total library expenditure in all the pre-1992 universities rose from £64.6 million in 1981–2 to £134.5 million in 1991–2, an increase of 103 per cent; this was in excess of the general increases in the Retail Price Index in the same period (78 per cent), but significantly less than the average increase in academic book prices, a far more important measure for these institutions, which was 121 per cent.[6]

Global figures for library budgets, however, are merely the statistical framework. The practical consequences are less easily stated and have to be more subtly analysed. Library managers and policymakers have, in effect, been forced to redirect income in order to satisfy new kinds of demands from users. Some of these demands are themselves generators of revenue, and some are even self-financing, but the provision of core services to the users of public and academic libraries has also created new financial pressures. Computer systems represent a massive commitment of both capital and recurrent expenditure, with the capital expenditure itself as a *de facto* recurrent item over an approximately five-year cycle. In 1991–2 university libraries in Britain spent £32.9 million on the purchase of computer equipment, an increase of 96 per cent in five years; the general RPI increased by 36 per cent in the same period, and total university income by 67 per cent.[7] Directly comparable figures are not available for public libraries, but some idea of the scale of the increase in expenditure can be gauged from the 226 per cent growth in computing costs between 1981–2 and 1991–2.[8] Such levels of expenditure inevitably affect the distribution of the budget; in university libraries in the five years up to 1991–2, there was only a 28 per cent increase in spending on binding and conservation; the equivalent public library figure was 27 per cent between 1982 and 1992.[9] This disparity in the growth of expenditure is perhaps the most vivid practical expression of how public-sector libraries are addressing the conservation issue; in real terms, expenditure has declined dramatically.

When we develop this statistical framework, we find some of the consequences of restraints in funding. In Chapter 3, we quoted a number of examples of preservation problems which clearly arose from neglect of building maintenance or the use of unsuitable buildings for storing library materials.[10] Capital building programmes have been particularly badly hit by restraints on public expenditure and high levels of inflation. Although there have been some major projects in all sectors, they have been few compared with the backlog of need.[11]

Given the requirements of new financial regimes, and of new professional and political contexts, it is no surprise that both public and academic libraries have been subjected to generalised scrutiny of their activities and their future directions. In the university sector, the Higher Education Funding Councils sponsored a major investigation into library provision in 1993; the report of this group (the Follett Report) made important recommendations, some of which are directly relevant to our concerns, and all of which have some impact on them.[12] Two sections are of particular importance. The first of these deals with the needs of researchers in the humanities and certain social sciences, where primary materials are essentially library-based. The essence of the proposal is that specialised research collections should be treated as a national rather than a purely institutional asset, and that universities which own such collections should have additional financial support in return for giving access to unique or exceptional materials.[13] This suggestion has been welcomed although there is some debate about the rigidity of the conditions which should be imposed upon owners in return for the support which they receive.[14]

The second aspect of the Follett review which critically impinges on our concerns is the discussion of electronic document supply, and developments in electronic journals in particular. It is this, of course, which is seen as a key part of the solution to the alleged conflict between preservation and access, as well as providing a cost-effective alternative to conventional provision of materials.[15] Again, reactions have been generally favourable, but there are major issues which remain to be addressed, not all of which are purely technological or financial; in particular, the legal dimension of electronic publishing, in terms of intellectual property, is still an uncleared minefield.[16] Meanwhile, the Funding Councils themselves are following up Follett's recommendation by supporting projects to consider electronic document delivery, electronic journals, digitization and on-demand publishing,[17] despite the reservation expressed by some librarians about the Review Group's definitions of the options available.[18] Doubts and uncertainties, however, are inevitable in such a rapidly developing field, and, whatever the precise outcomes, it is clear that the future provision of materials and information in university libraries will be critically influenced by the official recognition of the significance of technological innovation.

Although these are the two areas of Follett which directly touch upon preservation and access issues, almost everything in the Report of the Review Group has some implications for them. One which has not attracted much attention is the proposal to allocate an additional £140 million in 1994–7 for new buildings, to repair the neglect of the last 20 years, and to provide some relief for overcrowded storage space.[19] This has obvious implications for preservation, and also contextualises the move towards digitization and electronic document delivery: the age of the library as a storehouse of collections is not yet ended.

In the public library sector, many of the same issues have been articulated, although from a properly different perspective, in a review commissioned from independent consultants by the Department of National Heritage. In the draft version, there was a proposal for what are called 'regional hyperlibraries', which would, in effect, be the centre of regional document supply systems, and would have major holdings of material of secondary importance. This somewhat surprising initiative for the 1990s was subject to much criticism and eventually dropped. A disappointing feature of the review is that it generally gives little recognition to heritage issues except in acknowledging their existence. Although constrained by its Terms of Reference (which highlighted such political priorities as support for enterprise), the review could have addressed some of the issues which we have highlighted in Chapters 2 and 3, such as the decay of buildings and the danger to many important and unique collections of material of local interest (but national significance) held by public libraries. Such collections are often not a particularly high priority in their owners' scale of values; however, the evidence from recent studies suggests that only collective action will make it possible for them to continue to be a useful asset.[20]

In turning from the particular to the general, it is notable that the Public Library Review, like the Follett Report, sets its findings and recommendations firmly in a national context. In both documents, there is a recognition of the role of the British Library, and its central importance in the provision of comprehensive services at institutional or local level.[21] This is a perception shared by the British Library itself whose current strategic plan recognises that it 'underpins academic activity and scholarship in the UK', and more broadly (clearly incorporating the non-academic sector) that by the year 2000 'it will operate at the centre of the UK library and information network'.[22] This aspiration can be taken as an acknowledgement of the developing convergence between some parts of the formerly discrete sectors of academic and public library provision. The same range of problems confronts libraries in all sectors: all operate in harsh financial climates and under sceptical political regimes; most importantly, all are faced with a shift in their traditional forms of provision under the continuing (and probably continuous) impact of technological change.

THE TECHNOLOGICAL DIMENSION

We now turn to consider some of the general technological issues which have been implicit in the first two sections of this chapter, and which, in turn, will lead us back to some specific matters which have a direct impact on questions of access and preservation and on the development of appropriate policies in libraries. Both in the Follett Report and, to a lesser extent, in the Public Library Review, the possibility of electronic document delivery looms large. In association with electronic publishing, electronic document delivery has the potential to transform the attitudes of librarians towards stock. Indeed, in the most futuristic views, 'stock' would become a superfluous concept, as information is provided from a multiplicity of sources through digital communications systems. The site of the database from which the information is derived is of no interest to the end-user, and of importance only to the extent that different hosts may have different pricing regimes. This vision, although technologically feasible, is not one which can easily be reconciled with much of the practice which we have uncovered in our survey. We shall discuss at a later stage whether this is because of wilful or unwitting ignorance on the part of librarians, or a recognition of the long-term need for on-site stock for both immediate and longer-term use.[23]

Nevertheless, technological developments have directly affected on many matters of concern to us. The 'access' argument implicit in some responses which we have already quoted is largely, although not entirely, based on technological assumptions. At a fairly basic level, network access to OPACs in other libraries, both in the UK and abroad, has given both users and librarians the means to trace unusual or rare books in a new and more effective way, and has further increased the demands made on their owner. We have already noted how the Follett Report has suggested a strategy for addressing this particular issue in the university libraries. More specifically, however, the digitization of documents has been widely canvassed as a preservation strategy in its own right. Format conversion has been practised by librarians for over half a century, largely by the creation of microform substitutes for decaying or rare originals.[24] More recently, however, the creation of digital surrogates has come to be seen as an even more convenient technology which has the added advantage of conforming with other lines of development in information provision.[25] Funding has been provided for major projects in the UK and elsewhere to develop the essential input and editing devices and to devise methods of quality assurance which will guarantee the integrity of the digital surrogate.[26]

The obstacles to progress are manifold. Digitization (or indeed any format conversion) is expensive, because it makes economic and professional sense only on a large scale, as we shall see when we consider the work funded by the Andrew W. Mellon Foundation.[27] Nevertheless, some major libraries have concluded that digitization is a cost-effective alternative to microfilming as a long-term preservation strategy, and some work is in progress.[28] There are, of course, still some serious technical obstacles especially for graphic materials,[29] and materials in non-uniform fonts, such as handwriting and indeed much early printing. The output formats themselves present preservation problems; although this can be overcome by a continuing process of refreshment by recopying (which all the surrogate technologies easily permit), this merely adds to the costs.[30] Moreover, when the digitized document is commercially produced, there are legal issues involved in making copies, however technically simple this may be.[31] On the other hand, a digital copy is always a perfect reproduction of the original, unlike photographic copies, which suffer quality losses between generations.

Digitization is no longer at a purely experimental stage, although it is still in the process of development as a daily working tool. The use of microform surrogates, on the other hand, is so well established as to be an 'old' technology in its own right. That, however, has not been a deterrent to its widespread and continuing application as a preservation strategy. This has been particularly true in the preservation of newspapers, a notoriously difficult problem.[32] One of the most successful and well-known preservation projects in the UK is NEWSPLAN, a cross-sectoral cooperative project designed to identify and list the holdings of libraries throughout the country and to prioritise them for preservation microfilming. Those involved in NEWSPLAN argue convincingly for its success, not only in awareness-raising but in achieving practical results.[33] Microfilming is less expensive than digitization, but nevertheless needs funding. It was recognised from the beginning that, to make sense, NEWSPLAN had to be both cooperative in arrangement and national in scope. The pilot projects were funded by the British Library on that basis, and the scheme has subsequently been supported by the Library and Information Cooperation Council (LINC). On the ground, however, NEWSPLAN is often dependent on funding from local authorities through public libraries; the recommendation that they should spend the equivalent of 1 per cent of their book budgets on the project has fallen on deaf ears in most authorities.[34]

Since 1988, however, there has been substantial funding available for cooperative microfilming projects in the UK. This has come from the Andrew W. Mellon Foundation which provided an initial US$1.5 million to the British Library and an additional US$500 000 to each of the Bodleian and Cambridge University libraries to film appropriate parts of their own collections.[35] A second tranche of money is more widely available through the British Library; projects are eligible for support if they match the conditions of the Mellon Foundation grant. These conditions include the crucial ones of filming to archival standards,[36] and the submission of bibliographic data to the Register of Preservation Microforms (RPM) and thus to the European Register of Microform Masters (EROMM).[37] The significance of these and other conditions is twofold: they emphasise both the issue of the preservation of the microforms themselves, and the absolute necessity of national and indeed international cooperation to avoid unnecessary and wasteful duplication of effort.

There is still room for debate about the relative merits of digitization and microforming as surrogate media for preservation purposes. The current consensus certainly seems to be that the 'traditional' surrogate of microform is recommended by its familiarity, reliability and comparative cheapness, although digitization is not rejected as a longer-term solution.[38] Indeed, microforms themselves can form the basis of digitization, as a pioneering project funded by the British Library has amply demonstrated.[39]

Against this background of professional, political and technological development, we now return to an analysis of the data which we collected in our survey of preservation policies and practices in British libraries. How far are these developments apparent in practice? What priority is assigned to preservation by library managers? On what do they base this prioritisation? Can we trace the influence of changing attitudes, changing contexts and changing technologies in the design and implementation of preservation programmes? More specifically, what are the views (if any) of British librarians on the possibilities of digitization as a tool of preservation, and how are those views reflected in library practices? Above all, perhaps, to what extent is the often discussed and much vaunted capacity of microform being exploited to preserve the content of decaying paper documents? We address these and other questions in the next section of this chapter.

PRIORITIES: THE PERCEPTIONS OF MANAGERS

Although a whole chapter of the Ratcliffe Report was devoted to 'Priorities and Policies', the authors of the report seem to have made no serious attempt to assess the priority assigned by library managers themselves to the issues under review.[40] A recent study of New Zealand libraries, by contrast, addressed the issue in great detail, asking respondents to prioritise five issues (acquisitions, preservation, physical storage, use, access) both from their own perspectives as managers and from the perspective of their parent body.[41] We chose a slightly different approach, by asking the following question:

Please rank the following considerations on a scale of 1 to 7 according to their importance as factors in inhibiting the preservation/conservation of your stock.

The seven factors listed were:

- security
- suitably trained staff
- finance
- storage conditions
- heavy use of the collection
- organisational priority given to preservation
- general staffing levels.[42]

We approached the issue in this way in the hope of provoking more subtle answers than might be obtained by the more straightforward methods used in New Zealand. Each consideration was weighted by multiplying each ranking of 1 to 7 by the number of respondents giving it a particular ranking. These sums were then added together and the total was divided by 419 which was the number of respondents who fully answered this question.[43] We are thus able both to provide a simple numerical listing of perceived priorities, and a weighted list which provides a rather more sensitive analysis of them.

The numerical listings can be found in Table 4.1. Of the 419 respondents who answered this question in full, 198 (or 47 per cent) indicated that financial factors were the major inhibitor of preservation policy implementation. This is not a particularly surprising finding. The comparatively few comments which accompanied the answers to this question fairly consistently picked on the same issue. One shire county, for example, added that 'these [other matters] are minimal factors' compared with finance; another commented that the other priorities:

... will vary from time to time. The only constant is finance.

These comments seem to be borne out by the lack of uniformity in determining the next highest inhibitory factor; storage conditions, heavy use of materials and

Factor	1	2	3	4	5	6	7
Security	17	35	33	55	70	81	128
Lack of trained staff	16	28	76	90	85	72	52
Finance	198	81	48	44	24	19	5
Storage conditions	52	87	84	64	79	36	17
Heavy use of materials	52	45	40	55	53	68	106
Organisational priority of preservation	53	50	65	58	60	69	64
General staffing levels	48	98	73	71	46	56	27

Note: The total number of analysable responses was 419. Responses were *not* analysed if they were incomplete, e.g. by not prioritising all the factors. Two or more factors were equally weighted by some respondents.

Table 4.1 Factors Inhibiting Preservation Activities. Number of Libraries Placing Each Factor in Rank Order as Indicated

the priority given to preservation by the parent body all ranked approximately equal at about 12 per cent of respondents to this question. This we found a little more surprising, since we might have expected that organisational priorities would be a somewhat more prominent factor here. One reading of our findings is that, in the present financial climate, the lack of funding is acting as a brake on the development of policies so that even where there may be a desire to take initiatives they are not seriously considered. A further breakdown of the figures (Table 4.2) lends some support to this interpretation. Among the public libraries, 52 per cent regard finance as the most important single factor inhibiting preservation; special libraries (51 per cent) produced an almost identical response. The comparable figure for academic libraries is significantly different; of our respondents, only 38 per cent put finance as the highest inhibitory factor, while 17 per cent of them highlighted organisational policy priorities. We do not wish to put too much weight on this finding, but it could be argued that it supports the hypothesis that academic libraries are further advanced than those in other sectors in considering their policy priorities and in taking decisions about how to address (or to ignore) the preservation dimension.

We turn now to the more complex matter of analysing the weighted data in Table 4.3. Overall, finance is very clearly regarded as the most important single factor; moreover, in an analysis by sector (Table 4.4), the differences between academic and public libraries are less marked than in using the raw data. One noteworthy distinction which does emerge, however, is that academic libraries rate general staffing levels above storage conditions as a factor in inhibiting preservation activities, while the lack of suitably trained staff concerns them less than it does either the public or the special libraries. This seems logical: if there is a *general concern* about staffing, a *specific concern* is superfluous. All sectors rate security as the least inhibiting factor. In some cases, we know that this is because libraries believe that they have good security systems in place; this was admirably expressed by one college librarian who wrote that:

I have excellent security ... which most people are crying out for ...

Factor	Public	Academic	Special
Security	5	7	5
Lack of trained staff	5	6	5
Finance	61	57	78
Storage conditions	15	18	19
Heavy use of materials	15	24	13
Organisational priority of preservation	8	25	20
General staffing levels	10	19	19

Table 4.2 Most Important Factor Inhibiting Preservation. (Number of Respondents (of 417) Placing Each Factor in First Place, by Sector)

Factor	Weighting
Finance	2.26
Storage conditions	3.49
General staffing levels	3.58
Organisational priority of preservation	4.16
Lack of trained staff	4.49
Heavy use of materials	4.53
Security	5.10

**Table 4.3 Factors Inhibiting Preservation Activities.
(In Weighted Rank Order; See note 43)**

Public	Academic	Special
F/2.14	F/2.45	F/2.19
SC/3.31	GS/3.51	SC/3.37
GS/3.83	SC/3.77	GS/3.48
TS/4.37	HU/4.00	OP/3.91
HU/4.38	OP/4.13	TS/4.27
OP/4.51	TS/4.82	HU/5.13
S/5.22	S/4.94	S/5.14

F = Finance.
GS = General staffing levels.
HU = Heavy use of materials.
OP = Organisational priority of preservation.
SC = Storage conditions.
S = Security.
TS = (Lack of) trained staff.

**Table 4.4 Most Important Factor Inhibiting
Preservation. (In Weighted Rank Order (See
note 43, by Sector)**

We suspect that many others (whether justifiably or not) share this belief about the security of their libraries. It is also possible that security is not yet fully recognised as being an aspect of preservation management policy and indeed it could be argued that, like disaster preparedness planning, it is a distinct aspect of it deserving of fuller treatment.[44] At least one important international document, however, treats storage and security as two aspects of the same problem.[45]

In general terms, therefore, is seems that lack of money and, at least in the academic sector, lack of staff are seen as the major obstacles to the development and implementation of preservation policies. In less formal and less systematic ways, the same conclusions emerge from much of what we have reported and discussed in Chapters 2 and 3. There are also, however, some indications that the perception of the issues varies between the academic libraries and libraries in the other two sectors.

TECHNOLOGY AND PRESERVATION: ASPIRATION OR REALITY?

The search for technological solutions to preservation problems is not new. Microform, as we have seen, has been used as a surrogate medium for information preservation since the 1930s. Digitization has been the subject of serious discussion for at least the last 20 years and the subject of experimentation for the last ten. Technology has also been applied to the preservation of information in original formats, most obviously through the development of various systems of de-acidification of paper as a strategy designed to address the problem of embrittlement which looms so large in the concerns of preservation managers and conservators in the United States and, to a lesser extent, elsewhere.[46] All of this is widely understood, and much of it is known, at least in general terms, beyond the comparatively narrow bounds of preservation specialists or custodians of heritage collections. We, however, sought to discover to what extent surrogate media were really used in British libraries, how and by whom they were being created, and what formats were selected.

Just under one-third of our respondents (157 libraries, or 32 per cent) used microform as a surrogate medium for preservation purposes. Contrary to our expectations, and the emphasis in the literature, the heaviest use was claimed by the public libraries (Table 4.5), most of it as a means of providing access to newspapers. The other major use of microform surrogates in public libraries is for local history material, and, especially, for documents used by genealogists. These include census records, parish registers, Poor Law records, electoral registers and ecclesiastical records. Other archival material, such as the minutes of Council meetings and documents described simply as 'archives', also feature, but are less prominent. The overall picture is clear: microform (and more specifically microfilm) is the principal medium through which newspapers are preserved and consulted in British public libraries. This no doubt partly reflects the ten years of effort which have gone into NEWSPLAN,[47] but also vindicates both the vision of the progenitors of NEWSPLAN and the continuing support of its professional and financial sponsors.

Microform surrogates are significantly less common in academic than in public libraries, so far as we can judge from the data supplied by our respondents (Table

Sector	Number	Percentage
All	157	32.17%
Academic	38	21.47%
Public	83	62.88%
Special	36	20.34%

Table 4.5 Use of Microforms for Preservation Purposes.
(Respondents (out of 488) who use Microforms)

4.5). Where we have some details of the purposes for which they are used, news-papers are once again in the picture, but are not as dominant as in the public library sector. Other uses include copies of manuscripts and rare books (the classic paradigm of surrogate preservation), archives and official and statistical publications. Reference was also made by some respondents to the acquisition of research materials (such as the *Landmarks of Science* series) in microform, presumably to support teaching and research which could not be locally supported from original materials in the library. Some libraries are also acquiring newspapers and other material in CD-ROM format; in some cases, this includes back issues when they are available.

Special libraries, in this as in other matters, were less uniform. The most common application reported to us was the use of microform to preserve the parent body's own archival records. Libraries using microforms for this purpose included those of scientific and learned societies, professional bodies, govern-ment agencies and quangos, and libraries of historic significance in their own right. Some more specialised uses included filming large documents, such as manufacturers' drawings in a government-sector library, or the records of experi-mental procedures and findings in the library of a public sector scientific agency. In addition, there are some important sets of documents (such as British Standards, sets of archival documents, and back-runs of learned journals, for example) which are commercially available on microfilm or microfiche, and are in widespread use, especially in academic and special libraries, as substitutes for originals which the library never acquired.

Across all three sectors, there is an awareness of the potential of microform as a medium which can preserve both the context and the graphic appearance of the original, losing only the physical format and, sometimes, colour. In some cases (such as technical drawings, blueprints, and indeed newspapers) conversion to a physically smaller or less awkward format may even be advantageous for both storage and consultation. All of this is encouraging; more disturbing, however, is the apparent lack of awareness, among some of those who are using microforms for preservation purposes, of the standards of production and storage which are necessary for genuinely archival films.

Our question on this was specific, in referring to BS5699 as an example of appropriate standards for archival microphotography.[48] We chose this as our example because it was long established, having been published in 1980. This and other standards essentially embody recommendations for creating and storing microfilms (and other micrographic formats) to archival standards of per-manence, the only level which is acceptable as a surrogate preservation medium.[49] The formal standards are, of course, continuously evolving as the chemistry and physics of photography are further developed, but it is the general principle which is important.[50] In essence, this is that the camera negative should be made on film of the highest quality, and that it should be processed using the purest chemicals yielding the most permanent image. This negative should then be copied, and the original stored as a master. The copy negative then becomes the source for further copies which are used for consultation or sale.

It is clear that some librarians have some understanding of the technical issues involved. Several respondents referred to 'silver halide' film or 'silver' film, which shows at least a basic awareness. Many follow the example of the librarian of a 1960s university who wrote that:

We presume the microforms we buy are of archival quality.

A shire-county librarian told us that they:

... assume [that films are of archival standards] as all our microfilming is done by the British Library.

Another shire-county librarian, however, was less confident indicating that their libraries did *not* use archival-quality microfilm, with the following gloss:

Our microfilm is generally acquired from the Public Record Office, British Library, Bodleian Library, newspaper publishers.

This response, we suspect, represents a cautious approach rather than an informed criticism, but the contrast between these two replies, from very similar organisations and officers with similar functions in each of them, deters us from attempting any quantification of responses on this matter. These contradictions and confusions are reflected in many responses to this question. Professional librarians do not yet know enough about these matters, but it is also the case that the microform producers (in both the public and the private sectors) are not always sufficiently explicit about the standards to which they are working.

The production of microfilms is a very expensive business; a recent authoritative estimate is that the in-house production of a 100-metre reel of 35-mm film surrogate for a newspaper costs £120.00, compared with a typical £42.00 for the commercially available equivalent.[51] Libraries may seek to enter into partnership with a commercial producer, and thus share the costs of production, sale and distribution. Such partnerships between the public and the private sector are perhaps more fashionable now than when they were first proposed in this context,[52] and have facilitated some very important projects such as the filming of the Thomason Tracts at the British Library. Our respondents referred to a number of British and American companies with whom they worked on a joint venture or cooperative basis, including UMI, Research Publications and Chadwyck-Healey Ltd. It is no doubt because of the costs involved, and the interest of commercial microform producers, that so few libraries have their own production capacity. Of our 488 respondents, only 39 have such facilities, all of them major institutions. Other libraries wishing to create their own microfilms are therefore forced into the commercial sector, either by paying for access to libraries which do have appropriate production facilities, or by going to commercial microfilming bureaux, where standards can be a problem, and there may be a conflict between customers' needs, bureau practices and the formal standards.[53] A unique response to this problem has been the creation of the Scottish Newspaper Microfilming Unit within the National Library of Scotland. The Unit has widespread support from the library community and infrastructure in Scotland; its commercial objective is to become self-supporting by 1996.[54]

Collaborative projects, whether among libraries, between libraries and commercial organisations, or entirely in the private sector, dominate the production of microfilms. Indeed, the driving force behind them is often commercial; the preservation of the original by the creation of a surrogate is a consequence rather than a primary aim. There are, of course, important exceptions to this generalisation, and these are widely reflected by our respondents. Just under a quarter of them (111 or 23 per cent) are currently participating in cooperative microfilming projects. Again, there is particularly heavy involvement by the public libraries; in that sector over half of our respondents (68 or 52 per cent) gave a positive response, compared with only 14 per cent (24) of academic libraries and 11 per cent (19) of special libraries. Within the public library sector, it is newspapers which predominate in these projects, partly no doubt because of the mere existence of NEWSPLAN, and the financial support which some NEWSPLAN regions have generated, but also, in part, we assume that it is because of the perceived importance of microfilms of newspapers in providing services to users especially in local studies and local history collections.

Of the public libraries which gave us details of their involvement in collaborative projects, 37 mentioned NEWSPLAN by name, and a further 16 referred to 'newspapers', 'local newspapers', 'provincial newspapers' or some similar phrase. Not all the NEWSPLAN projects have reached the implementation stage, as one metropolitan district reminded us:

> In theory anyway! We are members of the [regional] NEWSPLAN project, but so far there have been no co-operative projects (although agreed in principle).

Despite such reservations and delays, however, there can be no doubt of the central importance of NEWSPLAN in making public librarians aware of the issues, and in providing a strategy for addressing them. It seems to have been one of the most influential and widespread preservation initiatives of the last decade, clearly responding to the real needs of librarians and their users. Perhaps more than anything else, it has brought the use of microfilms as preservation tools into the domain of the public librarian.

NEWSPLAN, however, is by no means the only collaborative or externally driven project in which some of our respondents are involved. We have several references to commercial ventures, such as the microform series of British books published between the fifteenth and the eighteenth centuries,[55] and other projects in which, we assume, the library receives some sort of royalty in return for making its (non-copyright) material available to microform publishers. There are also many individual projects of which details were supplied to us. These included the filming of medieval manuscripts (for both internal use and external sale), of musical manuscripts and scores, and of particular collections. Perhaps the most unusual was the special library which is:

... currently filming ledgers of motorcycle records in cooperation with owners clubs.

Inevitably, the Church of Jesus Christ and the Latter Day Saints (the Mormons) also put in an appearance. Several respondents referred to their long-term programme of filming parish registers and similar documents for their own religious purposes. The archival masters are, we understand, stored in allegedly nuclear bomb-proof bunkers in Salt Lake City, Utah; the earthly benefit to the owners of the originals is the supply of a free copy of a high quality microfilm for preservation and use.

The cost of large-scale microfilming projects has clearly been a serious deterrent for almost all libraries, even where the theoretical advantages of surrogate programmes are acknowledged. It is in this respect that the generosity of the Andrew W. Mellon Foundation has been so important.[56] A number of our respondents made specific references to Mellon, including some who were in the process of applying for funding for the first time. The extension of eligibility for grants beyond the original small group of research libraries, and the eligibility of NEWSPLAN projects for funding, has clearly met with a very positive response from the library community in Britain. In particular, the support for the microfilming of newspapers will allow public libraries to develop even further projects which they have supported, often from very inadequate resources, over a number of years. It is to be welcomed and commended that such support is now available, recognising both the needs of the public libraries and their importance as holders of research material of national, as well as local or regional, significance.

Microfilms are not, of course, an ideal medium. All photographic media, however high the standards to which they are made and processed, are vulnerable to decay and damage. Even in normal use, microfilm is in particular danger, not least because of the aging and often very badly designed equipment which most libraries are still obliged to make available to their users. User resistance is still to be found, and dislike of the medium seems to be widespread, even where it is accepted as an inevitability. We found that libraries generally recognise that proper storage is essential; there is perhaps less understanding of the conditions needed for truly archival preservation of microform, but there is evidence that the major generators of preservation microforms are taking their responsibilities seriously in this respect. The conditions on which Mellon grants are made will, no doubt, provide further impetus towards both an understanding of the issues and the implementation of appropriate strategies.

Technology, in the rather elderly guise of microphotography, has become an important element in preservation management in British libraries, offering, as it does, access to materials without damaging the originals. For newspapers, it would seem that microfilm is now the normal medium of consultation in many libraries, a fact accepted as a necessity by users, and one which even offers some unexpected benefits.[57] The use of digital technologies is far less advanced. As we have suggested, it has barely gone beyond the experimental stage,[58] and it may be some years yet before it can offer an economically viable technique for information preservation on a large scale. The major exception to this is the publication of some newspapers and certain other data sources (such as bibliographies and abstracts) on CD-ROM instead of, or in addition to, the traditional printed form. Some libraries regard the CD-ROM as the archival copy rather than the paper original. Data which is created, and exists, only in digitized form is, of course, a separate issue, with important implications for the future;[59] as a surrogate for information currently in printed formats it is not yet a major factor, although the current experimental projects have clearly demonstrated its technical feasibility. Despite the slow development and adoption of digital techniques, however, the use of non-traditional technologies in preservation is more than a myth. Microfilm is clearly embedded in the consciousness of British librarians as a means of preserving and making available large quantities of both textual and graphic documents. For some libraries, it is the highest priority in their preservation strategy, and in some cases the only strategy which they are able to adopt. The professional and financial support for the creation of microform surrogates is, in itself, a testimony to the recognition of their importance. This is not perhaps the most spectacular of responses to the radical changes which we noted at the beginning of this chapter, but it is not without significance.

CONCLUSIONS

In this chapter, we have ranged widely over many issues at several different levels. We have tried to provide both a professional and a political context for preservation management. We have also explored in more detail how library managers themselves see preservation in the broader context of their strategic vision, and examined closely the use of one particular technology which can help to overcome (by evasion) the inherent problems of preserving certain kinds of documents in a usable condition. In drawing conclusions from this mass of material, we suggest that library managers are still not always aware either of preservation needs, or of what can be done to meet them. We recognise that many libraries, particularly in the academic sector, have taken reasoned decisions about the place of preservation in reaching their avowed institutional objectives. We suspect, however, that there are still too many libraries, even in that sector, where decisions are being taken by default.

In the remainder of this book, we shall carry forward the argument and implications of the last paragraph, first by examining the policies which are actually in place in libraries and which underlie the findings presented in this and the previous two chapters, and secondly, by suggesting some means by which policies can be developed which are relevant to the context and objectives of individual libraries but which reconcile the superficially conflicting needs of preservation and use.

NOTES

1. See, for example, Patricia Battin, From preservation to access: paradigm for the nineties. *IFLA Journal*, 19: 4 (1993), pp. 367–73.
2. Margaret Henty. Resource sharing among Australian libraries. A distributed national collection. *Library Acquisitions: practice and theory*, 17 (1993), pp. 311–17.
3. Sheila Corrall. The access model. Managing the transformation at Aston University. *Interlending and Document Supply*, 21: 4 (1993), pp. 13–23.
4. Bernard Naylor. 'Just-in-case' vs 'just-in-time': a librarian ruminates about journals, technology and money. *Logos*, 5: 2 (1994), pp. 101–4.
5. John Sumsion, Helen V. Pickering and Pamela J. Berridge. *LISU Annual Library Statistics 1993. Featuring trend analysis of UK public and academic libraries 1982–92*. Loughborough: Library and Information Statistics Unit (Report 7), 1993, p. 18.
6. Ibid., p. 121.
7. John Sumsion. *Survey of Resources and Uses in Higher Education Libraries: UK, 1993*. Loughborough: Library and Information Statistics Unit (Occasional Paper, 6), 1994, pp. 140, 141.
8. Sumsion, Pickering and Berridge, op. cit., p. 14.
9. Ibid., p. 14; Sumsion, op. cit., p. 140.
10. See above, pp. 47–8, 64–8.
11. See above, pp. 64–8.
12. Joint Funding Council's Libraries Review Group. *Report*. Bristol: HEFCE, 1993. [Chair: Sir Brian Follett]. Cited hereafter as Follett Report.
13. Ibid., paras 223–8.
14. See, for example, J.K. Roberts. One librarian's reaction to Follett. *Relay*, 40 (1994), pp. 6–9. See also John Feather. Special collections in the university library. In: Colin Harris, ed. *The New University Library. Issues for the 90s and beyond*. London: Taylor Graham, 1994, pp. 19–30.
15. Follett Report, paras 55–70.
16. See, for example, John Davies. Follett Report implementation: response from the Publishers' Association. *Academic and Professional Publishing* (October 1994), p. 5.
17. Higher Education Funding Councils. Joint Information Services Committee. *Follett Implementation Group on Information Technology: framework for progressing the initiative*. [Bristol: HEFCE (JISC Circular 4/94)], 1994.
18. John Akeroyd. The Follett Report: another view. *Relay*, 40 (1994), pp. 5–6.
19. Follett Report, para 167 and Annex D (p. 83); see also the comments by Derek Law. The Follett Report: panacea or placebo? *Relay*, 40 (1994), pp. 3–4.
20. John Feather, Graham Matthews and Carolyn Pritchett. The management and use of reserve and special collections in public libraries: a study of the East Midlands. *Journal of Librarianship and Information Science*, 27 (1995), pp. 89–98.
21. See, for example, Follett Report, paras 202, 205, 235.
22. The British Library. *For Scholarship, Research and Innovation. Strategic objectives for the year 2000*. London: The British Library, 1993, pp. 10, 13.
23. See below, pp. 146–51.
24. John Feather. The preservation of information: the principles and practice of format conversion. *Library Review*, 40: 6 (1991), pp. 7–12.
25. Battin, loc. cit.; Michèle Valerie Cloonan. The preservation of knowledge. *Library Trends*, 41: 4 (1993), pp. 594–605.
26. See above, pp. 13–14, and the citations in Chapter 1, notes 135–46. See also, Cornell/Xerox/CPA Joint Study in Digital Preservation – progress report number 2. *The Electronic Library*, 10: 3 (1992), pp. 155–63; Rare works digitised. *Library Association Record*, 96: 2 (1994), Technology

Supplement, 12; Arthur Sheil and Roger Broadhurst. *Library Material Digitization Demonstrator Project.* London: The British Library (Library and Information Research Report, 94), 1994. For a recent review, see Claire Ashley-Smith. Digitization and the Preservation of Library Materials. (Loughborough University MA dissertation, 1994). We are grateful to Ms. Ashley-Smith for her generosity in allowing us to use her work. For a brief overview, see Anne R. Kenney and Lynne K. Personius, The future of digital preservation. *Advances in Preservation and Access*, 1 (1992), pp. 195–212.

27. See below, pp. 90–92.

28. See, for example, Barden, loc. cit., Paul Conway. Digitising preservation. *Library Journal*, 119: 2 (1994), pp. 42–5; and Richard Gartner. Digitising the Bodleian? *AV Librarian*, 19: 3 (1993), pp. 220–3.

29. A point discussed by Gartner, loc. cit., in the context of the possible use of photo-CD.

30. On this vital point, see Catherine F. Pinion. Preserving our audio-visual heritage: a national and international challenge. *AV Librarian*, 19: 3 (1993), pp. 205–19; on two specific aspects of this, see Clive Cochrane. An overview of trends in the collection and use of moving images in the United Kingdom. *Journal of Documentation*, 49: 3 (1993), pp. 278–91; and Brian C. O'Connor. Preservation and repacking of lantern slides within a desktop digital imaging environment. *Microcomputers for Information Management*, 9: 4 (1992), pp. 209–24.

31. For the UK, see Charles Oppenheim. *The Legal and Regulatory Environment for Electronic Information.* Calne: Infonortics, 1992, pp. 16–17, 48; for the USA, see Mary Brandt Jensen, Copying for the future: electronic preservation. *Document Delivery World*, 9: 4/5 (1993), pp. 29–31. See also Graham P. Cornish. Copyright issues in legal deposit and preservation. *IFLA Journal*, 20: 3 (1994), pp. 341–9; and on a different but relevant aspect, Ross Dixon. Legal admissibility and probative value of document images. *Information Management and Technology*, 27: 1 (1994), pp. 38–40.

32. On the general issues, see Feather, op. cit., pp. 76–9.

33. Geoffrey Hamilton. NEWSPLAN, the preservation microfilming of newspapers and beyond. In: National Preservation Office. *Microforms in Libraries. The untapped resource?* London: The British Library, 1993, 13-17; and Glynn Payne. NEWSPLAN achievements 1983-1993. In: Pat Wressell, ed. *Current Perspectives on Newspaper Preservation and Access. Report of the 2nd national NEWSPLAN conference.* Newcastle-upon-Tyne: Information North, 1994, pp. 1–3.

34. Hamilton, loc. cit., p. 16.

35. Marie Jackson. The Mellon Microfilming Project. In: National Preservation Office, *Microforms in Libraries*, pp. 9–12.

36. For which, see Valerie Ferris. The concern for quality in preservation microfilming. In: Wressell, op. cit., pp. 28–32.

37. See John Feather and Giuseppe Vitiello. The European Register of Microform Masters: a new bibliographical tool. *Journal of Librarianship and Information Science*, 23: 4 (1991), pp. 177–81. The database is now established at Göttingen University Library, Germany.

38. See, for recent views in a British context, Peter Fox. Microforms: still the best hope for preservation? In: National Preservation Office, *Microforms in Libraries*, pp. 91–5; and Geoff Smith. Digitization of newspapers – capabilities and limitations. In: Wressell, op. cit., pp. 54–8.

39. Arthur Sheil and Roger Broadhurst. *Library Material Digitalization Demonstrator Project: a project for the British Library Research and Development Department by Cimtech.* Hatfield: Cimtech, 1992.

40. Ratcliffe, op. cit., pp. 39–46.

41. New Zealand Library and Information Association. Heritage Responsibilities Group. *Heritage Collections in New Zealand Libraries: report of a survey.* Wellington: NZLIA, 1994, pp. 6-7. This work was conducted more or less simultaneously with our own; we were in touch with our New Zealand colleagues throughout, and are grateful for information which they supplied to us in advance of publication as well as for a copy of the document cited here. We are particularly grateful to Theresa Graham of Auckland City Libraries, who was our contact person.

42. This list of seven factors was developed by us, in conjunction with the Advisory Group for the project.

43. For example, to take finance, 198 respondents ranked it number 1 in importance, 81 ranked it

number 2, as so on (see Table 4.1). Thus its weighting was calculated as $[(1 \times 198) + (2 \times 81) + (3 \times 48) + (4 \times 44) + (5 \times 24) + (6 \times 19) + (7 \times 5)]/419 = 2.26$.

44. Which, in part, it has had in recent years. See Burrows and Cooper, op. cit., and, among a large and diverse literature, A.G. Quinsee and A.C. McDonald, eds. *Security in Academic and Research Libraries. Proceedings of three seminars organised by SCONUL and the National Preservation Office.* Newcastle-upon-Tyne: Newcastle-upon-Tyne University Library, 1991. We chose these two examples because, significantly, the National Preservation Office was involved in both. For an explanation of that involvement, see Marie Jackson. Conference reports. *Library Association Record*, 93: 6 (1991), pp. 394, 397.

45. David Thomas. *Study on Control of Security and Storage of Holdings: a RAMP study with guidelines.* Paris: UNESCO (PGI-86/WS/23), 1986.

46. See above, p. 16.

47. Hamilton, loc. cit., pp. 13–17.

48. British Standards Institution. *Processed Photographic Film for Archival Records.* 2 parts (BS5699 Part 1:1979; BS5699 Part 2:1979). London: British Standards Institution, 1979. Other relevant standards include BS5847:1980 (35-mm microcopying of newspapers), and BS6313:1982 (microcopying of serials). For a full list, see National Preservation Office. *Preservation Microforms.* London: The British Library, [1988], pp. 18–19.

49. See Valerie Ferris. The concern for quality in preservation microfilming. In: Wressell, op. cit., pp. 28–32.

50. On this point, see Ross Harvey. *Preservation in Libraries: principles, strategies and practices for librarians.* London: Bowker-Saur, 1993, pp. 171–2.

51. John E. McIntyre. Microfilm as one preservation option – costings and choices. In: National Preservation Office, *Microforms in Libraries*, 28–32, at p. 31. To provide the full context, it should be added that the cost of boxing the original is estimated at £330.00, and of binding at £380.00.

52. For an early iteration of the argument, see John Feather. Microforms and the scholarly library. *Microdoc*, 18 (1979), pp. 16–24.

53. See Nick Luft. Standards for newspaper preservation microfilming: improving library/bureau relations. In: National Preservation Office, *Microforms in Libraries*, pp. 38–43.

54. John Lauder. Conception, birth and first four months of the Scottish Newspapers Microfilming, Unit. In: Wressell, op. cit., pp. 33–7. The SNMU began work in November 1993, and hence does not feature in responses to our questionnaire.

55. These are based on the three short-title catalogues covering the periods 1475–1640, 1641–1700, and 1701–1800. For the first two periods the publisher (on 35-mm microfilm) is University Microfilms Inc.; for the eighteenth century (on microfiche), the publisher is Chadwyck-Healey Ltd.

56. See above, p. 13.

57. See Jeremy Black. The user's experience of newspaper collections and their services. In: Wressell, op. cit., pp. 4–6.

58. See above, pp. 82, 84.

59. See below, pp. 138, 142, 153.

5 Preservation Policy Guidelines

There can be no doubt that much preservation work and related activity is taking place in British libraries. When it is overtly described in that way, however, it tends to be focused on special collections, older materials, rare books, manuscripts and the like. Nevertheless, as we have suggested in Chapters 2 and 3, there are many libraries which, while they do not identify themselves as having a formal preservation policy, are undertaking preservation activities in a systematic way under other guises, usually as a part of their stock management or building management.

In Chapter 7, we shall build upon our analysis of preservation practice in British libraries, and suggest possible strategies for the development of formal preservation policies where these are thought to be desirable.[1] To provide a broader context, however, we turn first to the normative guidelines which have been published by various organisations and to others which have been suggested in the literature in an attempt to establish whether or not there is a commonly accepted understanding of what constitutes a preservation policy. We shall then consider the published literature which tells us more about the policies of particular libraries or library systems. Having examined both theory and practice in this way, we shall suggest the broad headings under which a preservation policy might be developed. This provides the framework for the detailed analysis which appears in Chapter 6,[2] in which we shall then try to identify how such policies work in practice, and how they can be developed; for this, we draw on the published literature, on the results of our survey, and on preservation policy documents which have been supplied to us by some of our respondents. Finally, we shall suggest the context for the policy development process, and analyse the priorities assigned to preservation issues by British librarians. By adopting this approach, heavily dependent upon the *practices* and not merely the aspirations of library managers, we hope to provide practical guidelines which will assist those who seek to develop preservation policies, or need evidence to support the cases for resourcing their implementation.

GUIDELINES FOR PRESERVATION POLICIES

There is no formal international standard for preservation policies, although there are a number of ISO and other standards which are indeed relevant to some aspects of preservation work; we shall return to some of these in due course. In recent years, however, a number of formal guidelines have been published by national and international bodies from which we can draw some conclusions about the extent to which a professional consensus has developed. Two key documents have the authority of international organisations; these are:

- Patricia Chapman. *Guidelines on Preservation and Conservation Policies in Libraries and Archives*. Paris: UNESCO (PGI-90/WS/7), 1990. (Cited as *UNESCO Guidelines*); and
- J.M. Dureau and D.W.G. Clements. *Principles for the Preservation and Conservation of Library Materials*. The Hague: International Federation of Library Associations and Institutions (IFLA Professional Reports, 8), 1986. (Cited as *IFLA Principles*.)

Both documents were published as a result of lengthy iterative processes involving large numbers of people in many countries. Part of that process is in public domain, and gives a useful insight into the international background against which the UNESCO Guidelines were compiled. This is:

- D.W.G. Clements. *Preservation and Conservation of Library Documents: a UNESCO/IFLA/ICA enquiry into the current state of the world's patrimony*. Paris: UNESCO (PGI-87/WS/15 rev). (Cited as *UNESCO Enquiry*.)

At a more parochial level, there are two documents from the United Kingdom which partly derive from the *IFLA Principles* and the *UNESCO Enquiry*, but which because of their origin suggest a more specific context. These are:

- Library and Information Services Council (Wales). *Conservation Guidelines. Survey and Action*. Aberystwyth: National Library of Wales, 1993. (Cited as *LISC (Wales) Guidelines*);[3] and
- National Preservation Office. *Preservation Guidelines*. London: National Preservation Office, 1991. (Cited as *NPO Guidelines*.)

National professional bodies have been less active, although the Library Association adopted and published a policy statement in 1987, which referred to the Ratcliffe Report and to the *UNESCO Enquiry*. In 1986 the Association reprinted the *IFLA Principles* as one of its own *Guidelines* documents.[4] We have also drawn on the American Library Association's draft policy where it seems relevant and helpful.[5] An earlier publication by the Association of Research Libraries is also a valuable source;[6] it is, however, most useful for the extended examples which it contains of preservation policy documents in American libraries rather than for general statements of principles.

We start, however, with two major documents: the *IFLA Principles* and the *UNESCO Enquiry*. Not surprisingly, they have many common characteristics. The *UNESCO Enquiry* identified seven 'major concerns' arising out of the responses of 417 institutions throughout the world:

- properties of documents
- buildings
- environmental factors
- biological pests
- use, handling and storage
- preservation and conservation resources
- information dissemination.

It then suggested an 'action programme' to deal with:

- awareness
- education and training
- policy development and implementation measures
- treatment options.

The *IFLA Principles* are somewhat differently organised, but cover much of the same ground:

- *Preservation* (storage, temperature, light, air pollution, dust and cleanliness, storage materials and equipment, buildings, standards).
- *Security* (fire, water, war and natural disasters, theft, disaster preparedness).
- *Use* (protection, storage, materials in transit, readers and reader facilities, copying, reprography policy, exhibitions, limiting use, substitutes).
- *Deterioration* (biological factors, micro-organisms, insects, chemical factors, damage to paper, damage to leather and parchment, damage to photographic film, nitrate film).

In the first instance, we shall take UNESCO's recommended 'action programme' and consider each action line in turn.

AWARENESS

The premise is that:

> The basis of any action programme should start from the necessity to increase aware-ness of preservation problems and the need for good practices among funding bodies, library and archival authorities, professional and non-professional staff and the general public.
>
> (*UNESCO Enquiry*, para. 40)

Specific actions which are proposed under this broad heading are:

- presentations, articles, posters, leaflets etc.;
- production of guidelines on specific aspects of preservation;

- production of audiovisual materials;
- exhibitions illustrating the problems and solutions; and
- the establishment of national focal points.

Appropriately, these recommendations are directed at national and international bodies rather than individual libraries, but clearly all of them also have implications at institutional level. In specific terms, the awareness issue is now reflected in the other documents which form the basis of this section. In effect, those documents could be argued to be examples of precisely the kind of awareness-raising activity which the authors of the *UNESCO Enquiry* advocated. Certainly, the National Preservation Office has always seen this to be one of its key roles, especially in the 1980s when it was establishing its presence in the British library scene.[7]

EDUCATION AND TRAINING

After commenting that education and training are an 'on-going requirement', the *UNESCO Enquiry* summarised its findings:

> The studies not only showed the need to improve the technical knowledge of conservators but the necessity of explaining the preservation problems, the options available and the need for good practices to library and archive professionals as well as providing basic training in good housekeeping practices to non-professional staff. Provision of such training could also be directed towards users, though this is more difficult to achieve.
>
> (*UNESCO Enquiry*, para. 41)

Nine elements of such a programme are proposed; in summary these are:

- courses for conservators;
- courses for conservation administrators and managers;
- inclusion of preservation in initial professional education programmes;
- in-service training programmes for professionals;
- training in the use of specific equipment by technicians and conservators;
- up-dating courses for existing staff;
- a review of existing curricula;
- in-service courses for non-professional staff;
- short courses for users.

This programme is apparently comprehensive, although it actually includes proposals which operate at several different levels. Some of these (such as library school curricula) clearly fall outside the scope of institutional policies, while others can probably only be effectively implemented at institutional level. This is particularly true of training aimed at technical or non-professional staff, where considerations of time and cost effectively dictate that only in-house provision is feasible for the majority of libraries.

The *IFLA Principles* lack specificity; under the heading 'Training' is the following statement:

> In order fully to understand preservation and conservation problems, any librarian responsible for these tasks should not only have some knowledge of the scientific bases and the techniques and materials involved, but also some feeling for the origin and history of the library materials in the collections, their physical composition as well as their information content. It is essential that librarians and conservators should recognise that … preservation and conservation should, as far as possible, be carried out in ways sympathetic to the originals. Librarians specially concerned with preservation should have training in these methods, but all students of librarianship should be acquainted with the importance of preservation within the library's overall function and policy.
>
> (*IFLA Principles*, para. 19)

This statement is perhaps even less relevant to the policies of individual libraries than that in the *UNESCO Enquiry*; apart from a general statement about the need for training, the only specific suggestion relates to initial professional education. There are, however, some interesting examples of library training practices, to which we shall return later.[8]

POLICY DEVELOPMENT AND IMPLEMENTATION MEASURES

This section is really the core of the proposals arising out of the *UNESCO Enquiry*, and is perhaps the most helpful section in making practicable proposals for actions which could be undertaken by institutions. Essentially, the proposal is that national policies are needed which are capable of application at institutional level. It is the latter which is our concern, although there has been some progress at national level both in Britain and elsewhere.[9] The first part of the process is defined as the

> … identification of national and institutional priorities for the collection and retention of materials and for preservation treatment. With insufficient resources it is essential to ensure that scarce conservation resources are not applied to unimportant items … The identification of national priorities must also take into account the holdings in libraries and in archives as in some areas their holdings overlap … The coverage of oral tradition is another aspect that must be included. One aspect that should not be omitted is the question of material held in private collections or by institutions outside the normal aegis of libraries or state archives …
>
> (*UNESCO Enquiry*, para. 42(b))

These broad statements, although they are aimed at an international audience of governments, national libraries and national archives, can nevertheless be transformed into more concrete proposals appropriate to individual institutions:

> Each library, having established its aims and objectives will need to define if, and to what extent, it will acquire material and retain items added to the collections …
>
> (*IFLA Principles*, para. 9)

There is also an important additional statement in the *IFLA Principles*, which can be applied to most, and perhaps all, of these generalised statements:

> There can be no general guidance on what material should be selected for acquisition and future preservation; this will depend on each individual library and its policy.
>
> (*IFLA Principles*, para. 11)

The authors of the *IFLA Principles* also deal, implicitly, with the broader issues of national strategy raised by the *UNESCO Enquiry*:

> ... it is essential that libraries work together on preservation policies at both national and international levels ... National library associations and national libraries have a responsibility for formulating national policies and promoting their acceptance ...
>
> (*IFLA Principles*, paras 16, 17)

Indeed, substantial sections of the *IFLA Principles* can usefully be read as a gloss on this section of the report of the *UNESCO Enquiry*. This includes several paragraphs which deal with the need for cooperation between libraries and non-library institutions such as archives:

> ... librarians should work in close cooperation with archivists ... in dealing with preservation policies and with practical technical problems.
>
> It is ... essential that librarians, scientists and conservators cooperate closely and decide jointly on methods of treatment, materials to be used, and techniques in dealing with specific items.
>
> (*IFLA Principles*, paras 20, 21)

The problem of prioritisation was addressed by the Working Party of LISC (Wales) which produced their *Guidelines*. They suggest that institutions should ask four questions in deciding which material ought to be preserved, and 'which is dispensable':

(a) Is the collection associated with the founding of the institution?
(b) Is it of local interest on account of its content or association?
(c) Is it likely to be used by another institution such as a university, college, library, museum, art gallery or record office?
(d) Has possessing it enhanced the reputation of your institution?

> (*LISC (Wales) Guidelines*, para. 1)

The issue of prioritisation is the key to the successful implementation of a preservation policy, and hence the necessary starting-point for the policy itself. The questions proposed by *LISC (Wales) Guidelines* provide a framework within which the priorities demanded by the international bodies can be determined by institutions.

The next stage of policy development and implementation proposed in the *UNESCO Enquiry* concerned the determination of specific conservation techniques to be used:

> Consideration must be given to the choice of preservation options that are available (e.g. boxing, minor repair or furbishing, binding, hand conservation treatment, bulk de-acid-

ification, transfer to microfilm or other media, leaving on the shelf, disposal) and their relative costs.

(UNESCO Enquiry, para. 42(c))

One particular option is given special prominence:

the role of reprography must be identified and accepted as it provides one of the cheaper and faster options ...

(UNESCO Enquiry, para. 42(d))

This point is also taken up by the authors of the *IFLA Principles*:

... it is impossible to keep all documents in their original format or even by the transfer of the 'intellectual content' to other media. It is therefore necessary to be selective in deciding what is to be conserved, substituted or boxed and to decide on priorities.

(IFLA Principles, para. 14)

The message of both documents is clear: determine priorities both among the materials to be preserved, and for the methods to be used to achieve that preservation. In particular, both imply that for some materials the preservation of the information they contain (the 'intellectual content' to use the phrase of the authors of the *IFLA Principles*) may only be achievable at the expense of the original format. For those materials where format preservation is desirable or essential, an order of priorities needs to be developed.

TREATMENT OPTIONS

Finally, the authors of the *UNESCO Enquiry* suggested ways in which various treatment options might be assessed. They noted the wide range which is available, and also the need to institute preventive as well as restorative measures. The list which they propose is therefore a mixture of several approaches. Some concern the overall library environment, both physical and human:

- ... good housekeeping practices and the application of appropriate standards in the storage and handling of documents.
- minimising the effects of excessive or inappropriate use ...
- minimising the deleterious effect of environmental factors ... by trying to avoid the worst effects of high temperature and humidity levels, atmospheric pollution, dust and excessive light.

(UNESCO Enquiry, para. 43(a),(b),(c))

Other action lines deal with preventive measures:

- use of protective measures such as boxing or protecting slip cases ...
- use of reprography and other substitution methods ...
- establishment of listing ... of microform masters ... to provide lists from which other institutions could select and order material ...
- development and implementation of disaster preparedness procedures ...

(UNESCO Enquiry, para. 43(d),(f),(g),(i))

The section ends with some recommendations for active intervention:

- use of appropriate conservation methods including furbishing, binding or the various types of conservation treatment ensuring that the methods used are appropriate ... archival quality materials are utilised, and that the best conservation principles are followed ...
- development of systematic policies and practices for disinfestation ...
- technical standards should be developed and disseminated ...

(*UNESCO Enquiry*, para. 43(e),(h),(j))

This is, in some ways, a bizarre mixture, especially in the original order of the sub-paragraphs. Nevertheless, it contains many important suggestions and observations, many of which are elaborated in other documents.

Environmental issues dominate much of the literature. The 'good housekeeping practices' are the principle subject of the brief *NPO Guidelines*,[10] which could be taken as a model exemplification of the actions proposed by the authors of the report of the *UNESCO Enquiry* by briefly sumarising all the essential principles for the benefit of non-specialist librarians. Moreover, the NPO has supplemented its printed document by producing a video intended for training and instructional purposes, which is, in effect, a set of guidelines in a different medium.[11] The 'appropriate standards' have also generated a large and important literature.[12] Specific recommendations for such standards, and for environmental controls, are, however, usefully summarised in the *IFLA Principles* (paras 25–8). In essence, these are that there should be a temperature range of between 16°C and 21°C and a relative humidity of between 40 and 60 per cent in areas where paper-based materials are stored, and that these conditions should be regularly monitored with suitable equipment. The *LISC (Wales) Guidelines* (para. 4) similarly emphasise the importance of an appropriate and stable environment, and make similar recommendations, as well as offering some very practical suggestions about the need to ventilate and clean storage areas and to monitor both the ambient conditions and the materials in the collections.

Preventive preservation appears in many forms in the literature. The *IFLA Principles* perhaps contain the clearest statement of the basic requirements:

... A good quality binding provides the best form of protection with sewing going through folded sections and care taken in regard to adhesives and materials used.

(*IFLA Principles*, para. 53)

This statement also has the merit of reminding us that, in the last analysis, it is individual items which have to be preserved, and that it is at that level that all preservation policies will ultimately have to be implemented. The *IFLA Principles* also make specific suggestions for storage systems for single sheets, the use of covers and boxes and the storage of large documents, as well as recommendations about the materials which should be used for repair work. This leads naturally into interventionist work, rather than preventative conservation. The half-way house of format conversion and surrogacy is, by contrast, surprisingly low-key in the *IFLA Principles*. The only substantial reference has already been quoted.[13]

Does a common international vision of a preservation policy emerge from these documents? There is certainly a framework, but it could be argued that there is very little more than that. Both UNESCO and IFLA built their preservation policy guidelines around the concepts of priority and prevention, first deciding what must be preserved and then creating the conditions in which preservation is possible. There is a broad measure of agreement that such an approach depends on the establishment of a formal policy framework which takes account of national and perhaps international priorities and obligations as well as having an institutional perspective. Of course, this whole attitude was determined by the intrinsically international nature of the two sponsoring bodies, but it is an insight which is also reflected in the academic and professional literature. Secondly, there is a recognition that there are several key elements in such a policy, perhaps rather artificially squeezed under four broad groupings in the report of the *UNESCO Enquiry*, and reflected in the subdivisions of this section. These elements clearly include:

- *awareness-raising* and training programmes for both staff and users;
- *a controlled and monitored environment* for the storage of prioritised materials;
- *format conversion* to facilitate the preservation of information;
- *guidelines for good practice* in the handling and storage of materials; and
- *appropriate materials and techniques* for repair and conservation work.

Although this represents a broad consensus of the scope of a formal preservation policy, such a policy cannot be seen in isolation. The various documents which we have described and discussed in this chapter were produced by individuals, groups and organisations with a strong commitment to preservation and a well-articulated mission to raise the awareness of their fellow professionals. Indeed, some of the documents we have discussed were produced as a direct consequence of the attitudinal changes of the early 1980s which we discussed in Chapter 1; some were intended to promote those changes; yet others fall into both categories. The danger was, and is, that preservation issues would be isolated from the mainstream of library policy, and be seen as a stand-alone and specialised aspect of institutional activity. Some of the examples we have used in Chapters 2 and 3 suggest that this fear was not ill-founded, and we shall see further examples in the policy documents themselves in Chapter 6.

The problem is fundamental and yet the broader context of preservation policy is barely addressed at all in these guideline documents. It is essential that such policies are contextualised if they are to be seen as anything more than esoteric luxuries. There is little sense in the various guidelines of the linkage between preservation policies in particular and stock management policies in general. In one sense, this is not a criticism of the authors and sponsors of these documents. Thinking has moved very quickly in the last ten years, and many of the documents which are still current date from the early and middle 1980s. Nevertheless, the recognition that a viable collection management policy must be fully integrated suggests that a different approach to the assessment of preservation policies may need to be developed.

In practice, action has been institutional rather than national. In Britain, we have barely begun the long journey down the road towards national collection and retention policies. The British Library reviewed its own practices in the late 1980s, with the intention of focusing more sharply on how it should fulfil its obligations as the primary focus of the national collections.[14] In psychological terms, perhaps the most important breakthrough here was the recognition that acquisition and long-term retention (and hence preservation) policies had to be considered as an organic and dynamic entity. It was accepted as axiomatic that it was impossible (physically as well as economically) to preserve everything, and then argued that a formal retention policy would ensure that there was selection for preservation which was as well directed as selection for acquisition has traditionally been. Implicit in this was the idea that not everything was worthy of preservation, and that whole categories of publication (not all of them ephemeral in the traditional sense) could be represented by a very small part of the output of the genre. The Enright review highlighted the fact that even the British Library could no longer aspire to be the sole provider of the materials and information legitimately requested by its clients. For other libraries, the recognition of interdependence was a matter of daily life, and had been for decades. In terms of collection retention, however, as opposed to collection development, there was little overt recognition of this until very recently. Only now, in the mid-1990s, are moves towards national policies for collection development and retention beginning to take shape.[15]

Even this, however, does not entirely describe the broader context in which preservation policy has to be developed and implemented. We have suggested in Chapter 4 how contemporary developments in librarianship and the delivery of information to users are having an impact on all aspects of professional activity. The greater reliance on interlibrary loans, on national and regional reserve collections, and the like, are all having the effect of diverting attention away from collections and towards information provision and document supply. The rapid development of both formal and informal systems for the electronic communication of information is taking the whole process outside the library itself directly to the user's desk. When considered together with the economic and technical obstacles to preservation in many libraries, this suggests both a more focused and a more selective approach is now appropriate, rather than the broad sweep recommended or implied in the various guidelines.

These are general issues which we do not find in the guidelines. There are also two specific issues which are increasingly associated with preservation which did not command the same prominence in the early 1980s as they do now. These are disaster control planning and security matters, both of which are now seen as integral to the overall development of preservation policies. The former is a specialised subject in its own right, which we have, deliberately, barely touched upon here.[16] The latter, however, is still neglected, despite the publicity generated by a recent investigation of the scale of theft from British libraries.[17] As we shall see, few libraries identify this as a major problem, despite the findings of the Home Office survey.[18]

In this chapter, we have deliberately confined ourselves to generalities. We now, however, turn to the policies and practices to be found in Britain's libraries in 1993. Can the grand aspirations of international and national planners really be achieved in small (or even not-so-small) libraries under the continuous pressure of users, funders and institutional policy makers? Indeed, do these aspirations really represent the needs of such libraries and their clients? Some answers to these and other questions, based on an analysis of practice, are the subject of Chapter 6.

NOTES

1. See below, pp. 143–52.
2. See below, pp. 111–25.
3. This document is bilingual; the parallel Welsh version is LISC (Cymru). *Canllawiau Cadwraeth. Arolwg a gweithredu.* Aberystwyth: Llyfrgell Genedlaethol Cymru, 1993. We shall be quoting from the English text.
4. The *Guidelines* document is a photographic reproduction of the IFLA document, with a joint imprint of the two organisations, published in 1986. The policy statement, 'Preservation and conservation', was issued in May 1987.
5. ALA President's Committee on Preservation Policy. Report including draft ALA policy and recommendations for its implementation. *ALCTS Network News*, 2: 1, 1991, published electronically and archived at LIS-RAREBOOKS@NEWCASTLE.AC.UK. Cited as *ALA Policy.*
6. Systems and Procedures Exchange Center. *Preservation Guidelines in ARL Libraries.* Washington, DC: Office of Management Studies, Association of Research Libraries (SPEC Kit 137), 1987. Cited as *ARL Guidelines.*
7. Valerie Ferris. The National Preservation Office: its role in the 1990s. *Aslib Information*, 21: 2 (1993), pp. 63–4; for earlier views, see David W.G. Clements. The National Preservation Office of the British Library. *IFLA Journal*, 12: 1 (1986), pp. 25–32; and Marie Jackson. The National Preservation Office. *Conservation Administration News*, 38 (1989), p. 14.
8. See below, pp. 115–16.
9. See John Feather, National and international policies for preservation. *International Library Review*, 22 (1990), pp. 315–27.
10. National Preservation Office. *Preservation Guidelines.* London: The British Library, 1991.
11. National Preservation Office. *Controlling Your Environment.* London: The British Library, 1992. (Video cassette.)
12. See below, pp. 111–13.
13. See p. 103, above.
14. Enright, Hellinga and Leigh, op. cit.
15. See below, pp. 153–4.
16. See above, pp. 54–5.
17. See above, p. 10.
18. See above, p. 21, n. 79.

6   Preservation Policies in Practice

In the previous chapter, we offered a brief description of some key documents produced by various national and international organisations. In the absence of agreed standards, or any kind of formal national policy, we have no other recourse if we are seeking some sort of norms against which to measure practice. In taking this approach, however, our intention is to analyse rather than to criticise. On the basis of a greater understanding of current practices in British libraries, we shall be better placed to suggest possible directions of development for libraries in all sectors which have not yet adopted formal policies in this aspect of their work, as well as how existing policies can be further refined.

We have already noted that written statements of preservation policy are still uncommon in British libraries, although less so than in the early 1980s.[1] The various documents which we have used in Chapter 5 suggest some of the issues which arise in considering such a policy, and in the next section we shall begin our analysis of the extent to which such issues have indeed been addressed in the compilation of some policy statements. We shall first, however, analyse in more detail the *UNESCO Guidelines*, which are explicitly intended to be 'guidelines for the preparation and implementation of a preservation policy' (*UNESCO Guidelines*, para. 1.3). This document claims to be of universal relevance, and is certainly the only attempt known to us to provide a *de facto* template for policymakers.

It is proposed that a preservation policy should deal with ten topics; these are:

- preventive measures
- housekeeping routines
- staff and user training
- security
- protective measures
- a substitution programme
- conservation treatments
- disposal programmes
- reprography policies
- exhibition policies.[2]

Each is discussed in some detail which, under each heading, normally combines a general statement of rationale, purpose and principle with some more specific recommendations. For example, the section on preventive measures begins with this statement:

> The physical environment in which materials are stored will have a significant effect on their life span. Environmental conditions such as temperature, humidity, light and atmospheric pollution can all affect the organic raw materials from which library and archive items are made.
>
> (*UNESCO Guidelines*, para. 4.2.1)

This is followed by both general and particular recommendations:

> Of prime importance is the maintenance of a stable environment ... Temperatures should be maintained within the range of 16°C and 21°C ... Thermometers and hygrometers should be installed ...
>
> (*UNESCO Guidelines*, para. 4.2.3)

Similar statements are made about light, as well as some more generalised statements about air-conditioning systems and dust control. This example is cited to show the thrust of the *UNESCO Guidelines*. It was designed as a highly practical document which would assist managers in policy development and implementation.[3] Its ten principal sections try to encompass the whole range of preservation issues. In effect, it is an attempt to translate the results of the *UNESCO Enquiry* into a series of practical recommendations for the development of an institutional preservation policy.

In practice, however, preservation policies do not stand alone. It is generally recognised that they have to be related to, and integrated with, broader collection-management policies.[4] The Association of Research Libraries, in launching its *Preservation Guidelines*,[5] noted that 'collection development personnel play a key role in deciding what to preserve'.[6] The *UNESCO Guidelines* similarly state that they deal with 'those aspects of collection management which directly affect the preservation of the items within the collection'.[7] The *ALA Policy* creates an even broader, but entirely legitimate context;[8] after enumerating the roles of various parts of the ALA in the development of the recommendations and guidelines, it adds that:

> ... the Intellectual Freedom Committee will, in its own words ... , 'assert the basic importance of preservation in regard to the public's right to the free flow of information ...'

This is a rare public statement of the need to preserve information in order to permit access, or, in other words, that preservation facilitates rather than inhibits the use of books and documents and the information which they contain.

At a more mundane, but no less significant, level the same integration of concepts and policies can be seen in the British Library's statement of its medium-term strategic objectives.[9] The Statement of Purpose includes an unequivocal declaration that 'we build, catalogue and conserve the collections',[10] a broad objective which is made more specific elsewhere in the document. The need for selectivity in determining which materials are to be permanently preserved is explicit, but within that there is a clear commitment 'to ensure comprehensive coverage, recording and preservation of UK and Irish publications in all subject fields'.[11] The contextualizing of preservation in the British Library's strategic plan can stand as an example of one approach to the integration of preservation and conservation issues into the overall management of a library.

PRESERVATION POLICIES IN PRACTICE

Against the background of the various documents which we have discussed in the first two sections of this chapter, we now turn to a detailed consideration of how British libraries actually approach preservation policy in practice. We have already noted that only 51 of our 488 respondents told us that they had written preservation policies, although, as we have suggested, it can be reasonably inferred that policies are in place in other libraries even though no such document was reported.[12] A number of libraries supplied us with copies of the relevant policy documents, and we shall draw heavily on these in this section. Again, we must maintain anonymity,[13] not least because of the security implications of some of the information about library practices. This does not, of course, apply in cases where documents, or descriptions of policies, are already in the public domain.

In order to achieve a systematic analysis, we shall consider the ten issues suggested as the main headings of a preservation policy by the *UNESCO Guidelines*. Not all of these are covered in all of the policies to which we have had access, and there are some matters which they cover with which the *Guidelines* did not deal. We noted the question of security at the end of Chapter 5,[14] and there are other matters, some relating to local circumstances, which can also properly be part of a preservation policy. We shall note some examples in the course of this chapter, but, nevertheless, the *UNESCO Guidelines* are as close as we can come to a normative measure. We shall use them for that purpose, although it is not our intention to assess or evaluate the individual policies which have been supplied to us. We merely seek to explore further the present practice of preservation in British libraries, and to use this analysis as the basis for some suggestions about best practice.

PREVENTIVE MEASURES

Preventive measures to minimise the rate of deterioration.

(*UNESCO Guidelines*, para. 4.1(i))

These measures are defined by the *UNESCO Guidelines* largely in terms of environmental control of storage and reading areas. As we have seen, such controls do exist in significant numbers of library buildings in Britain, although they are often less than ideal.[15] Policy documents do make some attempt to address the issue, although the real constraint here is, of course, the effectiveness of the environmental control systems which are in place. This is reflected in the policy documents. A major research library, in which the greater part of the collection in kept in closed access stacks, makes this statement:

> The following are the levels aimed at and the system is monitored by ... staff taking RH [relative humidity] and temperature readings at 19 points in the building each day. [Another building ...] is monitored at a central point by a buildings management computer system.

> Temperature 18°C
> RH 50–55 per cent

> Light levels are strictly controlled and the storage areas which have no windows are kept in darkness except when material is being placed or retrieved.

This represents something close to the ideal, but it will be noted that it also represents the consequence of a huge investment in sophisticated monitoring and control systems.

A university library with buildings of different ages spread over several sites exemplifies the problem which still exists even when the solution is identified and understood:

> Bearing in mind the topography of the Library, the environmental situation ... is varied, complicated and rarely adequate. [Preservation management staff have become ...] responsible for ... monitoring; ... making recommendations for improvements; and ... work towards implementing them.

> This work continues to grow, with ... the increasing age of buildings which lack adequate maintenance, decoration and cleaning.

The authors add the following comment at the end of this section; it conveys the very essence of the problem:

> [The environmental issue] is an extremely expensive element in the total equation ... Nevertheless, in terms of the long term preservation of the Library's collections, it is the area where the greatest returns can be achieved from any improvements.

That aspiration is reflected in almost all the policy documents we have seen, from many different kinds of libraries. There is evidence of a widespread understanding of the issues involved, and indeed of a knowledge of the ideal solutions. In a shire-county library, for example, a document aimed at staff working with local history materials states that:

> To a certain degree we simply need to rethink the way we handle and store these materials.

There then follow two paragraphs which make textbook-like statements about temperature, relative humidity, control of biological pests, light and the use of fragile materials on photocopiers. We do not criticise this approach, but we know that this particular library is unable to monitor or control either temperature or relative humidity in its principal local history collection; the result can only be frustration for staff at all levels. A pre-1960 university recognises the same problem; after enumerating the usual list of desirable conditions, the documents says:

> In the short-term, some (though not all) of these requirements could be met by utilising:
>
> (a) the strongroom within Special Collections; and
> (b) a further area to be determined.

Others have moved further down the same road; another pre-1960 university library policy has this statement:

> In the bookstacks, the acceptable standard of heating and humidity should be 50° to 60° [C] with relative humidity of 55 to 60%. New meters have been bought ... A regular check system has been initiated. In [another building] adjustment of temperature will not be so easy.

The importance of the issue, however, is fully recognised in this library:

> In planning for any future store, the achievement of such favourable conditions must be of paramount importance.

In other cases, however, there are different institutional priorities; one 1960s' university has the following statement:

> The Library sees a primary need to maintain open access and to provide a satisfactory environment for readers using the general working collection. This necessarily puts stock at risk in terms of temperature, humidity and physical lay-out of the open stack areas, where a compromise has to be struck between conservation and accessibility.

The last sentence of this paragraph is not elucidated in the rest of the document; nevertheless, we have here a succinct formulation of the central dilemma which underlies the development and implementation of good preservation practice. This library has clearly taken a deliberate (and entirely legitimate) policy decision that access is more important than preservation where the two are in conflict; the rest of the document deals almost entirely with very practical means of keeping the stock in working order for heavy student use. This is an exemplification of the various views which we quoted in Chapter 2 from librarians whose preservation policy was, in effect, not to have such a policy. Again, we do not criticise; we merely observe that a policy arrived at by a rational decision-making process, properly recorded and implemented, is better than no policy at all.

HOUSEKEEPING ROUTINES

> Housekeeping routines to clean, protect and extend the life of materials.
>
> (*UNESCO Guidelines*, para. 4.1(ii))

The cleaning of books is not the most inspiring aspect of library work, and yet it is an essential aspect of preservation. As the policy of a major university library states:

> Dust and dirt are among the prime enemies of books: maintenance of cleanliness in all areas of the library should be a high priority.

Another university is more prescriptive:

> Regular cleaning should ... be organised so as to ensure that dirt and dust on floors, shelving, etc., and on library materials, is kept under control.

There is, however, the additional dimension of how to clean books, especially those which are valuable and perhaps fragile:

> [Cleaning] is systematically carried out by the library's porters/messengers with general training under the control of [professional staff in collection management].

The very succinct guidelines produced by a small college library firmly address this issue, telling staff that they should:

- instruct cleaners on how to handle books
- dust books by brushing away from the spine
- dust shelves regularly
- use book ends to keep books tidy and upright.

There are, in fact, two issues here. The first is at a policy level, and concerns the need for planned regular cleaning of stock, especially perhaps in closed-stack areas where dust is more likely to accumulate among less regularly used (but often more permanently significant) materials. The second is at an implementation level, where cleaning staff need to be instructed in the specific methods which are appropriate to dealing with books and other library materials. The problem is that the gap between the two, both intellectually and (in almost all libraries) hierarchically, leads to the danger of a breakdown between policy and practice. Supervision may also be a problem, especially in large institutions with a large (and perhaps transient) cleaning staff, or in libraries where cleaning services are either contracted-out or are not under the administrative control of library management.

For material of special importance, however, it is imperative that this mundane aspect of library work is not neglected; we have some evidence that it is.[16] The reason for such neglect is perhaps to be found in a statement from a pre-1960 university:

> Additional attention is needed to ensure regular dusting and cleaning of such material, but this has a financial implication.

The need for resources to support the implementation of policies can never be ignored.

STAFF AND USER TRAINING

Staff and user training programmes to promote and encourage correct handling and transport of materials.

(UNESCO Guidelines, para 4.1(iii))

It has long been recognised that the training of both staff and users in how to handle library and archival materials is central to resolving the perceived conflict between preservation and access. So far as staff are concerned, there has been a number of national and international initiatives intended to ensure that professional librarians are aware of their responsibilities in this matter. Ratcliffe's findings about the neglect of preservation issues in the professional education of librarians, and the observations made upon them at the time, led to some improvements, and some measure of international agreement on appropriate syllabuses.[17] There has been less emphasis in the literature on the training of non-professional staff, although there is some evidence of a shift of emphasis.[18] The National Preservation Office has recently published a *Training Pack* designed to enable training officers in libraries to develop programmes suitable for their own non-professional staff.[19]

The library policy documents which we have seen lend support to the suggestion that preservation issues are more prominent in in-house staff training programmes than was the case some years ago. As we have seen,[20] some 20 per cent of our respondents offered some form of training for staff, and about 25 per cent included preservation issues in induction courses for newly appointed staff. The level and depth of this training no doubt varies greatly, partly because of the commitment of staff time which is necessary to deliver it effectively and partly because of the varying expertise of trainers. A realistic statement, from one of the most sophisticated policy documents known to us, succinctly expresses the central dilemma:

It is considered important to promote conservation awareness and information among library staff of the causes of deterioration … At the moment this is limited to presentations given to groups of new members of staff … It is intended to extend this programme to cover all members of staff.

The implementation of such good intentions is inevitably limited by the availability of human and material resources. In one large university library, one of the two professional librarians employed in preservation management has, as part of his/her job description what is called 'the "preservation education" of other members of the library's staff'. This statement is explicated thus:

… to become involved in the induction courses for new members of the library staff … and to instruct staff on good handling and housekeeping techniques …

Indeed, the inclusion of preservation awareness in induction programmes now seems to be widespread in the larger libraries.

In smaller libraries, however, there is the inevitable problem of economies of scale. To some extent, the fact that training cannot be cost effectively provided is ameliorated by the existence of the preservation policy documents themselves. A short document from a college library provides an admirable list of prohibitions:

Do not:
- overcrowd books onto a shelf
- squeeze books onto a shelf with insufficient headroom
- take books off shelf by pulling at the top of the spine ...

Five others, equally practical (including a ban on using books as mats for coffee mugs!), follow. At a more general level, a large university library includes the following statement in its policy:

All library materials must be handled in such a way that they are not damaged.

Local circumstances effectively dictate how such aspirations are embodied in policy statements and in implementation programmes. A metropolitan district library is very specific in identifying key areas:

The conservation unit will assist in training ... in the following areas:

Correct handling of items
Basic book repair techniques.

User education seems to be less well developed, but it may simply be that it is less prominent in the policy documents which we have seen. In general, these are concerned with the activities of the staff in the library, rather than directly with public services. One university library noted that:

For readers, a book mark giving suggestions for 'do's' and 'don'ts' has been issued.

Anecdotal evidence and our own (unsystematic) observations, suggest that posters and other material issued by the National Preservation Office are used by some libraries, and that most induction courses for new users do actually include some broad statement on the need to look after library materials for the general good. In addition, it is, of course, normal practice for more valuable materials to be read under supervision, in some cases with strict regulations about the use of pencils, book rests and so on.

SECURITY AND DISASTER PLANNING

Security measures and contingency plans for disaster control and recovery.
(*UNESCO Guidelines,* para. 4.1(iv))

Disaster preparedness planning, as we have suggested,[21] has so many ramifications and implications that it has become a significant subdivision of preservation management in its own right. There is a distinct literature, and there are elaborate national and international guidelines and standards.[22] Perhaps because of this, few preservation policies deal with this matter in any detail. One national institution records that one of the objectives of its preservation policy is 'to plan for salvage operations in the event of a disaster' and refers to a separate document for details. This seems to be a common practice, no doubt because of the complexity of disaster plans, and the need to keep them up to date. As one university library notes, they must be 'kept under constant review', not least because some of the key parts of the plan – such as the identification of facilities and expertise – are dependent on external organisations which may themselves change.

We have not seen a preservation policy document which gives any details of security arrangements, and only one which even refers to the issue. The former is not surprising; by definition, many of the details of security would be inappropriate in a document such as a preservation policy which is, by definition, intended for wide dissemination within the institution and perhaps beyond. The virtually complete absence of any references to security in this context, however, is both surprising and disturbing in view of recent findings on the loss of library materials.[23]

PROTECTIVE MEASURES

> Protective measures, such as boxing, binding, and wrapping, to reduce wear and tear on materials.
>
> (*UNESCO Guidelines*, para. 4.1(v))

This paragraph of the *UNESCO Guidelines* covers one of the major areas of preservation activity, and indeed one which is sometimes understood as being coterminous with preservation itself. All preservation policies have something to say on these matters, but some go into important details which prescribe specific requirements and prohibitions for both techniques and materials. The overall objectives of such a policy are described in a document from a post-1960 university:

> To determine which printed materials require binding, strengthening, rebinding or repair.
> To use both commercial and in-house facilities as appropriate.
> To ensure that work designated is carried out as quickly, efficiently and economically as possible …

All the essential elements of policy are in these three simple sentences: prioritisation of materials, choice of service provider, and quality control and monitoring. In practice, many complex decisions are concealed by these apparent simplicities.

Some policy documents attempt to address the wider issues in some detail. In particular, the selection of materials for treatment, and the determination of financially acceptable and professionally appropriate treatments, are dealt with in some detail. Two examples will illustrate this point. The first is from the policy of a major research library:

> In taking decisions about priorities for active preservation, the following factors must be taken into account:
>
> The importance of the item ... for heritage, scholarly or research purposes.
> The likely level of use ...
> The existing condition of the item ...
> The extent to which preservation responsibilities can be shared ...

On the basis of these broad criteria, the library has prioritised three categories of material for special attention:

> Printed materials that are part of the national heritage.
> Printed materials that are fragile and require special protection.
> Printed materials that are subject to heavy use.

The second example, from a university library, shows a similar conceptual approach:

> Since it is neither practicable nor desirable to keep all material indefinitely, differing levels of care are appropriate for ...
>
> Unique, rare and valuable materials needing permanent preservation ...
> Material expected to have long-term use, which may be kept in its original format or ... transferred to other media.
> Material intended for short-term use ...

The selection of an appropriate form of repair or substitution is also the subject of this aspect of preservation policy. Large libraries increasingly recognise the need for first-aid measures which, although they are theoretically temporary, are likely to become somewhat long-term in practice. These 'temporary measures' are described thus by one large library with important contemporary and historical research collections:

> The use of protective wrappers and boxes is the first step ... A box, folder, wrap-around or polyester pocket will protect an item from further damage ... repairs should be restricted to quick, simple procedures such as tipping-in loose sheets, mending tears on modern books and serials ... and applying leather dressing ...

We cite this as an example of the principles involved. The selection of methods and materials is a rather different matter. This document states that 'a protective casing must be made of high-quality permanent materials', but others go into more detail.

Boxing has clearly become a major element in preventive preservation work in many major libraries.[24] One classification which is of general interest is from a research library which divides its boxes into three categories. These are firstly, 'commercial boxes' bought in standard sizes and used for a wide range of materials; secondly, so-called 'phase boxes' made of acid-free card to the exact size of the item to be boxed; and finally, 'book boxes', described as 'superior permanent boxes', for items of special importance, which are made to a high specification and which may be covered in book cloth, contain special lining material to protect fine bindings, or be customised in other ways. In this case, the library has an expert staff which can select, design and make suitable boxes; the advantages of this are implicit in the policy document of a university library which states that:

> The conservation officer should be consulted where boxes, folders, or wrappers may be needed ... to ensure that materials of appropriate quality and design are employed.

When items are to be bound or rebound, there is also a need for clear guidelines on acceptable techniques, materials and standards. In some cases, this is very detailed. In one shire-county library, for example, the 'stock-care' policy deals with such matters as the retention of dust-jackets, the tipping-in of date labels, the placement of spine-labels with class or shelf numbers, the form of authors' names for spine lettering and the inclusion of tags for the electronic security system. There are additional rules for paperbacks, reference books and items from special collections. In this case, the library has no bindery of its own, and has developed these guidelines to ensure uniformity in dealing with commercial binderies. Such procedures are typical; the commercial binderies expect to receive detailed instructions, and in their promotional literature and presentations emphasise their importance. Moreover, many of them also stress their willingness and ability to adapt standard procedures to the requirements of customers; they regard this flexibility as an important selling point.[25] Where there is an in-house facility, workshop manuals normally prescribe all the details of acceptable procedures and materials.

The choice of bindery is one which is not open to many libraries; as we have noted in Table 3.4 (page 58),[26] only about 10 per cent of our respondents have their own binding facilities. The others must all make use of commercial binderies, whose standards are normally high, but which expect to receive explicit instructions from their customers. It is for this reason that such detailed guidelines as those cited in the last paragraph are thought to be necessary. Where there is a choice, however, there is a need for criteria by which it can be determined. One shire-county library has addressed it in this way:

> Most standard binding operations will be contracted out to commercial binderies ...
> The work [of the in-house unit] ... will consist of ...:

> Specialist binding of books unsuitable to be entrusted to a commercial bindery.
> Conservation [of] paper and parchment archives and maps, seals, etc.
> Polyester encapsulation ...

The intention of this policy (based on a fairly detailed analysis of the library's needs and resources) is to ensure that rare and valuable materials are given appropriate treatment, while not wasting specialist skills on ordinary work. There is also a security issue; in many libraries, the in-house bindery is always preferred for rare and valuable materials, as well as for items needing specialised treatment. At the same time, unique or rare items are more accessible, even when they are being treated in some way, if they are on the premises.

SUBSTITUTION PROGRAMMES

A substitution programme for replacing valuable or very brittle materials with surrogates such as microforms.

(*UNESCO Guidelines*, para. 4.1(vi))

Surrogacy programmes are now of major importance in implementing preservation policies, and have probably been one of the most important instruments in facilitating the shift of emphasis from preservation of books and documents towards the preservation of information for access by users.[27] Photographic reproduction (usually in microform) is the principal mechanism for surrogate preservation of information, as we have seen, despite the development of digitization. Many libraries are engaged in active programmes. As we have seen, two national initiatives, NEWSPLAN and the Mellon Programme, have driven developments in the UK (and indeed Ireland) in the last few years, to the point at which almost one-third of libraries use microforms for archival purposes, and nearly a quarter participate in one or more collaborative microfilming programmes; these we have already discussed.[28] We now seek to trace how the idea of surrogacy is reflected in library policies.[29]

Many libraries are acquiring microforms (and have done so for many years) because it is the most convenient format in which to make certain kinds of material available to users, and sometimes the only way in which acquisition is possible. In some cases, this has enabled libraries to make available to their local users rare or unique materials which would otherwise have to be consulted in other, sometimes very distant, libraries. This, however, is rather different from the conscious use of microforms as a preservation tool. The basic principles of the latter can be found in the policy document of a post-1960 university:

In a few cases periodicals on microfiche have been substituted for hard copy, saving binding costs, and most newspapers of archival interest have also been treated in this way. Here it is a question of substitution as an alternative to preservation.

Economic motives clearly predominate here, but in other libraries they do not. It has to be noted, however, that some of the 'policy' statements seem to be aspirations rather than realities:

In order to reduce wear and tear on heavily used, rare or fragile material, a programme of preservation microfilming should be undertaken.

Another university library offers a rather different approach, which is more specific and deserves quoting at some length:

There appears to be no role for bought-in microforms in preserving existing material. This would be seen rather as a space-saving measure ...

Eventually all theses ... will be transferred to microfiche. An on-going programme is under way ...

No archival material needs filming.

For local history material in demand ... a backup copy on film should be made ...

If any other rare material is found to be in constant demand either [locally] or on inter-library loan, microfilming should be considered as a preservation measure.

This is, however, a rare example of a well-developed policy statement. In most libraries, it seems that microforms are bought when they are the most convenient way of acquiring and storing materials. In the 1960s and 1970s, back runs of journals were often bought in microform, especially by new or rapidly expanding university and polytechnic libraries. Microforms are also very useful for 'awkward' items, such as long runs of newspapers. The purposeful generation of microform surrogates, however, is largely confined to participation in various cooperative schemes, although there are also examples of the use of institutional resources to protect rare or heavily used originals.[30] Given the cost of such operations, this is not surprising, and is indeed to be welcomed as a effective use of resources.

CONSERVATION TREATMENTS

Conservation treatments to repair damaged originals.

(UNESCO Guidelines, para. 41.(vii))

The author of the *UNESCO Guidelines* uses the word 'conservation' in its usual contemporary sense, to indicate the process of repairing individual items to a high standard for permanent preservation. By implication, such treatments are applied only to very important materials, which is normally understood to mean items of long-term or historical significance as artifacts. In practice, this means that for some libraries conservation is indeed an irrelevance, unlike preservation which is a universal (if variable) need for all libraries. Conservation policy derives from preservation policy, and is indeed an integral part of it; the extract quoted above from the policy document of a shire-county library exemplifies the relationship between the two.[31] The *conservation* element is the part which is concerned with the treatment of individual items and in that library system, as in many others, is considered appropriate only to items which are of special value or of a particular physical construction.

Conservation policies generally prescribe both techniques and materials. Again, this may be at a comparatively basic level, as in the university library whose conservation policy is summarised in this brief statement:

Fragile and valuable items ... [are to be] placed in acid-free wallets or boxes, as appropriate, to ensure longevity.

The essential problem for most libraries is implicit in the document from another university:

Treatment of all materials must be in accordance with professional advice.

121

That professional advice is, of course, available within some libraries from their own specialised staff; such institutions, are, however, in a small minority, although they do include the major national repositories and some of the many important public and university libraries.

In some of these libraries, the policy document itself outlines the treatments which are regarded as either mandatory or acceptable. An extract from one such document can be held to illustrate the level of detail which is, ideally, needed:

> Minor repairs are often quite adequate for old books printed on good quality paper; small tears repaired, hinges strengthened, leather refurbished and protective boxes made. Fuller treatment, where the book will be disbound, consists of dry-cleaning, washing, de-acidifying if necessary, paper repairs, strengthening of spine folds and rebinding in leather, cloth or vellum.

Such treatment can only be achieved at the cost of much time and money by the deployment of the very skills which are said to be in such short supply.[32]

For most libraries which recognise the importance of conservation to the long-term survival of their most valuable materials, perhaps the best advice is indeed to take advice.

DISPOSAL PROGRAMMES

> Disposal programmes for materials of no further use.
>
> (*UNESCO Guidelines*, para. 4.1(viii))

With a handful of exceptions, all libraries dispose of some materials. In public libraries, and in most academic and many special libraries, disposal is an integral part of the collection management process. The following extract from the stock retention policy document of the library of a public sector agency can be taken as typical of most scientific special libraries:

> All newly acquired texts are retained for a minimum of three years ... Books and pamphlets should therefore be considered for disposal if they
>
> 1. Are out of date and more up to date material is available.
> 2. Are seldom or not [*sic*] used.
> 3. No longer reflect the interests of either libraries or their parent organisations.
> 4. Are in poor physical condition.
> 5. Are over 10 years old.

This may be rigid, but it has the merit of being unambiguous (allowing for some infelicities of expression) and of clearly conveying how the library's stock is to be managed in line with its overall mission and strategy.

In public libraries, the following statement from a shire-county librarian may be taken as typical:

> The decision whether to withdraw a book ... must be taken by professional staff based on knowledge of physical condition, subject context or likely continued use.

This is almost a mirror image of what might be expected in a broad statement of acquisitions policy; the reflection actually locates disposal policies in the collection management process. All that needs to be added occurs a few lines further down in the same document, under the heading 'Non-current stock':

> Books in this category, *unless of historic value* [our italics], should be withdrawn.

The italicised phrase is, of course, the essence of the matter, and calls for the proper exercise of informed professional judgement.

In universities, policies are more diverse and perhaps less sharply defined. This is hardly a matter for surprise; as we saw in Chapter 2, attitudes to preservation in general vary greatly within the university library sector with great national institutions at one end of the scale seeking to preserve large parts of their stock in perpetuity and, at the other extreme, medium-sized libraries in which service to current users is the only significant determinant of policy. A broad statement, capable of wide interpretation (but no less useful for that), comes from one post-1960 university:

> The general policy is to retain all material which is considered of current or potential value ... the library has in hand a complementary programme of relegation to compact storage ... The criteria used for relegation are at the discretion of the subject librarians, but items relegated may include older material, less-used back-runs ...

Interestingly, this is in a library which theoretically adhered to the 'self-renewing' concept proposed in the 1970s, but which states that 'the balance has moved in favour of retention'. This raises issues to which we shall need to return, for this library, like many others, seems to be preserving by default, with very restrictive policies for disposal and relegation.

REPROGRAPHY POLICIES

> Procedures for reproducing originals.
>
> *(UNESCO Guidelines,* para. 4.1(ix))

The villain of the piece is the photocopier, whose flat-bed platen is a great destroyer of book structures. This was recognised many years ago in research libraries; indeed, one of the first public manifestations of a renewed concern with preservation was the imposition of restrictions on photocopying if the items in question were likely to be damaged. The British Library, the Bodleian and other libraries now regularly prohibit the copying of manuscripts and older printed books on such machines. Other processes can, also of course, be destructive or damaging. One library states in its policy document:

> The library exercises the right to refuse to allow filming or copying from material when this may subject the item to risk.

In any case, even when copying is allowed, it is not usually done by readers:

> No reproduction of archive material should take place, unless undertaken by library staff using formats with minimal disturbance or damage to the original ...

The meaning of this (as a later phrase makes clear) is that such copying shall normally be in microform rather than photocopy.

In a sense, policies on reprography are part of the more general rules and recommendations about the careful handling of materials, and in some policy statements are indeed incorporated into such rules.

EXHIBITION POLICIES

> Procedures for the exhibition of materials within the institution or whilst on loan to another organisation.
>
> (*UNESCO Guidelines*, para. 4.1(x))

Probably most libraries exhibit some of their material, if only in the form of dust-jackets of new acquisitions. For many libraries with heritage collections, exhibitions are perhaps the best way of bringing such collections to the attention of the majority of users of the library. For some libraries, exhibitions can also represent a source of revenue, either by entry charges or by the publication of catalogues or both, and perhaps from fees for lending materials for exhibition elsewhere. The latter point is one of great difficulty and great importance; in the heritage world, especially in the visual arts, international loan exhibitions have become an increasingly important feature of the public presentations of institutions. All major owners benefit, and most seek to participate, but they are inevitably faced with the problem of protecting their property both in transit and during the period of exhibition itself.

At a local level, the first priority is to ensure that materials are exhibited in an appropriate way. In one shire-county library, it was recommended that:

> Improvements could be made by ... rearranging furniture or equipment, acquiring new equipment ... placing UV [ultraviolet] filters on framed pictures or display cases ...

The work involved can be considerable; one large university library summarises it as follows:

> ... preparing [an exhibition] ... may involve repairing the materials ... creating suitable display units ... mounting the exhibition into cases.

This is only at the beginning:

> Subsequently, [there is] ... dismantling the exhibition and returning the items ... remounting, fasciculing, etc.

All the documents we have seen which deal in detail with matters relating to exhibitions, emphasise the importance of curatorial and conservation staff working together to ensure the safety and security of items whether on the premises or in transit to another site.

So far as actual exhibition practices are concerned, there are some clear recommendations in one library's policy:

> The environment of the exhibition area is monitored, and if necessary a micro-climate is established within the exhibition case … Lighting levels too have to be established and controlled … [as does] ambient heat.

When materials are lent to other institutions, owners normally expect that the display conditions will be comparable to their own, and it is normal practice to accompany exhibits of exceptional value to ensure that this is achieved. There are, of course, also security issues in the transport of materials; like other such matters, these are highly confidential.

SUMMARY

In this section, we have taken a prestigious international document and used it as a template for the analysis of preservation policy documents in certain British libraries. This analysis is, of course, only part of our overall study of current preservation practices. As we have already noted, many libraries have policies but no policy documents; there are documents which we have not seen; there is data from our survey to suggest that some, often incomplete, *de facto* policies are in place in libraries which do not describe them as such; and there are libraries in which some of the elements of a preservation policy are to be found in collection-management policies and the like. Nevertheless, this study of a selection of policy documents has provided some valuable and detailed insights into practice, and into some of the thinking which underlies practice.

Perhaps the most important overall conclusion to be drawn is that preservation is indissolubly linked to wider aspects of library strategy and policies. The key factor is the attitude of the library to its primary functions, and how those functions are related to the stock. This has emerged at several points in our analysis; for example, it is clear that in one of the universities whose policy statement we have used, the primary consideration is the provision of adequate services to undergraduates and others whose demand is for high volume, quick turnover and currency. In other cases, there is a different concern reflected in the wish to preserve parts of the collections for more permanent retention as part of a collection management policy which envisages the development and maintenance of stock in the long term. These differences, and many others, are as predictable as they are legitimate. They reflect the wide range of libraries which we surveyed and the huge differences between some of them. Such variety has to inform the final section of this chapter, in which we shall try to isolate best current practice in preservation in British libraries.

SOME OBSERVATIONS

Comparatively few British libraries appear to have developed formal preservation policies embodied in specific documents. Nevertheless, compared with Ratcliffe's findings in the early 1980s, there is an increased number of such documents, and many more libraries in which preservation and collection management issues have been systematically considered and developed. Libraries have had to work within narrow constraints of both human and financial resources; indeed the whole period under consideration (like the foreseeable future) has been a time of retrenchment combined with rapid institutional, technological and cultural change. Inevitably, the consequences of these changes are reflected in those preservation policies which are realistically located in the library world of the mid-1990s.

The alleged conflict between the demands of preservation and those of access is now being articulated in a different arena. The use of microform surrogates, and the advanced stages of development of cost-effective digitized surrogates for both textual and graphical data, are significant developments. The former is clearly reflected in some of the documents we have seen, as well as in responses to our questionnaire. The high capital costs of mass microforming, however, have led to the development of nationally and even internationally coordinated schemes in such key areas as surrogate preservation of newspapers. The potential impact of computer-based technologies is, however, even greater.

It is already apparent both from the literature and from many of the responses which we have received, that many librarians see the future of their libraries in terms of giving instantaneous access to information rather than as a long-term storage place for books and documents. In such libraries, preservation is a very minor concern, often not designated as such and essentially aimed at ensuring that current materials are available in sufficient quantities and in a usable condition, while drawing on external sources – both document supply services and network-based information services – for other materials and data. Each library will, of course, determine its own priorities in conjunction with its parent body. It is not our business to criticise, but rather to suggest mechanisms for ensuring that information and documents are indeed available when and where they are required. This certainly involves extending the traditional concept of 'preservation', and perhaps even some consideration of whether *preservation* is the word which best describes what we are discussing, but the underlying conceptual issue – the need to have an information store on which users can draw – remains essentially the same. We shall return to this issue in Chapter 7, where we shall also consider the broader issue of retention policies and the roles of national and regional cooperative schemes and document-delivery systems.[33]

It is clear from our findings and from the information which has been provided to us that the fundamental objective of making documents (in any medium) and their information content available is most likely to be achieved – and perhaps can only be achieved – in the context of a wide-ranging strategy which determines the institution's priorities in meeting the needs and legitimate demands of its users. We can take the British Library as an example of the process. The Library's Statement of Purpose includes the following sentences:[34]

> Our function is to serve scholarship, research and enterprise. Our purpose is to promote the advance of knowledge through the communication of information and ideas.

One of the five action lines intended to enable this to be achieved is:[35]

> We build, catalogue and conserve the collections.

A more detailed statement about preservation expands on this general statement of intent. The key passage defines the order of priorities:[36]

> … the Library's preservation policies will aim at preserving material in need of conservation in the following order of priority:
>
> - heritage material and unique or rare material including manuscripts, certain special collections, archives, rare printed material, materials of bibliographic or structural importance, or material classed as artifacts;
> - material comprising the national collection of British publications;
> - material that is heavily used now and has become fragile, or that may be expected to receive heavy use in the future and has already or is likely to become fragile;
> - material not available elsewhere;
> - material belonging to the research archives;
> - low-use material which is too fragile to be consulted or copied.

The British Library is unique, but so are all libraries, just as all libraries have some common characteristics. The strategic plan quoted in the last paragraph is a unique solution to a unique set of challenges, but it suggests a template for the basic development of preservation policies in very different circumstances. First, there is a clear vision of overall purpose, and a sense of the direction of development which the library is pursuing. Secondly, preservation is incorporated into the actions which will enable that vision to be realised. Finally, there is a clear prioritisation of specific issues which will enable resources to be consistently applied to the achievement of the action plan. It is this three-level approach – strategy, action plan, prioritisation – which forms the basis of any effective preservation policy. In many libraries, however, we have found that it is the link between the first and second stage which is missing; a mission statement envisages the need for information resources, many of which will be locally held materials, but there is no action plan to ensure that such materials will indeed be available. It is for this reason that we have implicitly commended libraries which have bluntly told us that they have no preservation policy because long-term preservation is not their objective. In a perverse way, that is, in effect, a policy which determines how the stock will be managed, provided that arrangements are in place which ensure that the stock survives in a usable condition for the period of time for which it is needed. These arrangements are as likely to include a policy for relegation or disposal as a preservation policy in the conventional sense. All, however, is grist to the mill of provision for users. The line between preservation and other aspects of collection management is imprecise and largely meaningless; the two are wholly interdependent, because the former – preservation – is merely a part of the latter.

When we turn from generalities to specifics, practice will inevitably be determined by local circumstances. It is clear, however, from the practices which we have found and from the policy documents which we have seen, that in most libraries the maintenance of the stock for use is the guiding principle of the preservation policy. The policy documents deal with a series of key issues, of which the most important is prioritisation. Exemplary guidelines are provided by one major institution:

> There are three major points to consider:
>
> whether the information could be copied, perhaps into a different format, with or without subsequent conservation of the original;
> whether an item warrants full conservation treatment or merely a protective wrapper or box;
> if conservation treatment is decided upon, which technique is the most suitable and how urgently it should be carried out.

The order of priority suggested here is instructive; the first task is to make the information content of documents accessible to potential users, while the actual format and material form is considered of lesser importance. Only when physical preservation is desirable for other reasons are the treatment options considered. This is, in some ways, a simplified version of the complex decisions which could be involved; in particular, it ignores the possibility that a surrogate might be made for purposes of consultation, and the original then preserved as an historical artefact protected from excessive (or perhaps any) handling and direct use.

The library whose document we have quoted in the previous paragraph has important research materials as well as a large working collection. For libraries for which the latter is the only major consideration, we note the following simple suggestions in the stock policy of a public library which were, in turn, adapted from a document produced for training and promotional purposes by a commercial binder:

Why and When to Re-bind and Bind

Why rebind?
- to save money
- to encourage issues
- to extract maximum life from pages
- to maintain worthwhile titles in active use

Considerations that influence the re-binding decision
- durability
- importance

- relevance
- degree of demand
- ease of replacement
- frequency of re-print
- cost of options
- availability of shelf space
- can it be re-bound?
    margins wide enough?
    paper quality good enough?
- book is not superseded

When to re-bind?
at *early* sign of deterioration in either dust jacket
or
the text is coming away from cover.

It is possible to make some technical criticisms of this, not least in the use of imprecise language ('pages' for 'text block', for example), but such criticisms would miss the point. This is a working document usable, and used, by paraprofessionals and non-professionals involved in circulation, shelving and other day-to-day activities in a wide range of central, district and branch libraries throughout the system. In effect, it enables such staff to operate a system of triage of apparently endangered books and to make the primary decisions on preservation priorities.

The selection of appropriate treatments is necessarily a more technically skilled task, and again dependent on institutional requirements and priorities. Typically, well-developed preservation policies prescribe what treatments are – and are not – acceptable, desirable or mandatory. In the most detailed documents we have seen, this is taken to the level of suggesting or requiring particular materials or techniques. We have quoted some examples in the previous section which illustrate the principles involved.[37] The compilation of such documents requires input from those with the appropriate technical expertise; as we have seen, that is not available in many libraries, and some turn to the binding industry for guidance, some (especially among public libraries) to local record offices, and others to the National Preservation Office.[38]

It is here, however, that the *LISC* (*Wales*) *Guidelines* come into their own; nine of the 16 numbered sections deal with treatments available for different categories of material: books, newspapers, ephemera, maps, manuscripts, archives, pictures and prints, photographs, and audiovisual material. As an example, we quote the section on maps:[39]

(a) Purpose-built cabinets can be obtained for standard size maps, e.g. Ordnance Survey maps.
(b) Tithe maps and estate maps are not standard in size and they are difficult to store. Ideally, they should not be rolled up but there seems to be little option when they are oversize. Extending tubes and linen bags are available for storing maps and they can be made to measure.

(c) Every effort should be made to photocopy heavily-used maps in order to minimise wear and tear on the originals.

(d) Map-conservation is a skilled operation and it should only be undertaken by conservators. However, everyone involved in the care of maps can ensure that they are properly stored, not rolled too tightly (a tube can be placed in the centre) and inspected regularly.

We find here that combination of practical advice and contact with reality ('there seems to be little option') which commends itself in the development of practical policies in libraries. These suggestions for particular types of materials, taken together with the generic housekeeping suggestions in the *NPO Guidelines*, and the NPO's more recent guidelines on security matters,[40] offer a very solid foundation for a preservation policy.

Policy, however, can only be fully developed and effectively implemented if the necessary information is available to planners and managers. As we have noted, only just over one-third of libraries in our survey have systematic stock survey procedures for preservation purposes.[41] No doubt there are others in which staff are expected, as a matter of course, to note defects as they become apparent, especially at the point of return of lending stock. Even so, it seems likely that most British libraries need to reconsider their attitude to stock surveys. For those parts of the collections which are regarded as being of exceptional importance, and worthy of permanent preservation, such surveys are the essential basis for action. Indeed, it was such surveys which first revealed the extent of the 'brittle books' phenomenon in American libraries, which some would see as one of the major starting-points of the modern preservation movement in the profession.[42]

Surveys inevitably start from samples, although even before the sample can be chosen there has to be some prioritisation between categories of materials. Various techniques have been used and recommended, but those which produce statistically valid samples are obviously to be preferred. One such survey, conducted in Trinity College Dublin in the late 1980s, has recently been described in print with a full statistical analysis.[43] A survey conducted in a wide range of libraries in Oxford University has also been described.[44] Other suggestions for sampling methods, including some very practical advice on how to work at the shelves, will be found in an NPO publication from the mid-1980s.[45] Having established the target collections, and the sampling method, the next stage is to conduct the survey itself. Interestingly, we find nothing in any documents which we have seen from British libraries which indicates how such surveys are actually handled even in those libraries which do conduct them regularly and systematically, although some comments from our respondents do give us some insights, and the methodology of the Oxford survey has been described in detail in a semi-published report.[46] In public libraries, the monitoring of stock is generally a part of the regular routine housekeeping; the statement that 'all lending stock [is] checked for condition on return' in one shire county library seems typical. Systematic surveys are largely confined to special collections and local history collections, and in a number of cases reported to us this in indeed undertaken systematically on an annual basis. One London Borough told us that it has a:

rolling programme of surveying archives and prioritising necessary conservation work.

This appears to be as exceptional as it is commendable!

For the most part, however, stock is *inspected* rather than surveyed; the basis may be systematic (as in the course of regular stock check) or effectively random (as, for example, when books are returned by borrowers). In this respect, academic and public libraries do not greatly differ. In several college and university libraries, there is some inspection as part of the annual shelf-check. We assume that in many cases, this is adequately described by the college librarian who told us of a 'rough survey undertaken with annual stocktaking'. We do, however, find more detailed procedures in place in a few libraries. One large library in London University, for example, undertakes annual conservation surveys of specific areas of the library, and there are indications of similar practices elsewhere. Nevertheless, such surveys are not a common feature of British library management practice, and models are therefore hard to find.

At a prescriptive level, there is a UNESCO document which is a useful point of reference.[47] The author recommends that the following characteristics should be inspected during the survey:

- appearance (general level of cleanliness, etc.)
- wear and tear
- soil and surface dirt
- stains
- acid damage (i.e. embrittlement and 'foxing')
- oxidation
- biological damage (mould, mildew, insects, rodents)
- light damage
- water damage

The study also contains a model pro forma for recording the results of the survey, which, with adaptations, could be used by many libraries. So could the software package which has been developed by the Research Libraries Group in the United States.[48] In the context of three British libraries, there are published proposals for conducting preservation surveys submitted for a competition organised by the National Preservation Office in 1989.[49] In general, however, systematic surveys, even at the most basic level are a major gap in British preservation management practice, and need to be addressed as a matter of urgency.

CONCLUSIONS

In this chapter we have taken a very broad sweep across the practice of preservation policy in the United Kingdom as it can be determined both from our own work and from the literature. We have also tried to suggest some approaches to the development of such policies in libraries which seek to do so. We have been able to draw heavily on prescriptive literature, both British and international, and have tried to relate it to practice. In particular, in our concluding observations, we have suggested at least the broad outlines of how a library might address the issues involved. We do not believe that a single template can serve for all libraries. Preservation, like all aspects of library policy, is properly driven by institutional considerations and by the mission of the library itself and its parent body. On the other hand, there are aspects of good practice, which we have tried to indicate and to explicate, which are capable of more general application, and we believe that these might be useful to others. In Chapter 7, we shall draw upon all of this, and particularly upon our analysis of practice, to suggest how policies might be developed in institutions which aspire to them.

NOTES

1. See pp. 52–3, above. There is some difficulty with this statement; Ratcliffe found that only nine libraries had written policy statements (four universities, two public, two government, one national); Ratcliffe, op. cit., p. 17. In 1986, it was reported that 18 per cent of universities (at that time meaning some 12 institutions) had compiled such policies; no polytechnics had done so (Ian R.M. Mowat. Preservation problems in academic libraries. In: R.E. Palmer, ed. *Preserving the Word. The Library Association Conference Proceedings, Harrogate 1986*. London: The Library Association, 1987, pp. 37–45, at pp. 38–9. In 1988, the number of universities (excluding the then polytechnics) with policy statements was 17 (Brenda E. Moon and Anthony J. Loveday. Progress report on preservation in universities since the Ratcliffe Report. In: National Preservation Office. *Preservation and Technology*, pp. 11–17, at p. 13). We have commented on this in Eden, Feather and Matthews, Preservation policies and conservation in British academic libraries in 1993, pp. 65–8.
2. *UNESCO Guidelines*, para 4.1.
3. In this sense, the example chosen is perhaps ironic. The predominance of environmental issues in the literature takes little account of the cost of installing, running and maintaining good environmental control systems. This is reflected in our findings in Britain (see above, pp. 64–68), and is even more true in the tropical and subtropical regions where developing countries are unable to fund such systems.
4. See, for a recent general discussion, Margaret Child, Preservation issues for collection development staff, *Wilson Library Bulletin* (November 1992), pp. 20–1, 106.
5. Chapter 5, note 6.
6. *SPEC Flyer*, 137 (September 1987), p. 1.
7. *UNESCO Guidelines*, para. 1.3.
8. See above, Chapter 5, note 5.
9. The British Library. *For Scholarship, Research and Innovation. Strategic objectives for the year 2000*. London: The British Library, 1993.
10. Ibid., p. 9.
11. Ibid., p. 21.

12. See pp. 52–4, above.
13. This has presented some additional problems in this section. The policy documents are specific to their own institutions, which means that there is a real likelihood of identification in discussing, for example, particular buildings. We have therefore made even greater use of ellipses, brackets and other devices while retaining as much as possible of the original wording of the documents. We hope that this has not made the text too difficult to read, nor too opaque in meaning.
14. See above, pp. 106–7.
15. See above, pp. 64–8.
16. See above, p. 62.
17. See above, pp. 6–8, and the references there; see also John Feather. *Guidelines for the Teaching of Preservation to Librarians, Archivists and Documentalists.* The Hague: IFLA (Professional Report, 18), 1990.
18. John Feather, Staff training for preservation. *Library Management*, 11: 4 (1990), pp. 10–14.
19. See above, p. 19, n. 47.
20. See above, p. 58.
21. See above, pp. 106–7.
22. See Graham Matthews, Disaster management: controlling the plan. *Managing Information*, 1: 7/8 (1994), pp. 24–7; Buchanan, op. cit., Tregarthen Jenkin, op. cit., and Harvey, op. cit., pp. 119–36. See also, pp. 8–10, above.
23. See above, p. 10.
24. See above, pp. 71–2.
25. We derive this statement from off-the-record conversations with senior managers in the binding industry, and from the promotional material which we have seen from a number of companies.
26. See p. 58, above.
27. See above, pp. 82–4.
28. See above, pp. 90–92.
29. For the various international standards for archival microforms, see above, pp. 89–90.
30. See above, pp. 90–92.
31. See above, p. 119.
32. See above, pp. 69–71.
33. See below, pp. 141–2.
34. British Library, *For Scholarship, Research and Innovation*, p. 9.
35. Ibid.
36. Ibid., p. 27.
37. See above, pp. 117–19, 121–2.
38. See above, pp. 72–3.
39. *LISC (Wales) Guidelines*, pp. 4–5.
40. See above, p. 10; National Preservation Office. *Security Guidelines.* London: The British Library [1990].
41. See above, p. 61.
42. For the general principles, see Gay Walker. Assessing preservation needs. *Library Resources and Technical Services*, 33: 4 (1989), pp. 414–19. See ARL Guidelines, pp. 71–109, for examples from five American libraries. For a general statement, see David C. Weber. Brittle books in our nation's libraries. *College and Research Libraries News*, 48: 5 (1987), pp. 238–40. There are (significantly) few published surveys from British libraries; for a key example, see Edmund King, Surveying the printed book collections at the British Library. *Library Management*, 11: 4 (1990), pp. 15–19, and, in a specialised area, Graham Matthews. *Preservation of Russian and Soviet Materials in British Libraries* (British Library Research and Development Report 6033). Liverpool: Liverpool Polytechnic Press, 1991.
43. Paul Sheehan. A condition survey of books in Trinity College Library Dublin. *Libri*, 40: 4 (1990), pp. 306–17.
44. Katherine Swift. The Oxford preservation survey. *The Paper Conservator*, 17 (1993), pp. 31–4. We are grateful to Mr Giles Barber for supplying us with a copy of Part 1 of the Report of this survey,

which gives details of the findings (Oxford University. Libraries Board Preservation Committee. *Preservation Report. Part 1, Report on the extent and condition of Oxford library holdings.* [Oxford: Oxford University Libraries Board, 1994.]

45. Issued as part of National Preservation Office. *Preservation. A Survival Kit.* London: The British Library, [1986]. See also the paper by King, cited in note 42, above.

46. See note p. 22, n. 100, above.

47. George M. Cunha. *Methods of Evaluation to Determine the Preservation Needs in Libraries and Archives: a RAMP study with guidelines.* Paris: UNESCO (PGI-/WS/16), 1988, pp. 31–45.

48. Research Libraries Group. *RLG Preservation Needs Assessment Package (Print Materials)* [Software package]. Mountain View, CA: Research Libraries Group, 1993.

49. National Preservation Office. *Keeping Our Words. The 1989 National Preservation Office competition.* London: The British Library, 1990. The three libraries were the William Salt Library Stafford (Thea Randall and Pauline Thomson), which won the competition, and St Catherine's College, Cambridge (Avril Pedley) and the BBC Central Music Library (Nazlin Bhimani and Janet Ogleby) which were commended by the judges.

7 Planning for Preservation

A snapshot is a two-dimensional, static and partial representation of an original which is three-dimensional, dynamic and holistic. Survey-based research, such as that which supports much of the factual superstructure of this book, is indeed a snapshot. But, like a snapshot, it has its purpose: it does convey, however imperfectly, something of the essence of the original more effectively, more accurately and more objectively than any interpretative and impressionistic representation can do. In the central chapters of this book, we have used the data which we collected in 1993 as the basis for an analysis of preservation policies and practices in a wide range of libraries in Great Britain, and have used the data as the basis for a presentation of our view of preservation management and related issues in those libraries. In this final chapter, we shall go beyond the data and comparatively simple interpretations of it. We shall suggest possible lines of development both for institutions and at a higher level, both professional and political, and we shall try to offer some practical guidelines of our own which will, we hope, prove valuable to librarians and others.

PRESERVATION IN BRITISH LIBRARIES: THE STATE OF THE ART

We have suggested that the evolution of attitudes to preservation, and of preservation policies, in British libraries has been largely driven by factors external to the great majority of institutions. The British Library led by example in the first decade of its own existence, not least by sponsoring the work undertaken by Ratcliffe and by housing and supporting the National Preservation Office. These initiatives, however, were themselves the product of a growing perception among the custodians of heritage collections that the preservation of those collections for the long-term future was approaching a point of crisis because of increased use, overcrowded storage areas and both internal and external environmental deterioration. The redirection of resources, and the infusion of some additional funding, made it possible to define and to begin to address these issues. In this book, we have, as one of our objectives, tried to assess the results of the intellectual, professional and managerial efforts which grew out of those initiatives.

It is clear that there is a greater awareness of the preservation issue than was the case 15 or 20 years ago, but it is far from clear that the perception is universally positive. We have reported and discussed the responses of many librarians in all sectors whose attitude is that preservation is none of their business. Those who see their libraries as being mechanisms for the supply of current information to current users may or may not dismiss preservation conceptually, but certainly in many cases they see it as wholly irrelevant to their own activities and priorities. The operational link between preservation and collection management and the logical link between the need to preserve information and the ability to provide it, although both loom large in the specialist literature, appear not to have entered fully into the professional thinking of many librarians.

As a consequence, we have found that the general professional approach to preservation is still very traditional. This is perhaps exemplified by the fact that most libraries identify paper-based materials as being their main preservation problem. In quantitative terms, this is, no doubt, true in almost all libraries, but there is some evidence of comparatively little understanding of the issues which surround this predictable, straightforward and largely accurate perception. Photographic and digitized materials are, in their different ways, at least as vulnerable as paper. Moreover, there is little suggestion that many of our respondents have fully considered the issue of selectivity for preservation, despite the best practice which we have identified in some institutions. In other words, a widespread problem (which is genuine) is seen as insoluble merely because of its scale. Little attempt has been made to take the analysis beyond that in many libraries. The almost entire lack of properly conducted surveys of collections exemplifies the problem: the statistical basis on which we could form a reliable estimate of the scale of the preservation needs of Britain's library collections *as a whole* simply does not exist. We shall return to this national issue later in this chapter.[1]

The comparative narrowness of perception is perhaps most obvious in the public library sector. As we have suggested,[2] the whole question of preservation policy was identified as an issue for local studies and special collections librarians by a large number of our public library respondents. We do not necessarily criticise this, and indeed it is encouraging that public librarians recognise the significance of the heritage collections which they have developed. On the other hand, we found little evidence that any connection was made between this aspect of the library's collection management and the equally important, and quantitatively far larger, issue of the management of current stock. Yet well-managed public libraries have well-established and constantly reviewed stock management policies; these include, in many cases, specific policies concerning, for example, binding and long-term retention. The link between these activities and public access is obvious; the same link exists between availability of materials and formal preservation policies for local studies and other special collections. In the public library sector, preservation is seen as a specialist activity, identified with other specialist activities. It may carry some prestige, but it has little real weight.

A more positive interpretation of the same findings can, however, be offered: that the limited human and financial resources available for preservation are being prioritised in key areas of the library. In many academic and special libraries this is certainly the case. Indeed, in some libraries in all sectors, there is evidence of a systematic consideration of preservation issues even where no preservation policy exists, and even in some cases where the very idea is specifically rejected. To some extent this is a semantic issue. Many practitioners and academics who have considered the preservation issue during the 1980s and 1990s have been making a conscious effort both to increase general professional understanding in this field, and simultaneously to widen the meaning of the word itself. It is argued (and has indeed been implicit throughout this book) that preservation is one element in a collection management policy which is designed to make materials and information available to users in response to legitimate and reasonable demand. It is clear, however, that, although there may be wider awareness of preservation, there is certainly not a universal acceptance of the wider definition of the term.[3]

This semantic point is not merely of academic interest. We have found evidence, some of which we have discussed, of systematic consideration of stock management issues in many libraries in all sectors. Indeed, there are few libraries where it is not considered in some form or other. Many libraries which specifically deny having a preservation policy in effect have taken a conscious decision *not* to preserve; they seek to determine the optimal life of their stock and to take whatever steps are necessary to achieve that. In the broader sense, that is a preservation policy designed to facilitate access and use. Nevertheless, we suggest that the time has come to recognise that such policies are not identified as *preservation* policies by many, perhaps most, library managers. What is important is not the vocabulary, but the ideas which the vocabulary is intended to convey. The need for systematic management of stock is widely recognised in all sectors of librarianship; the longer-term preservation both of heritage collections and of stock no longer needed on a regular basis is merely one aspect of this. We shall suggest later in this chapter some of the implications of this in terms of institutional, local, regional and national policies for the retention of stock and common access to it.[4]

The fairly narrow understanding of preservation partly explains why there are comparatively few written preservation policies in British libraries. Apart from the traditional British distrust of such documents, which is being rapidly eradicated in the face of demands for tighter management and monitoring of activities and resources, it is probably the case that many *de facto* preservation policies (in the wider sense) are embedded in stock management policies and not identified with preservation at all. Indeed, we have seen some such documents, which we have used in Chapter 6 and elsewhere, and believe that others exist.[5] It remains the case, however, that only 10 per cent of our respondents identified themselves as having a formal written preservation policy; even more disturbing is that barely 30 per cent have a disaster control plan. We have suggested that there are other libraries which have a *de facto* policy, unwritten or even unrecognised, but there are others where librarians expressed a recognition of the need for one, and indeed a wish to develop one, but felt they did not know how to proceed. We address this issue later in this chapter.[6]

In general, it is the case that preservation issues are understood in a very traditional sense, and that this aspect of library management is seen as being most relevant (and by some librarians as uniquely relevant) to books, manuscripts and archival documents in heritage collections. Despite this, however, there is some evidence, as we have suggested, for a growing awareness of preservation issues in relation to other media, and, in particular, digitized data. This takes several forms. One important aspect of it is that electronic document delivery systems are seen as the future alternative to holdings of stock. The 'just-in-time' approach to document delivery will inevitably become more common in libraries in all sectors, although especially in academic libraries and in special libraries with a clientele in the scientific research community. This development, of course, raises as many issues as it solves. Access to distant information sources presumes that such sources exist; digitized data, like the printed or written word, is ultimately dependent on the quality and permanence of the medium on which it is stored. That essential point is sometimes forgotten, and yet the intrinsic impermanence of electronic documents and digitized data is a critical consideration in assessing the long-term viability of information systems which depend upon them. Electronic data archives do exist; they have been largely outside the scope of this study, but they present their own preservation problems, recognised by their managers but not always by those enthusiastic for their further development.[7]

Even in libraries where the importance of preservation is acknowledged, and in the smaller number where that acknowledgement has been translated into a formal policy, there are still formidable obstacles to implementation. Financial factors were identified as being the most important of these. This is not surprising, but nor is it merely an automatic knee-jerk reaction. Where funding has been made available from external sources, preservation activities have indeed been undertaken. Wolfson Foundation funds administered through the British Library have enabled the custodians of dozens of smaller collections to undertake conservation work which would not otherwise have been possible.[8] More recently, and on an even larger scale, the generosity of the Mellon Foundation would have supported the realisation of the long-standing and widely expressed desire for mass microfilming for preservation purposes. The linkage between Mellon and NEWSPLAN would have enabled that project to achieve large-scale tangible results, particularly in helping public libraries, to fulfil the obligation (which they recognise) to play a part in the preservation of runs of local and regional newspapers of national importance.[9]

Lack of funds, however, is only one of the inhibitions on the implementation of preservation policies; there are unhelpful attitudes among some senior managers, leading to frustration at middle management level, and there is still a lack of knowledge and skills as well as, in some cases, commitment. The gaps in skills and knowledge are a particular concern. It is important, however, to understand the implications of our findings on this matter. In the early 1980s, Ratcliffe argued that there was a major crisis in the availability of binders and conservators.[10]

It is not immediately clear, in statistical terms, how this conclusion was formulated; nevertheless, it was certainly a general perception at the time, although one not shared by a distinguished and knowledgeable American analyst of the British preservation scene.[11] Undoubtedly, there was social change; apprenticeship was no longer an attractive proposition for school-leavers, and the binding trade was neither glamorous nor well paid. Skills did, however, survive, and a decade later there is little evidence of a serious skill shortage for either trade or craft binding.[12] Various colleges are producing conservation binders and conservators, who may not meet with approval of the international superstars of the conservation profession but are nevertheless able to undertake acceptable work on valuable books and documents. The real problem lies not in the shortage of skills, but in the shortage of jobs for skilled workers. Only a minority of libraries have their own binderies. The commercial binding industry is heavily dependent on work for publishers, and on standard library work such as strengthening of paperbacks and binding of periodicals. Specialised skills are indeed needed and used, but there is no evidence of a serious mismatch between the skill base and employment opportunities.

The knowledge base of professional librarians also gives cause for optimism mingled with residual concern. During the middle and late 1980s, there was a small, but detectable, revival of interest in preservation management among library educators, largely in the context of collection management courses. At the same time, the NPO began its outreach activities towards practising professionals, although with limited success. Few librarians, however, have the necessary knowledge to take detailed decisions about the work needed to repair and conserve individual items, especially where that involves the application of specialised conservation techniques to items of high value or great importance. The partial failure of the NPO to establish itself in professional consciousness as a referral and advisory centre is perhaps unfortunate. Librarians still turn to binders for advice; since the majority of libraries do not employ binders this means, inevitably, turning to those with a commercial interest in the advice which is proffered. We have not investigated the quality of that advice, but certainly have no evidence that it is flawed or skewed. Nevertheless, it must remain a matter of concern that British librarians, even those with specific responsibilities for heritage collections intended for long-term preservation, do not always have the requisite knowledge base on which to develop decisions about preservation policy in general or conservation of individual items of stock.

In turn, this raises further issues about the role of the NPO both now and in the future. The NPO clearly cannot (and probably would not wish to) compete with traditional sources of advice on individual books and documents. It can, and does, provide lists of binders and conservators, although these are for information only, and are not intended to carry any sort of 'seal of approval'. On the other hand, the role of the NPO in training and the facilitation of training, and in awareness raising, is well-established, although even those services are not used as widely as might once have been hoped. It is its role as a provider of information which needs to be re-assessed. It can provide general information, and perhaps should aim to work at that level. It may be that its own pages on the World Wide Web would be a move in the right direction if it seeks both to raise its profile and, so far as possible, to control its workload. These are matters for the British Library, as the host and sponsor of the NPO, and the National Preservation Advisory Committee, as its link into the library and conservation professions. We merely draw attention to the issue, and suggest that the valuable work which it has done in the last decade needs to be sustained and developed.

The 'state of the art', as we have called it in the title of this section, is mixed, and offers both encouragement and cause for concern. On the one hand, librarians are aware of the issues, sometimes more aware than they realise; moreover, when resources are made available, they are willing and able to take advantage of them. On the other hand, there are few formal policies even at institutional level and barely a hint of the development of regional or national policies. Issues raised by the electronic storage of important data sets are only beginning to be addressed when it may already, in some cases, be too late. There has certainly been progress, but there is no cause for complacency.

As we have argued in Chapter 4, these developments have to be seen against the background of professional, political and technological change which has characterised the 1980s and the 1990s in all aspects of British life. The issues which we have raised, and the conclusions which we have reached, cannot be meaningfully understood or interpreted in isolation. We now return to the broader canvas on which we began to paint in Chapter 4, and suggest some of the key issues which have emerged and strategies by which these issues might be addressed.

At the national level, as we have indicated, there have been major reassessments of both university and public libraries which were undertaken more or less contemporaneously with our own work. In the light of the recommendations of both Follett and the Public Library Review, and the somewhat earlier recommendations of Enright and his colleagues for the British Library,[13] we detect a real move towards recognising the practical implications of the idea that no library can stand alone. Although this has been a commonplace of librarianship for half a century, it is only under the financial pressures of the 1980s, and with the assistance of parallel developments in information and communication technology, that it has become possible to envisage how truly national collection, retention and access policies can be developed.

Some library collections are clearly of more than institutional or local interest. As we have seen, there is an awareness of this in libraries in all sectors, especially among the immediate custodians of the collections. One of the key recommendations of Follett was that the national significance of such collections should be recognised by the award of additional funding to universities which owned them, in return for servicing them and providing general scholarly access. At the time of writing, this proposal is being implemented by the Funding Councils. The authors of the Public Library Review were less imaginative in this respect; indeed, references to local history and other special collections are notable principally by their absence. On the other hand, the proposal for regional hyperlibraries, although it was not well received, shows an awareness of the need for interinstitutional collection and access policies; the original specific proposal may have been misguided, but the underlying principal addresses a real problem.

The key issue which is emerging is the need to develop a *national retention policy*. It is a reasonable interpretation of our findings that many librarians would welcome such a development. There is much unnecessary duplication of holdings of lesser used materials, and probably some loss of other materials which slip through the net as a consequence. The British Library, as the Enright Report argued, can no longer be expected to undertake the whole burden of retention for national use. Even in collaboration with the other copyright libraries (who are also currently investigating their own futures in the respect), the task is too great. There is clearly a case for collections of regional significance to be held in the region in which they are principally of interest; NEWS-PLAN perhaps provides a model which can be adopted for other categories of material.

Retention implies preservation. Materials held for regional or national use on a long-term basis will have to be maintained in a usable condition, and will have to be accorded a high priority for quality storage and, where necessary, physical preservation or format conversion. The special support being made available for special collections in some university libraries is a model which might commend itself in the public library sector. There is, of course, no agency for public libraries whose role is comparable with that of the Higher Education Funding Councils for university libraries. On the other hand, the Department of National Heritage has established a Library and Information Commission, with a brief which extends in some respects to Scotland, Wales and Northern Ireland as well as to England. There are two issues which the Commission needs to address in the field with which we are concerned: first, the financial implications for a public library of holding collections which it is obliged to preserve for long-term access and use because of their value as heritage material or as scholarly resources, or as both; and secondly, the need to provide a strong regional and inter-regional network to support the book and information needs of public library users, especially where these are not those typically provided through the British Library Document Supply Centre. In other words, a national collection, retention and access policy cannot be confined to a single sector. National, academic and public libraries all have their part to play.

Even more complex issues arise when we consider the special libraries. The special library sector is far less easily defined than the other two traditional categories of academic and public libraries. Our definition was effectively that it included everything that was *not* either academic or public and, while this was a useful practical device, it does mean that the term 'special libraries' covers an immense range from major public sector bodies to small private institutions. In many cases, the institutions, both large and small, are not primarily libraries; professional bodies and learned societies for example, have a far wider role, and their other activities often (rightly) take a higher priority. In many government bodies and throughout business and industry, a library or information centre is merely a part, and often a comparatively small part, of the organisation as a whole; its operation is instrumental in meeting institutional objectives, but not an objective in itself. Yet many of these libraries contain material whose historical significance extends beyond the parent body, and needs to be considered in a wider national context.

To some extent, this has been recognised by the support of conservation and cataloguing work in some of these libraries through the Wolfson Foundation money administered by the British Library. On the other hand, it is clear that the size and diversity of this sector creates different, perhaps unique, problems in every library. Owners and their librarians may be aware of their responsibilities but either unwilling or (perhaps more often) unable to meet them as fully as might be desired. There can be no public policy about the public use of private property, but public support should bring with it some obligations to preserve and make available materials of general importance. More importantly, however, it is the librarians in small special libraries who are often most isolated from the profession at large, and perhaps most in need of help and support. There is a clear role here for a national advisory centre or information service, such as the National Preservation Office.

Questions of retention and access are essential issues which relate to collections and materials; indeed, that is our main concern in this book. On the other hand, these issues cannot be seen in isolation from the whole question of document delivery and information service provision. As we have suggested, access to information is dependent upon the physical survival of the information medium, but not necessarily on the survival of the format in which the information was originally disseminated. Format conversion is indeed a major preservation tool. As we look to the future, it is clear that use of some materials will be facilitated by the use of technologies which actually provide more sophisticated access than is possible to the originals. Multimedia CD-ROM is only the latest, and probably by no means the last, development which exemplifies this.[14]

Preservation of originals becomes a wholly different proposition when they are to be preserved as objects rather than as information sources. Indeed, the whole question of the retention of originals when their information content has been converted into another format may need to be reconsidered. While certain books and documents will always be desirable as works of art or as heritage items, it can be cogently argued that we need preserve only representative samples of many classes of material. If we have a visual image of a newspaper, and can read its text in a digitized version which has far more powerful access tools than the original, the case for retaining the document, and spending money on its conservation and preservation, is, at best, minimal. This is not to argue for universal destruction of originals. Cases need to be treated on their merits, and especially in the light of user needs and demands. The reader of a novel does not (at least as yet) want it on optical disk, any more than the scholarly needs of an art historian or a bibliographer can be satisfied by a photographic or digitized version of a medieval manuscript or an eighteenth-century printed book. But some of the needs of some users may be better met in a format other than the original, and, in the long term, decisions about retention and access will be driven by balancing user demand, technology and resources. A preservation, retention and access policy has to be developed in this context. Moreover, it has to be supported on a base of information about the physical condition of the collections and media which it seeks to preserve. A national sample survey of the condition of collections, covering all sectors and a wide range of materials, is an essential element in the development of a national policy such as that suggested here.

In this section, we have tried to generalise from our findings, and to put them in the broader context of current professional practice and thinking. We have suggested some possible directions of development at national and regional level, to which we shall return at the end of the chapter.[15] In the end, however, preservation takes place in libraries not in the minds of policymakers. It is to that level that we now return, to consider how librarians and their institutions can formulate policies which will best ensure that their users have reasonable access to both the materials and the information which they need.

DEVELOPING POLICIES FOR PRESERVATION, RETENTION AND ACCESS

In Chapter 5 we analysed some of the available guidelines to the development of preservation policies, and in Chapter 6 we attempted an analysis of preservation practices in British libraries. We have identified both common themes and good practice, and such consensus as there is on the objectives, content and implementation of policies. In this section, however, as part of our conclusions, we approach these issues from a somewhat different perspective. Throughout this book, we have tried to reflect the views of our respondents as well as merely report and analyse the information with which they provided us. At the same time, however, we have also felt it important to put our findings into the broader context which informed the previous section of this chapter. This dual approach had led us to argue that preservation and access have to be seen together, and that the link between them is a retention policy which takes account of user demands, technological capacity and the availability of resources. In suggesting how such a policy might be developed, therefore, we have not attempted to duplicate the guidelines issued by UNESCO, IFLA and other authoritative bodies. Instead, we shall suggest some principles upon which a policy might be built, and the context in which those guidelines have to be understood as we approach the end of the twentieth century.

STRATEGIES

We have already suggested that a preservation policy (like any other policy) has to be evolved and can only be fully understood at three levels: strategy, implementation and prioritisation. It is the strategy which provides the framework, and it is there that we must begin.

The example of the British Library is perhaps the most explicit of those we have discussed in deriving a preservation and access policy from a formal strategic mission statement. Of course, such a derivation is implicit in many of the other policy documents, as well as in less formal comments which we have received from respondents in many libraries in all sectors. The key issues which emerge seem to be these:

- the role of the library as a custodian of collections;
- the role of the library as a provider of information; and
- the balance between the sometimes conflicting demands of different user groups.

The library as custodian is not a currently fashionable concept, but in developing a preservation and access policy, the first stage is to consider the extent to which a library is the owner of the materials which it provides to users. The balance between ownership and access has changed, often dramatically, in the last 20 years, and the trend is likely to continue. Even so, almost all libraries will continue to own substantial core collections of materials. These core collections will include some reference materials and the basic lending collections in both academic and public libraries. Not all of this will be print on paper. Indeed, in the reference section, it is more than likely that many of the most important sources will be found in an optical disc format. Similarly, at least some of the teaching and learning material in academic libraries will be in multimedia formats rather than simply be traditional textbooks. Nevertheless, as we have repeatedly emphasised, such materials, like the books which they partly replace, need to be preserved in a usable condition. The library as custodian is the essential prerequisite to the library as information resource.

As a provider of information, however, the library will, of course, need to search far beyond the resources which it owns. Traditionally, this has been understood in the context of document delivery services, which will continue to be important. Technologies will change; electronic document delivery, already technically feasible, may become economically feasible as well in the foreseeable future. Network access is already essential to the effective provision of services; both charged-for databases and the 'free' information on the Internet are used in many academic and special libraries as a matter of course, and will become increasingly common in public libraries as well. Access issues are rather different here, for they are essentially economic and political, crudely but effectively summarised by a single question: Who pays? At one remove, however, there is another question, which we have already raised, of where and how the data are held in an accessible form. As we become more dependent on digitized data held in databases over which individual service providers have little or no control, it becomes ever more important that the *owners* of these databases are aware of the need to ensure that their contents are properly protected against degradation. Like the owners of collections, the owners of databases need to take decisions about the long-term future of the information which they have collected and stored. Libraries need to be aware of these issues and their implications in considering how they can reliably provide the information services which their users require.

The users themselves lie at the heart of the matter. Whether the user seeks a medieval manuscript or up-to-the-minute financial information, the library exists only to provide it. This is not to deny the heritage function of libraries, so clearly recognised as a duty and a responsibility by so many of our respondents. The problem lies not in defining functions but in meeting needs. Libraries inevitably respond most readily to the largest groups of users and to those with the greatest economic power. In the public sector (whether in public or in academic libraries) the former probably predominates; but in private sector libraries (many of which, as we have suggested, have important historical collections) the user is clearly a customer and often, *de facto*, a proprietor.

A strategy for preservation, retention and access needs to take account of these partly conflicting and partly converging considerations. In both public and academic libraries, we have detected a trend towards a recognition that the conflict can only be resolved – if at all – by making clear and explicit distinctions between different parts of the collections. In both sectors, special collections – in the broadest sense – are the main subject of preservation policies. This seems inevitable, and, provided certain conditions are met, even desirable. The central condition is that it is recognised that all materials in the library need to be preserved for as long as they are needed by users. We have quoted the example of a university library which has been forced into recognition of this fact as its collection ages but remains useful.[16] In the same way, we have seen how public libraries, while developing detailed policies for their special collections of local and historical material, have also, in many cases, detailed polices in place for the maintenance of current stocks in the general collections.

The longer-term strategy builds upon the shorter-term desire to serve current users. We suggest, however, that the questions which must be addressed are themselves changing. The concept of a national collection, widely disseminated between multiple owners, is, in one sense, merely a development of long-established ideas about interlibrary cooperation. But when it is formalised, as it has been, for example in Australia,[17] it enters into a different dimension of professional consciousness. A national collection in Britain would, of course, be built upon and around the collections of the national and copyright libraries, but we have inherited vast resources of great importance in libraries of all kinds. The recognition that this is a common burden as well as a common heritage is essential if such collections are not to be endangered.

We have suggested that there are indications that this danger is indeed recognised. Libraries seeking to develop a preservation policy for themselves need to take into account their role in the regional and national context. It is very unlikely that late twentieth century Britain is going to develop vast new library institutions. What can be achieved is a renewal of the existing infrastructure, drawing on the great wealth of holdings inherited from the past. A national preservation and retention policy is the proper context for the development of institutional preservation strategies. Libraries must seek to define their own roles; for many this will be multifaceted, and will need different action plans for different parts of the library. We do not merely regard this as acceptable: we argue that it is essential. The preservation of the heritage, and retention of materials and information in an accessible form, are different expressions of the same set of issues, but the differences are real, and should be acknowledged by policymakers.

In developing a preservation, retention and access strategy, therefore, library managers need to address the following questions:

- What must be preserved as heritage?
- For how long must different categories of material be directly available to users?
- What materials must be retained for reasons of regional or national collection policies?
- What materials and/or information can more cost-effectively be obtained from other owners without disadvantaging local users?

Only when these questions have been asked and answered can an effective action plan be developed.

ACTION PLANS

A preservation strategy, however well developed it may be, can only be effective if it is translated into an operational plan. Conversely, but perhaps less obviously, discrete operations can be more effective if they are evolved and implemented in a strategic context. Our findings and analysis, especially as we have recorded them in Chapters 2, 3 and 6, suggest that there is a great deal of good practice in preservation management to be found in British libraries in all sectors and at all levels. What is often lacking is a clear and explicit link between the strategic overview of the institutional mission and the specific actions, often of the most mundane kind, which facilitate the retention and access policies which the library seeks to pursue.

In one sense, there is abundant literature to guide librarians seeking to develop preservation policies. Quite apart from the international and national normative documents which we have discussed,[18] there is a substantial academic literature,[19] and examples (mainly American) of published policies which can be used as models.[20] The direct influence of this body of published work may be thought to be somewhat limited, although it does provide the basis of understanding which is necessary for the development of effective action plans. In practice, however, action plans are driven by local circumstances, and local practices are evolved which meet those circumstances.

We do not aim to add to the existing prescriptive literature. It is, however, clear that there are examples of good practice which could usefully be considered by others, and we draw attention to some of these as elements in an action plan designed to implement a strategic preservation policy. We have suggested at the end of the previous section that the key strategic issues relate, in general terms, to the identification of classes of material which need to be preserved and retained in order to meet institutional missions. The action plan is designed to deal with those classes of material.

The first, and perhaps most important, element in the plan is to ensure the availability of high-demand material. In terms of a preservation and access policy, this involves the regular monitoring of stock to ensure that it is in a usable condition, and systems which ensure that problems are identified and rectified. In many libraries, in both the academic and public sectors, this monitoring is done by frontline staff when materials are returned by borrowers. A system of triage operated at this point can identify books in urgent need of repair before they are used again. Where archived data from circulation records can be retrieved, individual decisions can be based on the use a particular title receives. Such a decision might involve repair, replacement or even duplication. Such systems clearly operate most effectively in those libraries in which there are clear guidelines for the comparatively junior, and almost invariably non-professional, staff who are directly involved in the first instance.

Secondly, an action plan deals with the storage and condition of materials on the shelves and in the library. Much of this is mundane, but essential. Proper shelving practices, good practice in cleaning of both shelves and materials, and generally high standards of housekeeping can be achieved, but only if there are clear guidelines in place. We have noted that much of this work takes place at some remove from senior management in institutions which are, in many cases, still hierarchical in their organisation. Good practice, in the form of simple guidelines, is essential. We note and commend those libraries where cleaners *are* told that certain kinds of cleansing agents are not acceptable, that books should be dusted in a particular way and so on. Similarly, shelvers need clear instructions on spacing, and a feedback loop through which supervisors can be told of problems which are developing as stock increases and shelves become full. Library managers need to recognise that it is at this level that the intelligent observation which can prevent trouble is most effective, but staff cannot be expected to make such observations unless they are told what to look for and have some means of reporting what they see with the confidence that the report will lead to effective action.

A third element in an action plan is that concerned with the care of materials which are in use. Security is an essential element here, both in terms of monitoring use in the library and preventing illicit removal of materials. The former is labour-intensive, and it is clear that in most libraries supervision of users is fairly minimal. Best practice, however, suggests that even in some public libraries, and commonly in academic libraries and in special libraries with rare or historic collections, separate reading areas are set aside for special materials, especially those which are on closed access or not available for loan. Supervision of such areas is more intensive; in some libraries it is continuous, a practice to be commended whenever it is feasible even in comparatively small libraries. We also note that some libraries make specific requests (sometimes framed as instructions) to users about how they should handle and use special materials. Minimally, this includes simple rules (pencils only, no resting of notepads on open books, and so on), as well as special instructions about special materials (proper handling of photographic materials or manuscripts) and restrictions on access (such as limits on the number of books allowed to a reader at any one time, or a requirement to use a microfilm rather than an original). At this level of detail, only local circumstances can determine local needs, but the general principle of best practice is clear enough: materials with long-term significance need to be used in a way which ensures their preservation.

The issues raised above become more acute as the material becomes more important. Again, there are local decisions here, in the broad context of institutional missions. This might, for example, lead to the designation of a collection as being of high value *because it is a collection* rather than for the value of individual items. Many local studies collections probably fall into this category. When there has been a strategic decision that there are heritage items and collections which must, as far as possible, be preserved in perpetuity, more stringent arrangements will be needed. Such collections are typically kept in closed access storage; where they are not, libraries should consider the desirability of changing their arrangements. In a library with a broadly based long-term retention policy (such as many of the larger university libraries, for example), there will inevitably be greater selectivity of material for closed access storage, but the distinctions are usually clear enough. Special collections, physically vulnerable collections (such as manuscripts), items of real or apparent high monetary value (older books in particular, whose value is often overestimated by the uninformed), and so on, will be prioritised. Where special storage areas are created, and environmental control systems are in place, these need to be regularly monitored. Again, however, a feedback loop is needed to ensure that action is taken on the basis of the information which the monitoring reveals. This may be no more than occasional adjustments to thermostats, but even that cannot be achieved without creating a system in which responsibilities, and the lines of management, are clear. At the same time, libraries need to ensure that they have inventories and current valuations which will satisfy insurance companies and their loss adjusters in the event of damage or destruction.[21]

A related line of action concerns the use of materials – again most likely to be heritage materials – for exhibition purposes. Best practice, well represented in the literature and in a formal British Standard,[22] is to be found in a few large libraries where exhibitions (and the lending of materials for exhibiting elsewhere) is a major activity. Many libraries, however, mount exhibitions from time to time, or are asked to lend materials for external exhibitions. A framework document which lays down clear standards of security (for transport, storage and display), handling (at the standards applied by the owner) and exhibition conditions (in terms of lighting levels, environmental conditions inside cases and the like) is essential. BS5454 provides an ideal starting point for developing this aspect of the plan.

There are also standards being developed, and some common areas of agreement, about the fourth essential element in the action plan: how books and other materials shall be repaired or protected. The basic principles are well understood, but perhaps more so for special materials than for the bulk of the stock. For most of the stock, in all libraries, the objective is to maintain it in usable condition for a comparatively limited period of time (say 5 to 20 years, and in any case not permanently), and this can be achieved by comparatively cheap and familiar methods. We have found considerable evidence of good practice here, some of it emanating from the binding industry, where, at present, much of the expertise in this field is actually to be found. Solid library bindings and well-made shelves are adequate for all but a comparative handful of materials. Guidelines are needed to enable staff to determine what action is needed and when it is appropriate. Again much of this is very simple, dealing with such matters as when a book shall be sent for rebinding, and the quality of binding to be applied. We have quoted examples of good simple guidelines which enable staff to undertake this selection process quickly and uniformly.[23] For some materials, of course, more specialised plans are needed, which determine the acceptability and applicability of materials, techniques and equipment. These include instructions on, for example, what categories of books shall be boxed (such as pamphlets to be boxed rather than bound as an economy measure), the use of vertical files for storing single sheets, and so on. These practical matters are the essential foundation of a preservation policy which will ensure that materials are conserved in a way which facilitates retention and access.

The fifth element which we emphasise in the action plan underpins all the others. We have suggested three lines of action from the mundane to the specialised. Some, such as the regular monitoring of the condition of stock, are appropriate to all libraries; others are perhaps more rarefied. Nothing, however, will be achieved if staff are not made aware of what needs to be done. One of our most alarming findings was that so many respondents could not identify even the most rudimentary levels of training or awareness-raising in their induction programmes for new staff.[24] As we have suggested, the basic practices which will preserve stock for retention and access are in the hands of junior staff, many of them part-time, often with a high level of turnover, especially in the larger institutions in urban areas. Some form of rudimentary training is essential. The recently published *Training Pack* is a step in the right direction,[25] but managers need to consider even simpler approaches which will inform staff of their responsibility to ensure that the library's property is kept in a condition which makes it usable by the customers who have paid for it.

Operational plans are complex documents. We have done little more than suggest the levels of practicality at which they need to be developed, and some of the areas of concern which they should cover. We emphasise the essentially local nature of such a plan. Indeed, some aspects of it are specific to buildings or even parts of buildings, and may not even be of systemwide application in a multisite library. In other cases, constraints will be imposed by the very nature of the service which is being offered, and it is right that they should be so. Intensive use of material of immediate interest is not compatible with some aspects of longer-term preservation. It is precisely for this reason that the operational action plan can only be effectively developed and fully understood in the context of a wide-ranging but carefully-targeted strategy. There is some evidence to suggest that the activities of the preservation 'lobby', however worthy their motives may have been, have actually had a deterrent effect on some librarians who have responded either by dismissing preservation as being none of their concern, or have despaired at the gap between the ideals of the theoreticians and attainable objectives in working institutions.

There are, we suggest, five essential elements to be considered in preparing an action plan for the realisation of a preservation management strategy. The following questions have to be addressed:

- How can unimpeded access to high-demand material be guaranteed?
- How can the condition of items and storage areas be maintained and monitored, and how effective is the feedback between monitoring and action?
- How can the use of materials be monitored both inside and outside the library?
- How can appropriate valuations be made and standards set for the special maintenance of high-value items?
- How and by whom are staff to be appropriately trained?

The answers to these questions are complex, and some are institutionwide. Only when such answers have been formulated, however, can a preservation strategy be translated into effective action.

PRIORITIES

The action plan can only be operationally effective if priorities for action are clearly established. Such priorities derive from the same strategy as the action plan itself. Much of the action plan is concerned with the identification of need (for repair, for example) or the choice between particular technical solutions to problems (such as choice of binding style). Between the two, however, lies the critical area of matching needs to resources; it is this link which is addressed in determining an order of priority.

The traditional approach is to develop a matrix of value and use, which effectively provides a mechanism for prioritising collections or indeed individual books, with priority going to high value/high use items.[26] This is a valid approach, and can be useful, but the application of the matrix has to be related to the overall strategy. Among the policy documents we have seen, and in the comments of our respondents, we find some implicit recognition of this. To establish the primacy of a particular group of users effectively prioritises, both for acquisition and for availability, the materials which they principally need. Where this is unambiguous (as in some special libraries, for example) it presents no problems. In many cases, however, librarians do have to balance the conflicting claims of different user groups and different categories of material. The preservation strategy defines which categories of material are intended for permanent retention, and the rationale upon which that decision must be based. The prioritisation of the action plan determines how those principles are implemented.

Again local circumstances will determine institutional practices. Moreover, establishing an order of priorities does not create the resources needed to implement a policy. It does, however, permit the most effective use of resources, and ensure that the interests of all users can be considered, and the value of all materials appropriately recognised.

SUMMARY

In this section, we have tried to offer some general guidelines to librarians who are seeking to develop a preservation policy. It is not a manual of practice; such things do exist, although it may be that something different is needed. We have, however, drawn on our knowledge of current practice in British libraries to suggest how the essential links between strategy, action and prioritisation can be established. We suggest that the key to effective implementation is to ensure that preservation policies clearly make a contribution to the achievement of the library's mission and above all, to the fulfilment of its objectives in terms of making materials and information available to users. Only when such a strategy has been conceptually determined, can operational plans be developed within which prioritised actions can be implemented. Limited resources are thus applied in the most effective way which will facilitate access by preserving the information and the media which users want and need both now and in the future. It is indeed the future which is the main focus of preservation, even when it is concerned with objects from the past. We conclude by suggesting some ways forward, and identifying some issues which will determine the future direction of preservation policies.

THE FUTURE

We are not prophets, but we can build upon our work to identify issues and needs, and to suggest some of the ways in which those needs can be met. We shall first consider some of the issues which have arisen in analysing our findings, and in particular in relating them to the broader developments in the library and information world. We shall then turn to two key areas in which we have identified major gaps: standards and resources. Finally, we shall suggest some specific courses of action, both large and small, which would facilitate the development of preservation and access policies in Britain.

ISSUES

We have identified a number of general issues which clearly arise both from the practice of preservation management in Britain, and from the context in which that practice exists. In particular, the professional, political and technological changes which we discussed in Chapter 4 are having a profound influence on the future of all aspects of work in library and information services.

At the strategic level, Britain is beginning to develop a rudimentary, and still largely implicit, national information policy. The recognition by the British Library that even it can no longer be a universal library, which is the real subject of the Enright Report, is an important step in this direction. It forces the library and information community itself, and the politicians and policymakers who resource it, to reconsider the national dimension of access to information. The role of the Library and Information Commission in the Department of National Heritage is not yet clear; what is clear is that it will be critical in providing a national forum for the identification and determination of key issues. Perhaps the most important of these is that of access. It is clear from our findings that many librarians still perceive a conflict between access and preservation, or between retention and use. We see no such conflict: access can only be achieved when information is available, and that requires the existence of a usable medium in which it is stored. The problem is not to reconcile the conflicting demands of preservation and access (although such a conflict may, marginally, exist with exceptionally high value materials), but rather to consider the problems of long-term access to information stored in ephemeral media.

It is here that the national dimension is so important. Traditionally, in Britain as in other countries, a national legal deposit library (or several such libraries) has been the storehouse and guardian of the written and printed heritage. These libraries have, to some extent, adapted themselves to perform a similar role for the non-printed media, although only spasmodically and not with complete success. They have, moreover, long since accepted that their aspiration to universality is unrealistic, and have excluded either completely or selectively certain categories of material (such as ephemera) or certain classes of media (such as archived television programmes). Current and future information technologies highlight and exacerbate these problems. A few examples will illustrate the point. Refereed electronic journals, of which there are said to be more than 70 available on the Internet at the time of writing, will probably never wholly supersede the traditional printed journal, but they will be significant in some disciplines and will need to be retained for access for the foreseeable future. The creation of appropriate data archives for such journals, perhaps independently of their commercial producers and analogous with the legal deposit libraries, could be argued to be a matter of concern and some urgency. Moreover, the refereed journal is merely one example among many of the new conceptual demands being made on those who seek to preserve the products of the present as the heritage of the future. Information, data and text which exist only in electronic form present a new range of preservation and retention issues. Much of this material is inherently unstable, being designed for constant updating and current accuracy rather than as the basis of an historical record. It is impractical to store in perpetuity more than a fragment of the databases which we are creating; we can do so only by selection and sampling, and need to take steps to ensure that this is indeed done to create an on-going historical record. The comprehensive, although less than universal, preservation which has been the objective of research libraries in relation to printed publications, is simply unattainable in the electronic age.

More conventionally, it is clear that there is still a good deal of misunderstanding of the preservation issue among British librarians. Perhaps this should be expressed differently: practice has clearly not come into line with the recommendations and expectations of the more enthusiastic advocates of preservation. In practice, librarians seek to preserve selected materials deemed to be of particular interest and importance. The broader implication of this is that there is a need for policies which will ensure the retention of all materials for so long as they are needed. Such policies cannot be confined to individual institutions. The regional networks of public libraries, with their central stores of commonly accessible, or even commonly owned material, provide one model. The Follett proposals for support for nationally important collections in individual libraries is another. Indeed, no single model is needed. What is essential is the broad acceptance of the concept of a national retention policy, with access to the materials and information thus preserved.

STANDARDS AND RESOURCES

There is a real problem in relating normative standards to the realities of professional practice. This is, no doubt, generally true, but our work suggests that it is perhaps particularly acute in this field. The key to understanding the problem lies in the fact that the standards for the manufacture, storage, use, conservation and exhibition of materials have been, for the most part, based on the assumption that permanent preservation is a universal objective. It is now clear that it is not; even if this had not been self-evident, it is demonstrated by our findings about the practices which prevail in British libraries. As a result, the standards are dismissed by many librarians as being both generally impractical and specifically irrelevant to their own needs; yet there are no other sources to which they can turn. There is a clear divide between the need for advice and information and either their availability or knowledge of their availability. The emphasis on the highest standards (appropriate as they are for some materials) can be argued to have had the ironic effect of making many librarians ignore the challenges presented to them by the medium-term management of information resources and the materials in which information is actually contained. We are not arguing that standards should be lowered; but we do argue that the comparatively limited applications of the highest standards should be made more explicit.

The lack of resources was highlighted by many respondents as a major concern; this was, of course, predictable. We do, however, suggest that the resourcing issue also needs to be seen in a broader context. Money is not the only resource needed to implement a policy. Properly trained people are at least as important. We have already suggested some of the deficiencies in training at the most rudimentary level, and consider that action to remedy this is, in many libraries, more important than grandiose conservation schemes in ensuring continued access. Such an approach is no substitute for properly financed programmes of repair of damaged materials, or of preventative measures such as boxing or substitution. Nevertheless, the evidence is that active intervention is more effective in the long term if it is undertaken in parallel with appropriate initiatives to train staff so that they can monitor use and condition, together with the creation of managerial and administrative structures to facilitate the work. We return here, of course, to the whole issue of prioritisation. Perhaps the greatest single success which we can identify in the last decade has been the recognition, through the national initiative of NEWSPLAN, of the need for local action to ensure long-term access to newspapers, and the direction of funding to support that clearly defined objective.

THE WAY FORWARD

Like all research, ours has identified gaps in our knowledge even as it remedied other gaps which were already known to exist. By examining current practices, it has become clear that there is much that is *not* being done partly because it is not known whether or not it needs to be done. In other cases, it is only from such research as ours that long-term needs can indeed be identified. In this final section, we shall suggest some directions for future work where research and practice can meet.

The need for a national strategy emerges very strongly from our work. There are many libraries with effective preservation policies in place, and many more in which the need for them is recognised. All of them, however, would be strengthened by a properly identified national context. The problem which emerges can perhaps be expressed most succinctly as the need for a *national access policy*, which will ensure that users can indeed gain access to the information, books and other materials and media which they need or can reasonably expect. In the academic sector, the British Library has effectively provided such services for many years; the inevitable and desirable growth in cooperation between the national and institutional libraries will enhance the provision of such services to universities at a time when their information provision strategies are under so many technological and financial strains.

For the general public, however, the situation is less happy. Assuming that it continues to be policy to provide a public library service of which a substantial part is uncharged at the point of access, it is clear that such libraries will continue to prioritise the provision of that core service. We have, however discovered some alarming facts. Public libraries contain important heritage collections which some of them, despite the will to do so, probably cannot maintain in the long term. Where these directly relate to the library's mission, as is clearly the case with local studies and local history collections, the situation may be somewhat less strained, but there is a need to recognise that some public libraries, like some university libraries, have collections of national importance. These are a national resource; no national access policy can ignore them, and some support, along the lines of that envisaged by Follett for some university collections, could be argued to be justified.

Access, retention and preservation cannot be separated from each other. Moreover none of them is specific to any one sector of libraries, nor to particular categories of materials and media, although the problems are, of course, more acute in some areas than in others. We do not advocate universal preservation, nor even the universality of preservation as an issue for library managers. We do, however, conclude that if libraries are to meet their obligations to provide information to their clients, library managers must consider the integrity and survival of the material sources from which that information is derived. Preservation by benign neglect is not a policy; preservation in isolation is not a viable option. There will, in the end, be no substitute for a clear understanding that it is part of the professional obligations of a librarian to ensure the existence of the resources which users need. The context, however, is the recognition, which is developing slowly but perceptibly, that this can only be achieved if there is a broad professional and political acceptance of this as a national issue, which needs to be addressed at national level.

NOTES

1. See below, pp. 152–4.
2. See above, pp. 32–3.
3. An anecdote may help to exemplify this. When this book was in the final stages of preparation, one of us was talking to one of our respondents in a different context. She commented that she – despite being very much aware of preservation as a major issue in her large university research library – had understood it entirely in the context of special collections, and had not taken account of the issues of access to general collections by the majority of readers. See also Margaret Child. Preservation issues for collection development. *Wilson Library Bulletin*, 67: 3 (1992), pp. 20–1, 106; Ellen Cunningham-Kruppa. The preservation officer's role in collection development. Ibid., pp. 27–9, 107; and Gay Donnelly. The collection development officer as part of the preservation team. Ibid., pp. 30–4.
4. See below, pp. 141–3.
5. At the time of writing, a small working party established by an *ad hoc* national meeting of preservation administrators called by the British Library in November 1994 is addressing this issue further. One of us (J.F.) is a member of that group, so that it will, in effect, be able to build on our findings.
6. See below, pp. 146–51.
7. Richard E. Barry. Electronic document and records management systems: towards a methodology for requirements. *Information Management and Technology*, 27: 6 (1994), pp. 251–6.
8. British Library. *British Library Grants for Cataloguing and Conservation*. London: The British Library, 1994.
9. See above, pp. 83–4, 90–94.
10. See above, p. 69.
11. David H. Stam. *National Preservation Planning in the United Kingdom: an American perspective.* (British Library Research and Development Report 5759). London: The British Library, 1983, p. 3.
12. See also, pp. 69–70.
13. See above, pp. 20, 29.
14. See, for example, Medieval multimedia. *Initiatives for Access News*, 2 (December 1994), pp. 4–5. This is a newsletter published by the British Library.
15. See below, pp. 152–4.
16. See above, p. 123.
17. See above, p. 79.
18. See above, pp. 98–105.
19. Discussed in Chapter 1.
20. See above, p. 98.
21. A number of these points arise out of the aftermath of the fire at Norwich Central Library in 1994, which destroyed much of the Norfolk reserve stock.
22. See above, pp. 124–5.
23. See above, pp. 128–9.
24. See above, pp. 57–60.
25. See above, pp. 7–8.
26. In National Preservation office. *Preservation: A Survival Kit*, for which see Chapter 6, note 45.

Appendix 1 The survey

We reproduce here the text of the questionnaire which was used for data collection (see pp. ix–x, above) and the covering letter sent to recipients.

PRESERVATION POLICIES AND CONSERVATION IN BRITISH LIBRARIES: A TEN YEAR REVIEW 1983-1992

Questionnaire

PRESERVATION: the managerial, financial and technical issues involved in preserving library materials in all formats - and/or their information content - so as to maximise their useful life.
CONSERVATION: the maintenance and/or repair of individual items.

Please answer questions by ticking boxes where appropriate

1. Name of organisation: _____

   Address: _____

   _____ Telephone number: _____

   Contact name: _____ Position: _____

2. (a) Estimated size of total holdings (items or linear measurement): _____

   (b) What percentage (approximately) of these holdings is intended for permanent retention? _____

   Not known ☐

	Yes	*No*
3. (a) Do you have a written preservation policy?	☐	☐
(b) Do you have a disaster control plan (written or otherwise)?	☐	☐

4. Is there a member/are there members of staff responsible for the management and implementation of:

	Yes	*No*
(a) preservation activity?	☐	☐
(b) disaster control planning?	☐	☐

   If you answered 'yes' to either of the above please give job titles (and/or grades):

   (a) _____ (b) _____

	Yes	No
5. Do you have any in-house training programmes in preservation awareness for existing staff?	☐	☐

   If yes, please describe briefly indicating level(s) of staff involved: _____

   _____

	Yes	No
6. Is preservation/conservation awareness included in training programmes for newly appointed staff?	☐	☐

   If yes, please give details: _____

   _____

Project funded by The Leverhulme Trust

		Yes	No
7.	Do you provide guidance to library users in the handling of library materials?	☐	☐

If yes, please describe briefly the method(s) used: _____

_____

8. Have you experienced preservation/conservation problems with any of the following media? (please tick box if yes):

(a) printed books ☐   (b) video tapes ☐   (c) vinyl records ☐   (d) microfilm ☐

(e) filmstrips ☐   (f) journals ☐   (g) compact discs ☐   (h) photographic prints ☐

(i) microfiche ☐   (j) 35mm slides ☐   (k) manuscript materials ☐   (l) optical discs ☐

(m) microcard ☐   (n) newspapers ☐   (o) audio cassettes ☐   (p) photographic negatives ☐

(q) other ☐   If other, please specify _____

Please describe briefly any problem(s) encountered (using additional sheets if necessary):

_____

_____

_____

_____

_____

9.	Do you have any systematic procedure(s) for:	Yes	No
	(a) surveying stock for conservation purposes?	☐	☐
	(b) cleaning/treating stock at the shelves?	☐	☐

If yes, please specify frequency of procedure(s) and type(s) of treatment: _____

_____

10. Which, if any, of the following environmental conditions are you able to monitor and/or control?:

	Monitor		Control	
	Yes	No	Yes	No
(a) Relative humidity	☐	☐	☐	☐
(b) Temperature	☐	☐	☐	☐
(c) Light	☐	☐	☐	☐
(d) Pollution	☐	☐	☐	☐

Please give brief details (using additional sheets if necessary): _____

_____

_____

		Yes	No
11.	Do you have any special storage equipment and/or facilities for special collections (excluding microform)?	☐	☐

If yes, please give brief details: _____

_____

_____

		Yes	No
12.	(a) Do you have an in-house bindery?	☐	☐

If yes, how many binders do you employ? _____

	Yes	No
(b) Do you have a conservation workshop/laboratory?	☐	☐

If yes, how many conservators do you employ? _____

	Yes	No
(c) Do you have any difficulties in recruiting suitably trained conservation staff?	☐	☐

If yes, please specify: _____

	Yes	No
(d) Do you have any difficulties in obtaining materials or products for use in conservation work?	☐	☐

If yes, please specify: _____

13. Do you make use of commercial binderies/conservators for:

	All	Some	None
(a) specialised conservation work (for example, paper repair)?	☐	☐	☐
(b) craft/hand binding?	☐	☐	☐
(c) standard/machine binding?	☐	☐	☐

		Yes	No
14.	Do you use any other means of protecting library materials as alternatives to binding (for example, acid-free boxes, wrappers and tapes)?	☐	☐

If yes, please specify: _____

_____

		Yes	No
15.	(a) Do you use archival-quality microform for preservation purposes (for example, microform quality which conforms to BS5699)?	☐	☐

If yes, please specify format(s) and main areas of usage: _____

_____

	Yes	No
(b) Do you have archival-quality microform production facilities?	☐	☐
(c) Do you have special storage facilities for microform?	☐	☐

<table>
<tr><td></td><td></td><td align="center">**Yes**</td><td align="center">**No**</td></tr>
<tr><td>(d) Do you participate in any cooperative microfilming preservation initiatives?</td><td></td><td align="center">☐</td><td align="center">☐</td></tr>
</table>

If yes, please specify: _____

		Yes	**No**
16.	Does your library subscribe to any preservation/conservation journals?	☐	☐

17. (a) What was your total expenditure on all preservation/conservation activities during the last financial year (approximately)?

£_____

(b) What is your total acquisitions budget (for comparative purposes)? £_____

18. Which, if any, of the following sources of advice and expertise have you made use of? (please tick box if yes):

(a) industrial laboratories ☐   (b) museums ☐   (c) university departments ☐

(d) government departments ☐   (e) private conservators ☐   (f) commercial binders ☐

(g) other libraries ☐   (h) record offices ☐

19. Which, if any, of the following services provided by the National Preservation Office have you used? (please tick box if yes):

(a) advisory/referral service ☐   (b) training videos ☐   (c) free leaflets ☐   (d) seminars ☐

(e) courses ☐   (f) priced publications ☐

(g) other ☐   If other, please specify: _____

20. Please rank the following considerations on a scale of 1 to 7 according to their importance as factors inhibiting the preservation/conservation of your stock. The most important should be ranked number 1 and the least important number 7:

(a) security ___

(b) suitably trained staff ___

(c) finance ___

(d) storage conditions ___

(e) heavy use of the collection ___

(f) organisational priority given to preservation ___

(g) general staffing levels ___

THANK YOU FOR YOUR TIME AND COOPERATION

Should you have any queries please contact Paul Eden on 0509 223064

Please return to: Department of Information and Library Studies, Loughborough University, Loughborough, Leics. LE11 3TU

**PRESERVATION POLICIES AND CONSERVATION IN BRITISH
LIBRARIES: A TEN YEAR REVIEW 1983-1992**

**Please use this additional sheet should you wish to make any further comments or raise any
specific preservation/conservation issues**

Loughborough University

LOUGHBOROUGH, LEICESTERSHIRE, LE11 3TU
Telephone: 0509 263171   Telex: 34319

DEPARTMENT OF INFORMATION AND LIBRARY STUDIES
Head of Department: Professor John Feather

Direct Line: 0509 22 3064
Fax: 0509 223053

13 May 1993

Dear Colleague

PRESERVATION POLICIES IN BRITISH LIBRARIES
A TEN YEAR REVIEW, 1983-1992

In 1982 the British Library Research and Development Department funded a major investigation into preservation in libraries in Britain. The results of this investigation were published as *Preservation policies and conservation in British libraries* (British Library, LIR Report 25, 1984), known generally as the Ratcliffe Report.

Preservation emerged as a significant aspect of resource management because of its importance in maximising useful collection life and improving user access to information. As these concerns have assumed even greater significance because of both technological change and the severe financial constraints within which libraries now operate, we are assessing the current situation and likely future developments. Our investigation is funded by The Leverhulme Trust.

We are sending the enclosed questionnaire to all public library authorities, university libraries and selected 'special' libraries. We should be most grateful if you would complete and return it (in the enclosed s.a.e.) *by 11 June 1993*. We hope that you will be able to reply in terms of your library system as a whole and not only with reference to special collections. All replies will be treated in the strictest confidence.

I realise that there are many demands on your time but firmly believe that the results of this research, which will be widely disseminated, will have major implications for future funding in many spheres of professional practice. Your help would be greatly appreciated. Thank for your assistance and cooperation.

Yours sincerely

John Feather

Project team: Paul Eden, John Feather, Graham Matthews

JANET e-mail DILS @ UK.AC.LUT.(Personal e-mail   P.EDEN @ UK.AC.LUT.)

165

Appendix 2 Chronology

The Ratcliffe Report is generally felt to have had a seminal effect on preservation in the United Kingdom and it is accordingly from 1982 when work on the project began, that this chronological outline begins.

1982 Library Association Professional Development and Education Committee set up Sub-Committee on Preservation; later became Library and Information Services Sub-Committee on Preservation and Conservation.

Alex Wilson's paper ('For this and future generations') published in *Library Review*, Autumn 1982.

NEWSPLAN established.

1983 *Library Conservation News* first published.

News of British Library Grant of £22 000 for Cambridge University 'Conservation' Project in LCN (word 'preservation' does not appear in this notice).

David A. Stam's, *National preservation planning in the United Kingdom: an American perspective*, published.

1984 Ratcliffe Report published.

National Preservation Office established at British Library.

National Preservation Advisory Committee, first meeting.

IFLA Core Programme in Preservation and Conservation (PAC) established.

SCONUL established Working Party on Preservation.

Paper Conservation Centre established at UMIST.

National Library of Wales sponsors its first conservation conference: Paper, parchment and bindings; conservation problems in public repositories in Wales.

1985 National Library of Scotland *Planning manual for disaster control in libraries* published.

Register of Microform Masters begun.

NEWSPLAN pilot study completed.

NPO video, *Keeping your words* released.

*Permanence of paper for printed library materials.*US standard.

IFLA PAC Programme launched.

Committee on Library Co-operation in Ireland ran first national seminar on preservation – designed to raise awareness.

Initial Wolfson Foundation and Wolfson Family Charitable Trust grants to the British Library for awards for Conservation projects.

1986 National Preservation Office, first annual seminar, *The conservation crisis: our Achilles heel?*

IFLA guidelines, Principles for the preservation and conservation of library materials, published.

Library Association Annual Conference, Preserving the word: past imperfect, future imperative.

Los Angeles Central Library, fire.

Joint Conference of the Directors of National Libraries, IFLA and UNESCO on preservation of library materials, held in Vienna.

Domesday Book rebound.

Two leaflets under general title, *Preservation guidelines*, produced by NPO; and *Survival kit*; and booklet on permanent paper.

1987 *UNESCO guidelines, Methods to determine the preservation needs in libraries and archives* published.

Preservation first afforded a full chapter in *British librarianship and information work*.

LA Sub-Committee agreed its terms of reference.

Library Association policy statement on preservation and conservation.

NPAC Education Panel first meeting.

Museums and Galleries Commission Conservation Unit established.

IFLA International Symposium on Newspaper Preservation and Access, held in London.

British Library's 'Adopt a Book' Appeal launched.

New journal from IFLA, *International Preservation News*.

LISC Wales' Working Party on Conservation and Preservation established.

1988 Report, *Education for conservation in British library schools*, published.

Leningrad, Academy of Sciences Library, fire.

First NPO annual competition (preservation policy).

1989 Enright report, *Selection for survival*, published.

Mellon Microfilming Project begun.

National Manuscripts Conservation Trust launched.

NPO releases video on disaster control planning.

NPO takes on remit to advise on security.

NPO holds national conference on library security.

1990 NPO video on library security available.

1991 First contemporary UK textbook, *Preservation and the management of library collections*, published.

Reading guide to preservation published.

NPO conference on security.

Mellon Foundation/BLR&DD Digitization Demonstrator project started.

1992 Home Office/National Preservation Office report on theft from libraries published.

NPO conference on microfilming in libraries.

1993 Textbook with international coverage, *Preservation in libraries: principles, strategies and practices for libraries, and companion volume of readings*, published.

1994 Norwich Central Library, fire.

Preservation policies and management in British Libraries: a ten-year review, 1983–92, research completed and results disseminated.

National preservation policy reviewed; first national meeting of Preservation Administrators.

Index